GEOProcessing 2019

The Eleventh International Conference on Advanced Geographic Information Systems, Applications, and Services

February 24 – 28, 2019

Athens, Greece

GEOProcessing 2019 Editors

Claus-Peter Rückemann, Leibniz Universität Hannover / Westfälische Wilhelms-Universität Münster /North-German Supercomputing Alliance (HLRN), Germany
Yerach Doytsher, Technion - Israel Institute of Technology, Haifa, Israel

Printed from e-media with permission by:

Curran Associates, Inc.
57 Morehouse Lane
Red Hook, NY 12571

CURRAN ASSOCIATES INC. proceedings.com

Some format issues inherent in the e-media version may also appear in this print version.

Printed by Curran Associates, Inc. (2019)

International Academy, Research, and Industry Association (IARIA)
412 Derby Way
Wilmington, DE 19810

Phone: (408) 893-6407
Fax: (408) 527-6351

petre@iaria.org

Additional copies of this publication are available from:

Curran Associates, Inc.
57 Morehouse Lane
Red Hook, NY 12571 USA
Phone: 845-758-0400
Fax: 845-758-2633
Email: curran@proceedings.com
Web: www.proceedings.com

Table of Contents

GEOProcessing 2019

Forward

The eleventh edition of The International Conference on Advanced Geographic Information Systems, Applications, and Services (GEOProcessing 2019), held in Athens, Greece, February 24 - 28, 2019, addressed the aspects of managing geographical information and web services.

The goal of the GEOProcessing 2019 conference was to bring together researchers from the academia and practitioners from the industry in order to address fundamentals of advances in geographic information systems and the new applications related to them using the Web Services. Such systems can be used for assessment, modeling and prognosis of emergencies

GEOProcessing 2019 provided a forum where researchers were able to present recent research results and new research problems and directions related to them. The topics covered aspects from fundamentals to more specialized topics such as 2D & 3D information visualization, web services and geospatial systems, geoinformation processing, and spatial data infrastructure.

We take this opportunity to thank all the members of the GEOProcessing 2019 Technical Program Committee as well as the numerous reviewers. The creation of such a broad and high-quality conference program would not have been possible without their involvement. We also kindly thank all the authors who dedicated much of their time and efforts to contribute to the GEOProcessing 2019. We truly believe that, thanks to all these efforts, the final conference program consists of top quality contributions.

This event could also not have been a reality without the support of many individuals, organizations, and sponsors. We are grateful to the members of the GEOProcessing 2019 organizing committee for their help in handling the logistics and for their work to make this professional meeting a success.

We hope that GEOProcessing 2019 was a successful international forum for the exchange of ideas and results between academia and industry and for the promotion of progress in geographic information research.

We also hope that Athens provided a pleasant environment during the conference and everyone saved some time for exploring this beautiful city.

GEOProcessing 2019 Chairs

GEOProcessing Steering Committee
Claus-Peter Rückemann, Leibniz Universität Hannover / Westfälische Wilhelms-Universität

Münster / North-German Supercomputing Alliance (HLRN), Germany [Chair]
Yerach Doytsher, Technion - Israel Institute of Technology, Haifa, Israel
Monica De Martino, Consiglio Nazionale delle Ricerche - Genova, Italy
Thierry Badard, Centre for Research in Geomatics - Laval University, Quebec, Canada
Jianhong Cecilia Xia, Curtin University, Australia
Timofey Samsonov, Lomonosov Moscow State University, Russia
Thomas Ritz, FH Aachen, Germany

GEOProcessing Industry/Research Advisory Committee
Mete Celik, Erciyes University, Turkey
Katia Stankov, Synodon Inc., Canada
Lena Noack, Free University of Berlin, Germany
Baris M. Kazar, Oracle America Inc., USA
Petko Bakalov, Environmental Systems Research Institute (ESRI), USA
Olivier Dubois, OSCARS, France
Albert Godfrind, Geospatial technologies/Oracle Server Technologies - Sophia Antipolis, France
Cidália C. Fonte, University of Coimbra/INESC Coimbra, Portugal

GEOProcessing 2019

COMMITTEE

GEOProcessing Steering Committee

Claus-Peter Rückemann, Leibniz Universität Hannover / Westfälische Wilhelms-Universität Münster / North-German Supercomputing Alliance (HLRN), Germany [Chair]
Yerach Doytsher, Technion - Israel Institute of Technology, Haifa, Israel
Monica De Martino, Consiglio Nazionale delle Ricerche - Genova, Italy
Thierry Badard, Centre for Research in Geomatics - Laval University, Quebec, Canada
Jianhong Cecilia Xia, Curtin University, Australia
Timofey Samsonov, Lomonosov Moscow State University, Russia
Thomas Ritz, FH Aachen, Germany

GEOProcessing Industry/Research Advisory Committee

Mete Celik, Erciyes University, Turkey
Katia Stankov, Synodon Inc., Canada
Lena Noack, Free University of Berlin, Germany
Baris M. Kazar, Oracle America Inc., USA
Petko Bakalov, Environmental Systems Research Institute (ESRI), USA
Olivier Dubois, OSCARS, France
Albert Godfrind, Geospatial technologies/Oracle Server Technologies - Sophia Antipolis, France
Cidália C. Fonte, University of Coimbra/INESC Coimbra, Portugal

GEOProcessing 2019 Technical Program Committee

Mohd Helmy Abd Wahab, Universiti Tun Hussein Onm Malaysia, Malaysia
Al Abdelmoty, Cardiff University, Wales, UK
Diana F. Adamatti, Universidade Federal do Rio Grande, Brazil
Ayman Ahmed, GIS unit Kuwait Oil Company, Kuwait
Nuhcan Akçit, Middle East Technical University, Turkey
Zaher Al Aghbari, University of Sharjah, UAE
Amen Al-Yaari, INRA | UMR 1391 ISPA Interactions Sol Plante Atmosphère, France
Rafal A. Angryk, Georgia State University, USA
Francisco Javier Ariza López, Universidad de Jaén, Spain
Thierry Badard, Centre for Research in Geomatics - Laval University, Quebec, Canada
Petko Bakalov, Environmental Systems Research Institute (ESRI), USA
Fabiano Baldo, Santa Catarina State University, Brazil
Fabian D. Barbato, ORT University - Montevideo, Uruguay
Melih Basaraner, Yildiz Technical University, Turkey
Itzhak Benenson, Tel Aviv University, Israel
Michela Bertolotto, University College Dublin, Ireland
Deepak Raj Bhat, Gunma University, Japan
Mehul Bhatt, University of Bremen, Germany
Shrutilipi Bhattacharjee, Technical University of Munich, Germany
Thomas Blaschke, University of Salzburg, Austria
Soukaina Filali Boubrahimi, Georgia State University, USA

David Brosset, Naval Academy Research Institute, France
Benedicte Bucher, French National Institute of Geographic and Forest Information (IGN), France
Mete Celik, Erciyes University, Turkey
Yao-Yi Chiang, Spatial Sciences Institute | University of Southern California, USA
Dickson K.W. Chiu, University of Hong Kong, Hong Kong
Sidonie Christophe, IGN/LaSTIG/COGIT, France
Theodoros Chondrogiannis, University of Konstanz, Germany
Christophe Claramunt, Naval Academy Research Institute, France
Konstantin Clemens, Technical University in Berlin, Germany
Alexandre Corrêa da Silva, HEX Geospatial Technologies, Brazil
Helio Cortes Vieira Lopes, Pontifícia Universidade Católica do Rio de Janeiro, Brazil
Christophe Cruz, Université de Bourgogne, France
Giovanni De Amici, NASA Goddard Space Flight Center, USA
Monica De Martino, Consiglio Nazionale delle Ricerche - Genova, Italy
Vivian de Oliveira Fernandes, Universidade Federal da Bahia - UFBA, Brazil
Anselmo C. de Paiva, Universidade Federal do Maranhão, Brazil
Cláudio de Souza Baptista, Federal University of Campina Grande, Brazil
Mahmoud R. Delavar, University of Tehran, Iran
Sergio Di Martino, Università degli Studi di Napoli 'Federico II', Italy
Jiaxin Ding, Stony Brook University, USA
Jean-Paul Donnay, University of Liege, Belgium
Yerach Doytsher, Technion - Israel Institute of Technology, Haifa, Israel
Suzana Dragicevic, Simon Fraser University, Canada
Olivier Dubois, OSCARS, France
Surya Durbha, Indian Institute of Technology Bombay, India
Emre Eftelioglu, Cargill Inc., USA
Süleyman Eken, Kocaeli University, Turkey
Javier Estornell, Universitat Politècnica de València, Spain
Jamal Ezzahar, Ecole Nationale des Sciences Appliquées | Université Cadi Ayyad, Maroc
Jose Antonio F. de Macedo, Universidade Federal do Ceará, Brazil
Nazli Farajidavar, University of Surrey, UK
Gábor Farkas, University of Pécs, Hungary
Brittany Terese Fasy, Montana State University, USA
Marin Ferecatu, Conservatoire National des Arts et Metiers, France
Paolo Fogliaroni, Vienna University of Technology (TU-Wien), Austria
Cidália C. Fonte, University of Coimbra/INESC Coimbra, Portugal
Michael Foumelis, French Geological Survey (BRGM), France
Jérôme Gensel, Université Grenoble Alpes, France
Alba German, National University of Cordoba / Gulich Institute - Spatial Agency of Argentina (CONAE) / Ministry of Water and Environment, Cordoba, Argentina
Mauro Gaio, LIUPPA - University of Pau, France
Zdravko Galić, University of Zagreb, Croatia
Georg Gartner, Vienna University of Technology, Austria
Birgit Gersbeck-Schierholz, Leibniz Universität Hannover, Germany
Albert Godfrind, Geospatial technologies/Oracle Server Technologies - Sophia Antipolis, France
Flavio Gomez, National University of San Agust́ın, Arequipa, Peru
Enguerran Grandchamp, Université des Antilles – LAMIA, France, Guadeloupe
Carlos Granell Canut, Universitat Jaume I of Castellón, Spain

William Grosky, University of Michigan, USA
Cédric Grueau, Escola Superior de Tecnologia de Setúbal, Portugal
Gheorghi Guzun, San Jose State University, USA
Hatem Halaoui, Haigazian University, Lebanon
Abdeltawab Hendawi, University of Virginia, USA
Stefan Herle, RWTH Aachen University, Germany
Erik Hoel, Esri, USA
Bo Huang, The Chinese University of Hong Kong, Hong Kong
Qunying Huang, University of Wisconsin - Madison, USA
Yan Huang, University of North Texas, USA
Sergio Ilarri, University of Zaragoza, Spain
Xunfei Jiang, Earlham College, USA
Shuanggen Jin, Shanghai Astronomical Observatory, China
Didier Josselin, Université d'Avignon, France
Levente Juhasz, University of Florida, USA
Katerina Kabassi, TEI of Ionian Islands, Greece
Hassan A. Karimi, University of Pittsburgh, USA
Izabela Karsznia, University of Warsaw, Poland
Jean-Paul Kasprzyk, University of Liège, Belgium
Baris M. Kazar, Oracle America Inc., USA
Tahar Kechadi, The Insight Centre for Data Analytics, UK
Shahid Nawaz Khan, Institute of Geographical Information Systems (IGIS) - National University of Sciences and Technology (NUST), Islamabad, Pakistan
Margarita Kokla, National Technical University of Athens, Greece
Mel Krokos, University of Portsmouth, UK
Vineet Kumar, Indian Institue of Technology Bombay, India
Robert Laurini, INSA Lyon | University of Lyon, France
Dan Lee, Esri, USA
Lassi Lehto, Finnish Geospatial Research Institute (FGI) | National Land Survey of Finland, Finland
Ragia Lemonia, Technical University of Crete, Greece
Xian-Xiang Li, Singapore-MIT Alliance for Research and Technology (SMART), Singapore
Thomas Liebig, TU Dortmund University, Germany
Jugurta Lisboa Filho, Universidade Federal de Viçosa, Brazil
Zhi Liu, University of North Texas, USA
Cheng Long, Queen's University Belfast, UK
Qifeng (Luke) Lu, Sapient, USA
Dipankar Mandal, Indian Institute of Technology Bombay, Mumbai, India
Ali Mansourian, Lund University, Sweden
Jesús Martí, Universitat Politècnica de València, Spain
George Mavrommatis, University of Thessaly, Volos / Hellenic Open University, Greece
Abeer Mazhar, CSIRO, Australia
Michael P. McGuire, Towson University, USA
Grant McKenzie, McGill University, Canada
Ludovic Moncla, Naval Academy Research Institute, France
Beniamino Murgante, University of Basilicata, Italy
Ahmed Mustafa, University of Liège, Belgium
Saswata Nandi, Indian Institute of Technology Bombay, Mumbai, India
Aldo Napoli, MINES ParisTech - CRC, France

Gerhard Navratil, Technical University Vienna, Austria
Benjamin Niedermann, Department of Geoinformation/Institute of Geodesy and Geoinformation/University of Bonn, Germany
Lena Noack, Free University of Berlin, Germany
Javier Nogueras-Iso, University of Zaragoza, Spain
Daniel Orellana, Universidad de Cuenca, Ecuador
Marco Painho, NOVA IMS | Universidade Nova de Lisboa, Portugal
Xiao Pan, Shijiazhuang Tiedao University, China
Shray Pathak, IIT Roorkee, India
Kostas Patroumpas, Athena Research Center, Greece
Jian Peng, University of Oxford, UK
Shangfu Peng, University of Maryland, USA
Satish Puri, Marquette University, USA
Viktor Putrenko, World Data Center for Geoinformatics and Sustainable Development | International Council for Science (ICSU) | National Technical University of Ukraine "Igor Sikorsky Kyiv Polytechnic Institute", Ukraine
Lemonia Ragia, Technical University of Crete, Greece
K. S. Rajan, International Institute of Information Technology Gachibowli, India
Chris S. Renschler, University at Buffalo, USA / The University of Tokyo, Japan
Antonio M. Rinaldi, Università degli Studi di Napoli Federico II, Italy
Thomas Ritz, FH Aachen, Germany
Armanda Rodrigues, NOVA LINCS | Universidade NOVA de Lisboa, Portugal
Ricardo Rodrigues Ciferri, Federal University of São Carlos (UFSCar), Brazil
Claus-Peter Rückemann, Westfälische Wilhelms-Universität Münster / Leibniz Universität Hannover / North-German Supercomputing Alliance, Germany
André Sabino, NOVA LINCS | Universidade Nova de Lisboa, Portugal
Ahmed Saidi, Spatial Agency of Algeria - Center of spatial techniques Arzew, Algeria
Timofey Samsonov, Lomonosov Moscow State University, Russia
Markus Schneider, University of Florida, USA
Dennis Schobert, ESA - ESTEC, The Netherlands
Raja Sengupta, McGill University, Canada
Shih-Lung Shaw, University of Tennessee Knoxville, USA
Ingo Simonis, Open Geospatial Consortium (OGC), South Africa
Spiros Skiadopoulos, University of the Peloponnese, Greece
Dimitris Skoutas, Information Management Systems Institute | Research Center "Athena", Greece
Francesco Soldovieri, Istituto per il Rilevamento Elettromagnetico dell'Ambiente - Consiglio Nazionale delle Ricerche (CNR), Italy
Alexandre Sorokine, Oak Ridge National Laboratory, USA
Mudhakar Srivatsa, IBM T. J. Watson Research Center, USA
Cristian Stanciu, University Politehnica of Bucharest, Romania
Katia Stankov, Synodon Inc., Canada
Leon Stenneth, HERE (BMW, Audi, Daimler), USA
Christos Stentoumis, up2metric P.C., Athens, Greece
Kazutoshi Sumiya, Kwansei Gakuin University, Japan
Matei Stroila, HERE Technologies, Chicago, USA
Ruby Y. Tahboub, Purdue University, USA
Muhammad Ali Tahir, Institute of Geographical Information Systems (IGIS) - National University of Sciences and Technology (NUST), Islamabad, Pakistan

Copyright Information

Challenges in Evaluating Methods for Detecting Spatio-Temporal Data Quality Issues in Weather Sensor Data

Douglas E. Galarus
Computer Science Department
Utah State University
Logan, UT 84322-4205, United States
douglas.galarus@usu.edu

Rafal A. Angryk
Department of Computer Science
Georgia State University
Atlanta, GA 30302, United States
angryk@cs.gsu.edu

Abstract—**There is a need for robust solutions to the challenges of near real-time spatio-temporal outlier and anomaly detection. Yet, there are many challenges in developing and evaluating methods including: real-world cost and infeasibility of verifying ground truth, non-isotropic covariance, near-real-time operation, challenges with time, bad data, bad metadata, and other quality factors. In this paper, we demonstrate the challenges of evaluating spatio-temporal data quality methods for weather sensor data via a method we developed and other popular, interpolation-based methods to conduct model-based outlier detection. We demonstrate that a multi-faceted approach is necessary to counteract the impact of outliers. We demonstrate the challenges of evaluation in the presence of incorrect labels of good and bad data.**

Keywords-Data Quality; Spatial-Temporal Data; Quality Control; Outlier; Inlier; Bad Data; Ground Truth

I. INTRODUCTION

In our research, we address near-real-time determination of outliers and anomalies in spatiotemporal weather sensor data, and the implications of quality assessment on computation from the perspective of the data aggregator. Data might not reflect the conditions they measure for a variety of reasons. The challenges go beyond identifying individual outlying observations. A sensor might become "stuck" and produce the same output over an extended period. A sensor's output may conform to other nearby observations and fall within an acceptable range of values, but not reflect actual conditions. A sensor may drift, reporting values further from ground truth over time. A sensor may report correct values, but the associated clock may be incorrect, resulting in bad timestamps. An incorrect location may be associated with a site. These and related problems cause challenges that are far more complex than simple outlier detection.

Sensor-level quality control processes often utilize domain-specific, rule-based systems or general outlier detection techniques to flag "bad" values. NOAA's Meteorological Assimilation Data Ingest System (MADIS) [1] applies the range [-60° F, 130° F] to check for air temperature observations [2] while the University of Utah's MesoWest [3] uses the range [-75° F, 135° F] [4] for validity checks. These ranges are intended to represent the possible air temperature values in real world conditions, at least within the coverage area of the provider. If an observation falls outside the range, then the provider flags that observation as having failed the range test and the observation will, for all practical purposes, be considered "bad". Range tests are not perfect. The record high United States temperature would fail MADIS's range test, although it would pass MesoWest's test. Both MADIS and MesoWest further employ a suite of tests that go beyond their simple range tests. "Buddy" tests compare an observation to neighboring observations. MADIS uses Optimal Interpolation in conjunction with cross-validation to measure the conformity of an observation to its neighbors [2]. MesoWest estimates observations using multivariate linear regression [5]. A real observation is compared to the estimate, and if the deviation is high, then the real observation is flagged as questionable.

These approaches are flawed in that they do not account for bad metadata, such as incorrect timestamps or incorrect locations. They do not account for chronically bad sites which produce bad data including data that may sometimes appear correct. Of even greater concern, they may not do a good job in assessing accuracy and may be incorrectly labeling bad data as good and good data as bad.

The consequences of ignoring data quality are great. How can we trust our applications and models if the inputs are bad? In turn, how can we better assess data for quality so that we can be confident in its use?

In this paper, we present new evaluation results for our previously-published method including evaluation with several new data sets. These results are significant in that they demonstrate the challenges of evaluation of methods for data quality assessment of spatio-temporal weather sensor data. The rest of this paper is organized as follows: Section II presents relevant literature, Section III identifies general challenges, Section IV defines our approach, Section V documents evaluation results, and Sections VI gives our conclusion.

II. LITERATURE REVIEW

The data mining process includes data preprocessing and cleaning as critical components. Outlier analysis, is addressed within these headings by Han, et al. [6], and the impact of outliers is covered by Nisbet, et al. [7]. Robust regression techniques are employed in data mining to overcome outliers and low quality data in the process of data cleaning by Witten, et al. [8]. The handling of errors and missing values is presented by Steinbach and Kumar [9], along with quality attributes, such as accuracy and precision, as well as the adverse impact that outliers, can have on clustering algorithms. Such examples demonstrate the chicken-egg nature of the problem in which a method used to identify outliers is adversely impacted by outliers.

Aggarwal [10] presents a number of useful, general observations: Correlation across time series can help to identify outliers, using one or multiple series to predict another. Deviations between predicted and actual values can then be used to identify outliers. When used on temporal snapshots of data, spatial methods can fall short because they do not address the time component. Decoupling the spatial and temporal aspects can be suboptimal. Neighborhoods can be used to make predictions, yet it is a challenge to combine spatial and temporal dimensions in a meaningful way. Domain-specific methods can be used to filter noise, but such filtering can mask anomalies in the data.

Shekhar, et al. [11] present a unified approach for detecting spatial outliers and a general definition for spatial outliers, but they do not address the spatio-temporal situation. Klein, et al. [12]–[16] present work on transfer and management challenges related to the inclusion of quality control information in data streams and develop optimal, quality-based load-shedding for data streams in. A missing component is the spatial aspect.

The weather and road-weather communities employ detailed accuracy checks for individual observations. The Oklahoma Mesonet uses the Barnes Spatial Test [17], a variation of Inverse Distance Weighting (IDW) (see Shepard [18]). MesoWest [3] uses multivariate linear regression to assess data quality for air temperature, as described by Splitt and Horel in [19] and [20]. MADIS [1] implements multi-level, rule-based quality control checks including a level-3 neighbor check using Optimal Interpolation / kriging [2][21][22]. These approaches (IDW, Linear Regression, kriging) can be used to check individual observations for deviation from predicted and flag individual observations as erroneous or questionable if the deviation is *large*. But if interpolated values are erroneous, then the quality assessment will be bad too. If metadata, such as location or timestamps associated with a site, is erroneous, then the quality control assessment may be bad because of comparison with the wrong data from the wrong sites. None of these approaches identify incorrect location metadata and one provider, Mesowest, attempts to identify bad timestamps, yet their approach only identifies one of the most obvious timestamp-related problem – timestamps that cannot possibly be correct because they occur in the future relative to collection time.

Many spatial approaches use interpolation for quality assessment, so it is useful to examine work that compares and enhances traditional interpolation methods. Zimmerman, et al. [23] use artificial surfaces and sampling techniques, as well as noise level and strength of correlation, to compare Ordinary kriging (OK) and Universal kriging (kriging with a trend) (UK) and IDW. They found that the kriging methods outperformed IDW across all variations they examined. Lu and Wong [24] found instances in which kriging performed worse than their modified version of IDW, where they vary the exponent depending on the neighborhood. They indicate that kriging would be favored in situations for which a variogram accurately reflects the spatial structure. Mueller, et al. [25] show similar results, saying that IDW is a better choice than OK in the absence of semi-variograms to indicate spatial structure.

In prior work, we proposed a modification of IDW that used a data-based distance rather than geographic distance to assess observation quality [26][27]. That work focused on the use of robust methods to associate sites for assessment of individual observations. In [28][29][30], we extended the mappings to better account for spatio-temporal variation and observation time differences when assessing observations. In [31] and [32], we developed quality measures that extended beyond sites, to help evaluate overall spatial and temporal coverage of a region.

IDW is widely applied, including applications which involve outlier detection and mitigation. Xie, et al. [33] applied it to surface reconstruction, in which they detect outliers using distance from fitted surfaces. Others extend the method in different ways including added dimensions, particularly time. Li, et al. extend IDW in [34] to include the time dimension in their application involving estimated exposure to fine particulate matter. Grieser warns of problems with arbitrarily large weights when sites are near in analyzing monthly rain gauge observations [35], and mitigates the problem in a manner that Shepard originally used by defining a neighborhood for which included points are averaged with identical weights in place of the large, inverse distance weights.

Kriging and Optimal Interpolation were developed separately and simultaneously as spatial best linear unbiased predictors (blups) that are for practical purposes equivalent. L. S. Gandin, a meteorologist, developed and published optimal interpolation in the Soviet Union in 1963. Georges Matheron, a French geologist and mathematician, developed and published kriging in 1962, named for a South African mining engineer, Danie Krige, who partially developed the technique in 1951 and later in 1962. For further information, refer to Cressie [36].

Kriging is easily impacted by multiple data quality dimensions and its applicability is hindered unless data quality issues in the inputs are addressed. Kriging will downweight observations that are clustered in direction, as indicated by Wackernagel, et al. [37]. This may be beneficial. However, a near observation can also shadow far observations in the same direction, causing them to have small or even negative weights. This is problematic in the case that the near observation is bad.

Kriging is typically used to interpolate values at locations for which measurements are unknown using observations from known locations. As such, covariance is typically estimated. This estimate usually takes the form of a function of distance alone and is determined by the data set. A principal critique of kriging is that while it does produce optimal results when the covariance structure is known, the motivation for using kriging is questionable when the covariance structure must be estimated. Handcock and Stein [38] make such an argument. Another critique is that kriging will yield a model that matches data input to the model, giving the (false) impression that the model is perfect, as stated by Hunter, et al. [39].

Unfortunately, none of these approaches alone directly addresses outlier and anomaly detection for spatio-temporal data in a robust and comprehensive manner that meets our needs. None identify bad sites and metadata in a comprehensive manner. However, the data quality attributes presented are of some benefit and the methods used by the weather data providers appear to be state of the art for assessment of accuracy.

III. CHALLENGES

Our research involves (fixed) site-based, spatio-temporal sensor big data, acquired and evaluated for data quality with real-time potential. There are many computational challenges associated with our problem. We focus subsequent evaluation on scalability and accuracy.

Scalability. Our data sets include thousands of sites, with potential to expand to tens of thousands of sites. Sites have varying reporting frequencies ranging from every minute to hourly or longer. These sites collectively generate millions of observations daily. We desire to run our algorithms in near real-time, and scalability is key to achieving this goal.

Accuracy. The underlying data has many data quality challenges. Accurately modeling the data is challenging, because the modeled data will inherently include errors. We desire robust, accurate models that can be used to assess the quality of individual observations.

There are many indirect issues causing challenges that must be overcome. These all influence or are influenced by computation in one way or another.

Real-World Cost and Infeasibility of Verifying Ground Truth. Agencies cannot verify ground truth on a regular basis across hundreds or thousands of sites. Human-required resolution processes can be focused if problems are identified automatically. Third-party data aggregators have no control over original data quality. Assessment of quality is essential for use.

Non-Isotropic Covariance. Distance cannot be treated equally in all dimensions nor in all directions. There are differences between the time dimension and spatial dimensions. Elevation, proximity to the ocean, terrain, microclimates, prevailing weather patterns, the diurnal effect, seasonal change, etc. also cause differences in covariance.

Near-Real-Time Operation. We intend for our processes to run in near-real-time when observations are acquired. We store and use only the most recent observations for near real-time presentation and comparison. We do not intend to store third-party historical data on our production systems. This does not preclude the potential for offline preprocessing and analysis that makes use of historical data. Even if providers apply their own quality control measures, near-real-time operation may require us to use observations that have not been fully quality-checked.

Further Challenges with Time. Sites report observations at discrete times resulting in granularity and non-uniformity. Observation frequencies and reporting times vary across sites. Network latency and batch processing further disrupt timeliness.

"Bad" Data. Bad data includes but is not limited to erroneous observation data – individual observations that differ from ground truth; "bad" sites – sites that chronically produce erroneous data; and "bad" metadata including incorrect locations and/or incorrect timestamps. Bad data may include items that are not individually considered outliers.

Other Quality Factors. There are many other quality factors including reliability (site, sensor, communication network), timeliness of data, imprecision of data, and imprecision of metadata.

IV. DEFINITIONS AND APPROACH

A. General Definitions

An individual site refers to a fixed-location facility that houses one or multiple sensors that measure conditions. A measurement and associated metadata are referred to as an observation. The set of all sites, represented by S, is the set of sites for which observations are available for a time period and geographic area of interest.

An observation, obs, is represented as a 4-tuple, $obs = \langle s, t, l, v\rangle = \langle obs_s, obs_t, obs_l, obs_v\rangle$ consisting of the site/sensor s, timestamp t, location l (spatial coordinates), and an observed value v. We investigate observations from a single sensor type, so we assume that s identifies both the site and sensor. The set of all observations, represented by O, consists of observations from sites in S over a time-period of interest.

Ground-truth is the exact value of the condition that a given sensor is intended to measure at a given location and time. Ground-truth will rarely be known because of sensor error, estimation error, and high human costs, among other reasons. Human cost is a huge challenge, with agencies struggling to accurately inventory assets and technicians unable to service and maintain all equipment, including situations where they may not even be able to find the equipment.

We wish to evaluate observations to determine if they are erroneous. To do so, we compare observations to estimates of ground-truth. For our purposes, these estimates will be determined via interpolation, which is commonly used in the GIS community, as well as in the weather and road-weather communities.

B. Approach

Identification of Outlyingness and Outliers. We measure outlyingness as the absolute deviation between an observed value and ground truth. Ground truth may not be known, so we estimate outlyingness as the absolute deviation between an observation and modeled ground truth corresponding to the observed value in time and location. Given the degree of outlyingess (exact or estimated), we identify outliers using a threshold. If the degree of outlyingness for an observation meets or exceeds the threshold, then we flag the observation as an outlier. Otherwise, we flag it as an inlier. The degree of outlyingness is more informative than an outlier/inlier label.

Our approach is consistent with general model-based approaches for outlier detection found in Han, et al. [6], Tan, Steinbach and Kumar [9] and Aggarwal [10], and follows the general data-mining framework of Train, Test and Evaluate.

C. *Interpolation to Model Ground Truth*

IDW estimates ground truth as the weighted average of observation values using (geographic) distance from the site for which an observation is to be estimated as the weight, raised to some exponent h. If ground truth is known, a suitable exponent h can be determined to minimize error. Isaaks and Srivastava [40] indicate that if $h=0$, then the estimate becomes a simple average of all observations, and for large values of h, the estimate tends to the nearest neighboring observation(s). This simple version of IDW does not account for time, so it is assumed that observations fall in temporal proximity.

Least Squares Regression (LSR) estimates observed values using the coordinates of the sites. We only use *x-y* coordinates in our experiments for LSR. There could be benefit in using elevation and other variables including time. However, doing so compounds problems related to bad metadata, such as incorrect locations, bad timestamps and inaccurate elevations.

UK estimates observed values using the covariance between sites, the coordinates of the sites, and the observed values. In our experiments, we used a Gaussian covariance function of distance and estimated the related parameters to minimize error relative to ground-truth for our training data using data from the present time window. Refer to Huijbregts and Matheron [41] for further information on UK. We implemented a fitter/solver for the estimation of the covariance function parameters using the Gnu Scientific Library (GSL) non-linear optimization code [42]. Refer to Bohling [43] for additional covariance functions.

These methods can be applied using a restricted radius or a bounding box to alleviate computational challenges and to focus on local trends. Other interpolators could be applied in a similar manner. There are obvious risks in using interpolators. Outliers and erroneous values will have an adverse impact on interpolation, causing poor estimates. Lack of data in proximity to a point to be estimated can also result in a poor estimate. For these reasons, we developed our own robust interpolator in prior work.

D. *Our SMART Approach*

In prior work, we developed a representative approach for data quality assessment of site-based, spatio-temporal data using what we call Simple Mappings for Approximation and Regression of Time series (SMART) [26-32]. We used the SMART mappings to identify bad (inaccurate) observations and "bad" sites/sensors, so that they can be excluded from display and computation, and to subsequently estimate (interpolate) ground truth.

Site-to-Site Mappings. Let an observation be represented as $obs = \{(t, v): t = time, v = value\}$, pairing the value with the reported time. Let obs_i be the set of observations from site i and obs_j be the set of observations from site j. For a given time radius r we pair the observations from sites i and j as $obs_{pairs_{i,j}} = \{(x, y): (t_1, x) \in obs_i, (t_2, y) \in obs_j, |t_2 - t_1| \leq r\}$. We then define a site-to-site mapping l as a linear function of the x-coordinate (the observed value from site i) of the paired observations $obs\_pairs_{i,j}$: $l_{i,j}(x) = a + bx$. We determine this function to minimize the squared error between the values of the function and the y-coordinates (the observed values from site j) for the paired observations.

We next determine a quadratic estimate q of the squared error of the linear mapping relative to the time offset between the paired observations. We expect an increased squared error for increased time differences. This model estimates the squared error and accounts for time offsets between observations. Our method does not require a complex, data-specific covariance model.

These simple mappings are the core elements of our approach, and we must overcome the potential impact of the erroneous data in determining them. LSR suffers from sensitivity to outliers. We use the method from Rousseeuw and Van Driessen to perform Least Trimmed Squares Regression [44]. Least Trimmed Squares determines the least squares fit to a subset of the original data by iteratively removing data furthest from the fit. Before applying least trimmed squares to determine the linear mapping, we select the percentage of data that will be trimmed. We can interpret the trim percentage either as our willingness to accept bad data in our models or our estimate of how much data is bad. We used a trim percentage of 0.1 throughout.

For the quadratic error mappings, we experienced problems with local minima when attempting quadratic least trimmed squares. Instead we group data into intervals, determine the trimmed mean for each group, and then compute the least squares quadratic fit for the (*time difference, trimmed mean*) pairs.

We then check the coefficients and derived measures of the linear and quadratic mappings for outlying values relative to all other mappings. If we find outlying values, we flag the mapping as unusable. For instance, if the axis of symmetry of the quadratic error mapping is an outlier relative to that for another pairing, then there may be a problem with the timestamps of at least one of the two sites.

SMART Interpolator. Our SMART interpolator uses these mappings. Formally: Let S be the set of all sites. Let $s \in S$ be a site for which we are evaluating observations. Let $\langle s_1, \ldots, s_n | s_i \in S, s_i \neq s \rangle$ be the set of sites other than site s. We want to estimate $obs_s(t_s)$, the value of the observation at site s at time t_s using the most recent observations from the other sites relative to time t: (t_i, v_i).

Our SMART interpolator is like IDW, using our quadratic error estimates instead of distance given the time lag between observations and using our SMART linear mappings to yield estimated ground truth producing an estimate. Neither distance nor direction are directly used. The linear mappings and quadratic error estimates account for similarity between sites. No attempt is made to down-weight clustered sites, although there may be benefit in doing so.

We determine the exponent g by minimizing error relative to ground truth, if available, or estimated ground truth. Prior to computing the weighted estimate, we examine the weights and, if necessary, "re-balance" to reduce the potential influence of single sites on the outcome. We found it useful to restrict the maximum relative weight a site can be given to 0.25 to reduce the risk that a bad value from one site will overly influence the resulting average. Rather than take a simple weighted average, we use a trimmed mean to further reduce the influence of outliers.

E. Artificial Data Set

We developed a weather-like phenomenon representing temperature as approximate fractal surfaces produced using the method of Successive Random Addition. For further information on Successive Random Addition, refer to Voss [45], Feder [46], and Barnsley, et al. [47]. Fractional Brownian processes were used by Goodchild and Gopal to generate random fields representing mean annual temperature and annual precipitation for the purpose of investigating error in [48]. We used a similar approach to model time series in [49]. A 513x513 approximate fractal surface, $surface(x,y)$, was generated with Hurst Exponent H=0.7 and $\sigma^2 = 1.0$, representing elevation. A 1025x513x513 fractal-like weather pattern, $weather(x,y,t)$, was also generated with Hurst Exponent H=0.7 and $\sigma^2 = 1.0$. The larger x-coordinate allowed us to simulate motion/flow. We generated one surface and eight weather patterns, allowing us to train on one weather pattern and test on those remaining.

We generated time series of "ground truth" data by combining the surface data with the weather data, a periodic effect and a north-south effect to simulate a weather-like phenomenon like the diurnal effect and general north-south variation in the Northern Hemisphere respectively. We added the weather data as is, with varying offsets in the x-coordinate to represent a west to east flow in the weather pattern. The surface value is subtracted so that low points are "warmer" than high points. The periodic effect represents warming during the day and cooling at night. The north-south effect yields warmer points to the south and cooler points to the "north". Our approach yields a time series of length n=513 for each (x, y) on the 513x513 surface.

We selected 250 "sites" using random uniform x-y (spatial) coordinates. For each site we assigned a reporting pattern with a random frequency and offset. We added errors to the observations from 25 sites via: random noise added to ground truth (NOISE), rounding of ground truth (ROUNDING), replacement of ground truth with a constant value (CONSTANT), replacement with random bad values with varying probabilities (RANDOMBAD), or negation of ground truth. The remaining 225 sites were left error-free.

V. EVALUATION

We evaluated the performance of the various interpolators including our SMART Method in-depth, in terms of computation and ability to identify bad data. We compared our SMART method, IDW, LSR, UK and OK. We measured performance and scalability using run-time in milliseconds. We measured accuracy using mean-squared-error (MSE) between estimated and known ground-truth. We compared means using t-tests when multiple runs were available. We used Area Under the ROC Curve (AUROC) analysis to evaluate accuracy of outlier classification given varying "threshold" values for outlier/inlier determination.

We analyzed our artificial data set, MADIS air temperature for Northern California from December 2015, MADIS air temperature for Montana from January 2017, and Average Daily USGS Streamflow for Montana from 2015, 2016, 2017.

A. Evaluation Using our Artificial Data Set

We performed an in-depth comparison of the various algorithms using our artificial data set. We enhanced the standard algorithms by randomly choosing neighboring sites using set inclusion percentages (0.1, 0.2, 0.3, ..., 0.9, 1.0). For instance, a 0.9 inclusion percentage corresponds to selecting neighboring sites individually with 0.9 inclusion / 0.1 exclusion probability. We varied the radius (50, 75, 100, ..., 175, 200) over which sites were included relative to the location of the site whose observation we were testing. We repeated this procedure 10 times for each parameter combination (inclusion percent and radius) and used the median of the resulting estimates as the estimate for that parameter combination. By randomly holding out sites, bad data will be held out in some of the resulting combinations. By taking the median of the results, we eliminate the extreme estimates, particularly those impacted by bad data, and ideally determine a robust estimate.

We ran the methods in aggregate over the eight time periods spanning 512 time units. For each time period, there are 37,293 observations total from the 250 sites. We iterated through the observations in order by time and estimated ground truth for each observation as if computing in real time as the observations become known. Only observations that occurred at the same time as or prior to each observation were used for prediction, simulating real-time operation of the system. We averaged the MSE and run time for each configuration (inclusion radius and inclusion percent). We compared the results of the various runs of the methods. The run time for the SMART method was 6336.6 ms, and the MSE was 0.1026. The SMART method was comparable in run time to IDW, but the accuracy achieved was far better than for any of the other methods.

We measured the ability of each method to distinguish increasing percentages of the bad data from good data using an AUROC analysis. True outliers were defined as data that differs from ground-truth – i.e., data that was modified to be erroneous. Predicted outliers were data that differed from estimated ground truth by a given threshold. We varied thresholds for outlier/inlier cutoffs and compared results with the actual labels identifying whether the data was truly an outlier or inlier. The AUROC (area under the ROC curve) values are shown in Table I. The AUROC values show better discriminative power for the SMART method versus the other methods. No method will be perfect in identifying all errors. Some errors are small and impossible to distinguish from interpolation error. Known ground truth and known error from ground truth yields perfect labels.

TABLE I. AUROC VALUES FOR ARTIFICIAL DATASET

Method	SMART	UK	LSR	IDW
AUROC	0.827	0.740	0.739	0.708

Our SMART method's computation time is comparable to IDW and is far better than LSR and UK, but we still should account for the preprocessing computation time required for determining the linear mappings and quadratic error functions. The overall amount of preprocessing time required to determine the linear mappings and quadratic error functions was comparable to run time required for UK. This was encouraging. Generation of the mappings will be done as an offline, batch process, so the observed time required is still within reason to help facilitate the faster and more accurate, online process. Additional benefits, such as identification of bad sites and bad metadata, come from these mappings, further justifying the effort required. Optimization can reduce the overall time needed to compute the mappings. The benefits and potential to improve the run time outweigh the amount of required preprocessing time.

B. December 2015 MADIS California Data

We analyzed Northern California December 2015 ambient air temperature data from the MADIS Mesonet subset. We used a bounding box defined by $38.5° \leq latitude \leq 42.5°$ and $-124.5° \leq longitude \leq -119.5°$, yielding 888 sites. We excluded observations that failed the MADIS Level 1 Quality Control Check. This range check restricts observations in degrees Fahrenheit to the interval [-60°F,130°F]. Many values failing this check fall far outside the range and can have a dramatic impact on the interpolation methods. Our SMART method performs very well in the presence of extreme bad data, and it would have easily out-performed the other methods in the presence of the range-check failed data.

There were over 2 million observations. MADIS flagged 73.5% of these observations as "verified" / V, slightly less than 4% as "questioned" / Q, and 22.5% as "screened" / S, indicating that it had passed the MADIS Level 1 and Level 2 quality checks, but that the Level 3 quality checks had not been applied.

Training. Verified (V) observations from the first week in December 2015 were used to train all methods, including our SMART method. In the absence of range-failed data, the "enhanced" (iterated subset) versions of the other algorithms showed little improvement in accuracy while consuming excessive computation time, particularly "enhanced" UK. In some cases, it would have taken days to compute results. Because of this, we used the methods directly, without enhancement. We also tested OK (refer to Bailey and Gatrell [50] for further information). Since we do not know "ground truth" for this data, the verified data is the closest to ground truth. We trained all methods on this data to MSE of predicted versus actual. We used a 50-mile inclusion radius due to the density of sites to avoid excessive computation time for the kriging approaches.

The SMART mapping coefficients and derived values were examined for outliers, and ranges were determined for valid mappings. If any coefficient or derived value for a given SMART mapping fell outside these ranges, then the SMART mapping was considered bad, and that mapping was not used for predictions.

Our SMART method produced significantly better results than all other methods for the training data in terms of estimation of ground truth measured by MSE, as shown in Table II. A paired, one-sided t-test was used for significance testing using paired squared errors from predicted values. Only the verified (V) data was used in this comparison since it best approximates ground truth. The SMART method was compared pairwise with the other methods and results were aggregated over instances where both methods produced predictions.

TABLE II. MSE FOR MADIS CALIFORNIA TRAINING DATA

Method	**MSE**	**Method**	**MSE**
SMART	2.8322	IDW	7.6212
SMART	2.8322	LSR	17.1446
SMART	2.8046	OK	18.4989
SMART	2.8046	UK	16.5289

Testing. Testing was conducted using all data from the entire month of December 2015, minus the range-check-failed data. We computed the MSE for the verified (V) data since it best represents ground truth, but all observations were used in making estimates. The testing results indicate the robustness of methods in the presence of bad data. In comparisons across all other methods, the SMART method significantly out-performed all other methods in terms of MSE, as shown in Table III.

TABLE III. MSE FOR MADIS CALIFORNIA TESTING DATA

Method	**MSE**	**Method**	**MSE**
SMART	4.4611	IDW	9.1306
SMART	4.4611	LSR	16.5223
SMART	4.3360	OK	16.0868
SMART	4.3360	UK	14.2086

We conducted an AUROC analysis to compare classification ability of the methods based on the MADIS quality control flags. We considered the following flags from MADIS to be good/inlier data: V/verified, S/screened, good. The Q/questioned, was treated as bad/outlier data. Recall that we excluded the observations having a QC flag of X, those that failed the range test, from our evaluation. Even if we accept the MADIS quality control flags as being correct, and we do not, this approach is problematic. The MADIS QC flag S corresponds to data for which not all the QC checks have been run. While this data had not failed any quality control checks that have been applied, it possibly would have failed the higher-level checks.

TABLE IV. AUROC FOR MADIS CALIFORNIA TESTING DATA

	AUROC
IDW	0.7906
LSR	0.7578
SMART	0.7317
OK	0.6458
UK	0.6062

In terms of AUROC, IDW, LSR and SMART were comparable, with IDW finishing slightly ahead, as shown in Table IV. While these AUROC values seem reasonable, they are affected by incorrect outlier/inlier labels, and our SMART method suffers the greatest impact because the distance-based methods approximate the MADIS Level 3 quality control check. OK and UK fall short because they fail to make predictions for many observations.

C. *December 2017 MADIS Montana Data*

We investigated ambient air temperature for Western Montana / Northern Idaho from the MADIS Mesonet and the MADIS HFMetar subset in January 2017. We added the HFMetar data set to account for aviation AWOS/ASOS sites that had previously been included in the Mesonet data set. We used a bounding box defined by $44° \leq latitude \leq 49°$ and $-116° \leq longitude \leq -110°$, resulting in observations from 497 sites. This bounding box is comparable in size to the one used for Northern California, although the density of sites is less. We excluded observations that failed the MADIS Level 1 Quality Control Check.

All total there were over 1 million observations. MADIS flagged 71.2% of these observations as "verified" / V; 10.3% of as "screened" / S, indicating that they had passed the MADIS Level 1 and Level 2 quality checks, but that the Level 3 quality checks had not been applied; and a relatively large 18.5% of the data as "questioned" / Q. This is over four times the percentage of questioned data as there was for the California data set.

Training. Verified (V) observations from the first week in January 2017 were used to train all methods, including our SMART method. We used a 100-mile inclusion radius due to a low density of the Montana/Idaho sites. The SMART mapping coefficients and derived values were examined for outliers, and bad mappings were identified as any mapping associated with such values. The quality of the mappings as measured by MSE was noticeably less than that for the Northern California data set. We found problems with many of the timestamps in this data set. Recognizing that much of the Idaho data comes from the Pacific Time Zone while the Montana data comes from the Mountain Time Zone, there appeared to be many sites for which the conversion to UTC time was not consistent. The Northern California data all falls within Pacific Time, and we did not see this problem in that data set. In terms of MSE, the SMART method produced significantly better results than each of the other methods for the training data, as shown in Table V.

TABLE V. MSE FOR MADIS MONTANA TRAINING DATA

Method	MSE	Method	MSE
SMART	8.1513	IDW	16.7217
SMART	8.1513	LSR	29.8039
SMART	10.6726	OK	47.0028
SMART	10.6726	UK	33.9863

Testing. Testing was conducted using data from the remainder of January 2017. All data was used for this test except for the observations that failed the MADIS Level 1 range test. The SMART method significantly outperformed all other methods in terms of MSE, as shown in Table VI.

TABLE VI. MSE FOR MADIS MONTANA TESTING DATA

Method	MSE	Method	MSE
SMART	21.4714	IDW	38.3208
SMART	21.4714	LSR	38.5063
SMART	23.1496	OK	50.5078
SMART	23.1496	UK	36.6762

We conducted an AUROC analysis to test classification ability based on the MADIS quality control flags in the same way as described for the Northern California data set in the previous section. As noted in that section, many of the MADIS QC flags are incorrect. In terms of Area Under the ROC curve, LSR, IDW and SMART were comparable, with LSR finishing ahead, as shown in Table VII. These AUROC values are less than those for the Northern California data set at least in part because all methods adversely affected by incorrect outlier/inlier labels.

TABLE VII. AUROC FOR MADIS MONTANA TESTING DATA

Method	LSR	IDW	SMART	OK	UK
AUROC	0.6900	0.6697	0.6393	0.5432	0.5476

This data set includes a large percentage of observations (18.5%) that are flagged as "questionable" by MADIS. These were considered "bad" / outliers for the purposes of our analysis. It also includes a large percentage (10.3%) that are flagged as "screened" by MADIS, indicating that not all QC checks have been conducted. These are considered "good" / inliers for our analysis.

There were many observations flagged as "questionable" / outliers in the HFMetar subset that should have been flagged as "good" / inliers. This data alone accounts for most of the questionable data in the data set. Aviation weather sites are well-maintained and regularly calibrated, so it is hard to believe that these sites would produce data that is entirely bad. We checked this data against predicted values, as well as neighboring sites, and it was very close, so it is unclear why the data was labeled as questionable.

Numerous sites were flagged by our SMART method as "bad" and all observations from those sites were labeled as bad. MADIS flagged some observations from these sites as good when they were close to predicted values. In some cases, this may have been reasonable, but in others it was a random occurrence. There were some sites that produced bad data for the training period but then produced good data for at least a portion of the test period. One could argue that for such sites all associated observations should be questioned. If a site was identified as bad by the SMART method, then the V and S observations would adversely impact the SMART method in the AUROC analysis. The chance situations in which the other methods came close to the "good" values and far from the "bad" values improved their performance.

D. December 2015-2017 USGS Streamflow Data

Mean daily streamflow (ft^3/sec) was downloaded for all sites in Montana from the USGS [51] for every day from January 1st, 2015 through April 24th, 2017. There were 145 sites having data than spanned this period, and these sites were analyzed. This data set is far different from the air temperature data used for prior analysis. Since daily averages were used, there is no visible diurnal effect. There is a seasonal effect which varies with elevation and location relative to watersheds. Due to the dramatic fluctuations that occur in this data during times of peak runoff, the base-10 logarithm of the data was used for analysis.

This data set includes quality flags. Daily values are flagged as "A", approved for publication, and "P", provisional and subject to revision. Values may further be flagged as "e" for estimated. Values transition from provisional to approved after more extensive testing is conducted, so provisional values aren't necessarily bad. These flags were of limited use to us and we did not use them for analysis. We treated the data as being all good and subsequently introduced errors into some of the observations, making them known bad. There were 122,380 total observations.

Training. All data from 2015 was used to train all methods, including our SMART method. We assume this data, which was mostly "approved", to be ground truth. We trained over this data to minimize MSE of predicted versus actual. We used a 200-mile inclusion radius. The SMART mapping coefficients and derived values were examined for outliers. If any coefficient or derived value for a given SMART mapping was an outlier, then the SMART mapping was considered bad, and it wasn't used for predictions. In terms of MSE, the SMART method produced significantly better results than the other methods for the training data, as shown in Table VIII.

TABLE VIII. MSE FOR USGS TRAINING DATA

Method	MSE	Method	MSE
SMART	0.0174	IDW	0.8751
SMART	0.0174	LSR	0.9611
SMART	0.0174	OK	0.9431
SMART	0.0174	UK	0.9617

Testing. Testing was conducted using the 2016-2017 data. The SMART method significantly out-performed all other methods in terms of MSE, as shown in Table IX.

TABLE IX. MSE FOR USGS TESTING DATA (NO ERRORS)

Method	MSE	Method	MSE
SMART	0.0429	IDW	0.9031
SMART	0.0429	LSR	0.9869
SMART	0.0429	OK	0.9755
SMART	0.0429	UK	0.9874

Testing was then conducted using the 2016-2017 data, with errors introduced into 10% of the observations. A random normal value with mean zero and standard deviation one was added to each of the observations in the 10% group. The MSE was computed relative to the known, original observations which represent ground truth, and all observations (including bad observations) were used in making estimates. The testing results help to indicate the robustness of methods in the presence of bad data. The SMART method significantly out-performed all other methods in terms of MSE, as shown in Table X.

TABLE X. MSE FOR USGS TESTING DATA (WITH ERRORS)

Method	MSE	Method	MSE
SMART	0.0453	IDW	0.9103
SMART	0.0453	LSR	0.9907
SMART	0.0453	OK	0.9776
SMART	0.0453	UK	0.9914

We conducted an AUROC analysis to test the methods on classification ability based on whether observations had been altered to be erroneous by our process of randomly selecting 10% of the observations and adding a normal random variable with mean 0 and standard deviation 1 to those observations. The altered observations were labeled "bad"/outlier and the unaltered observations were labeled as "good"/inlier. Our SMART method performed far better than all the other methods, achieving an AUROC value of 0.8722, as shown in Table XI. The other methods had values between 0.6 and 0.63.

TABLE XI. AUROC VALUES FOR USGS TESTING DATA

Method	SMART	IDW	OK	UK	LSR
AUROC	0.8722	0.6241	0.6136	0.6046	0.6031

E. Evaluation Summary

For all four data sets and for every training and testing instance compared, our SMART method performed significantly better in terms of accuracy (MSE) than all other methods. Its computational performance was competitive even though no effort was made to optimize it. For the two MADIS data sets, its performance for AUROC analysis of classification and discrimination capability showed it to be competitive with the best of the other methods. This comparison and evaluation made use of MADIS data quality labels for which we have found numerous problems. As such, all methods underperformed, and the SMART method was penalized most by mislabeling. For the other two data sets (artificial and USGS) in which ground truth is known or assumed and errors were introduced relative to ground truth, the SMART method outperformed the other methods by a wide margin. This further supports our assertions regarding the impact of bad labels on the MADIS data, and the need for better methods and benchmark data sets for data quality assessment.

OK and UK both failed to produce estimates for many observations, likely due to singular matrices. They were not competitive in terms of run time and their accuracy was no better than the other methods. UK and LSR are prone to occasional very large errors if the predicted surface slopes in an extreme manner.

Our SMART method identifies "bad sites" that chronically produce bad data, and does not use data from these sites in estimating ground truth for other sites. Similarly, data from these "bad sites" is labeled as all bad. The SMART method falls short in cases where a site exhibits chronic behavior during training but recovers to produce good data during a testing period.

The USGS streamflow data exhibits correlation between sites, but the correlation corresponds to sites close to each other and in the same river/stream. Correlation will not necessarily be high for sites that are close but in different rivers. For rivers that have dams and other features that may influence streamflow in unusual ways, sensors will be correlated on each side of such features, but not as much on opposite sites, and certainly not as much with sites on rivers that do not have similar features.

The SMART method identifies like sites, yielding better correlations. IDW and LSR will not perform well in this circumstance. And, the kriging methods will not perform well either if a stationary, isotropic covariance function is used. Such an assumption is typical, and we used this assumption in determining the covariance matrices for the kriging tests.

VI. CONCLUSION

While our SMART method out-performed the other methods in nearly all instances, it was not our intent present it as the "best" method. Instead, we present it as representative of the type of approach needed to overcome challenges of spatio-temporal data quality assessment.

It makes no assumption of isotropic covariance and does not require the determination of a specific covariance function. While it requires preprocessing time, it is suitable for near-real-time, online use. It accounts for disparate reporting times and frequency of reporting across sites. It not only helps to identify "bad data", but it also works well in the presence of bad data. It helps to identify and mitigate erroneous observations, "bad sites", and bad metadata. It uses multiple, robust methods to mitigate the impact of bad data on its estimates. Other methods, such as LSR and the various kriging approaches, could (and should) be modified in s similar manner to produce better, more robust results. Further, it is important to recognize the impact of bad data quality labels on evaluation. It is necessary to develop and use benchmark datasets with known, correct data quality labels.

In this research, we investigated relatively simple situations and data sets involving ambient air temperature. We intend to expand our work to further examine other measures including wind and precipitation, as well as CCTV camera images. Departments of Transportation use CCTV camera images to verify road weather conditions reported by sensors. Yet, these images also suffer from poor data quality. Further research is needed to develop methods for detecting bad CCTV image data and for using CCTV image data to confirm sensor conditions and vice-versa. We intend to further develop benchmark datasets with known, good data quality labels.

REFERENCES

[1] NOAA, "Meteorological Assimilation Data Ingest System (MADIS)." [Online]. http://madis.ncep.noaa.gov/. [Accessed: 15-Dec-2018].

[2] NOAA, "MADIS Meteorological Surface Quality Control." [Online]. https://madis.ncep.noaa.gov/madis_sfc_qc.shtml. [Accessed: 15-Dec-2018].

[3] U. of Utah, "MesoWest Data." [Online]. http://mesowest.utah.edu/. [Accessed: 15-Dec-2018].

[4] U. of Utah, "MesoWest Data Variables." [Online]. http://mesowest.utah.edu/cgi-bin/droman/variable_select.cgi. [Accessed: 26-Dec-2015].

[5] M. E. Splitt and J. D. Horel, "Use of multivariate linear regression for meteorological data analysis and quality assessment in complex terrain," in *Preprints, 10th Symp. on Meteorological Observations and Instrumentation, Phoenix, AZ, Amer. Meteor. Soc*, 1998, pp. 359–362.

[6] J. Han, J. Pei, and M. Kamber, *Data mining: concepts and techniques*. Elsevier, 2011.

[7] R. Nisbet, G. Miner, and J. Elder IV, *Handbook of statistical analysis and data mining applications*. Academic Press, 2009.

[8] I. H. Witten, E. Frank, M. A. Hall, and C. J. Pal, *Data Mining: Practical machine learning tools and techniques*. Morgan Kaufmann, 2016.

[9] P.-N. Tan, M. Steinbach, and V. Kumar, *Introduction to data mining*. Pearson Education, Inc., 2006.

[10] C. C. Aggarwal, *Outlier Analysis*. Springer Publishing Company, Incorporated, 2013.

[11] S. Shekhar, C. T. Lu, and P. Zhang, "A unified approach to detecting spatial outliers," *Geoinformatica*, vol. 7, no. 2, pp. 139–166, 2003.

[12] A. Klein and W. Lehner, "Representing Data Quality in Sensor Data Streaming Environments," *J. Data Inf. Qual.*, vol. 1, no. 2, pp. 1–28, 2009.

[13] A. Klein and W. Lehner, "How to Optimize the Quality of Sensor Data Streams," *Proc. 2009 Fourth Int. Multi-Conference Comput. Glob. Inf. Technol. 00*, pp. 13–19, 2009.

[14] A. Klein, "Incorporating quality aspects in sensor data streams," *Proc. {ACM} first {Ph.D.} Work. {CIKM}*, pp. 77–84, 2007.

[15] A. Klein, H. H. Do, G. Hackenbroich, M. Karnstedt, and W. Lehner, "Representing data quality for streaming and static data," *Proc. - Int. Conf. Data Eng.*, pp. 3–10, 2007.

[16] A. Klein and G. Hackenbroich, "How to Screen a Data

Stream." [Online]. http://mitiq.mit.edu/ICIQ/Documents/IQ%20Conference%202009/Papers/3-A.pdf. [Accessed: 15-Dec-2018].

[17] S. L. Barnes, "A technique for maximizing details in numerical weather map analysis," *J. Appl. Meteorol.*, vol. 3, no. 4, pp. 396–409, 1964.

[18] D. Shepard, "A two-dimensional interpolation function for irregularly-spaced data," *23rd ACM Natl. Conf.*, pp. 517–524, 1968.

[19] M.E. Splitt and J. Horel, "Use of Multivariate Linear Regression for Meteorological Data Analysis and Quality Assessment in Complex Terrain." [Online]. http://mesowest.utah.edu/html/help/regress.html. [Accessed: 15-Dec-2018].

[20] U. of Utah, "MesoWest Quality Control Flags Help Page." [Online]. http://mesowest.utah.edu/html/help/key.html. [Accessed: 15-Dec-2015].

[21] NOAA, "MADIS Quality Control." [Online]. http://madis.ncep.noaa.gov/madis_qc.html. [Accessed: 15-Dec-2018].

[22] S. L. Belousov, L. S. Gandin, and S. A. Mashkovich, "Computer Processing of Current Meteorological Data, Translated from Russian to English by Atmospheric Environment Service," *Nurklik, Meteorol. Transl.*, no. 18, p. 227, 1972.

[23] D. Zimmerman, C. Pavlik, A. Ruggles, and M. P. Armstrong, "An experimental comparison of ordinary and universal kriging and inverse distance weighting," *Math. Geol.*, vol. 31, no. 4, pp. 375–390, 1999.

[24] G. Y. Lu and D. W. Wong, "An adaptive inverse-distance weighting spatial interpolation technique," *Comput. Geosci.*, vol. 34, no. 9, pp. 1044–1055, 2008.

[25] T. G. Mueller, et al., "Map Quality for Ordinary Kriging and Inverse Distance Weighted Interpolation," *Soil Sci. Soc. Am. J.*, vol. 68, no. 6, p. 2042, 2004.

[26] D. E. Galarus, R. A. Angryk, and J. W. Sheppard, "Automated Weather Sensor Quality Control.," *FLAIRS Conf.*, pp. 388–393, 2012.

[27] D. E. Galarus and R. A. Angryk, "Mining robust neighborhoods for quality control of sensor data," *Proc. 4th ACM SIGSPATIAL Int. Work. GeoStreaming (IWGS '13)*, pp. 86–95, Nov. 2013.

[28] D. E. Galarus and R. A. Angryk, "A SMART Approach to Quality Assessment of Site-Based Spatio-Temporal Data," in *Proceedings of the 24th ACM SIGSPATIAL International Conference on Advances in Geographic Information Systems (GIS '16)*, Nov. 2016, pp 1-4.

[29] D. E. Galarus and R. A. Angryk, "The SMART Approach to Comprehensive Quality Assessment of Site-Based Spatial-Temporal Data," in *2016 IEEE International Conference on Big Data (Big Data)*, 2016, pp. 2636–2645.

[30] D. E. Galarus and R. A. Angryk, "Beyond Accuracy - A SMART Approach to Site-Based Spatio-Temporal Data Quality Assessment,". *Intell. Data Anal.*, vol. 22, no. 1, 2018, pp 21-43.

[31] D. E. Galarus and R. A. Angryk, "Quality Control from the Perspective of the Real-Time Spatial-Temporal Data Aggregator and (re)Distributor," in *Proceedings of the 22nd ACM SIGSPATIAL International Conference on Advances in Geographic Information Systems (SIGSPATIAL '14)*, 2014, pp. 389–392.

[32] D. E. Galarus and R. A. Angryk, "Spatio-temporal quality control: implications and applications for data consumers and aggregators," *Open Geospatial Data, Softw. Stand.*, vol. 1, no. 1, p. 1, 2016.

[33] H. Xie, K. T. McDonnell, and H. Qin, "Surface reconstruction of noisy and defective data sets," in *Proceedings of the conference on Visualization '04*, 2004, pp. 259–266.

[34] L. Li, X. Zhou, M. Kalo, and R. Piltner, "Spatiotemporal interpolation methods for the application of estimating population exposure to fine particulate matter in the contiguous US and a Real-Time web application," *Int. J. Environ. Res. Public Health*, vol. 13, no. 8, p. 749, 2016.

[35] J. Grieser, "Interpolation of Global Monthly Rain Gauge Observations for Climate Change Analysis," *J. Appl. Meteorol. Climatol.*, vol. 54, no. 7, pp. 1449–1464, 2015.

[36] N. Cressie, "The origins of kriging," *Math. Geol.*, vol. 22, no. 3, pp. 239–252, 1990.

[37] H. Wackernagel, *Multivariate geostatistics: an introduction with applications*. Springer Science & Business Media, 2013.

[38] M. S. Handcock and M. L. Stein, "A Bayesian analysis of kriging," *Technometrics*, vol. 35, no. 4, pp. 403–410, 1993.

[39] G. J. Hunter, A. K. Bregt, G. B. M. Heuvelink, S. De Bruin, and K. Virrantaus, "Spatial data quality: problems and prospects," in *Research trends in geographic information science*, Springer, 2009, pp. 101–121.

[40] E. H. Isaaks and R. M. Srivastava, *An introduction to applied geostatistics*. Oxford University Press, 1989.

[41] C. Huijbregts and G. Matheron, "Universal kriging (an optimal method for estimating and contouring in trend surface analysis)," in *Proceedings of Ninth International Symposium on Techniques for Decision-making in the Mineral Industry*, 1971.

[42] M. Galassi and Et-al, *GNU Scientific Library Reference Manual (3rd Ed.)*. Free Software Foundation.

[43] G. Bohling, "Introduction to Geostatistics and Variogram Analysis." [Online]. http://people.ku.edu/~gbohling/cpe940/Variograms.pdf.

[44] P. J. Rousseeuw and K. Van Driessen, "Computing LTS regression for large data sets," *Data Min. Knowl. Discov.*, vol. 12, no. 1, pp. 29–45, 2006.

[45] R. F. Voss, "Random fractal forgeries," in *Fundamental algorithms for computer graphics*, Springer, 1985, pp. 805–835.

[46] J. Feder, *Fractals*. Springer Science & Business Media, 2013.

[47] M. F. Barnsley *et al.*, *The science of fractal images*. Springer Publishing Company, Incorporated, 2011.

[48] M. F. Goodchild and S. Gopal, *The accuracy of spatial databases*. CRC Press, 1989.

[49] D. E. Galarus, "Modeling stock market returns with local iterated function systems," 1995.

[50] T. C. Bailey and A. C. Gatrell, *Interactive spatial data analysis*, vol. 413. Longman Scientific & Technical Essex, 1995.

[51] USGS, "USGS Water Data for the Nation." [Online]. https://waterdata.usgs.gov/nwis/. [Accessed: 15-Dec-2018].

Using Unsupervised Learning to Determine Geospatial Clusters in Municipalities to Improve Energy Measurements

Italo F. S. Silva*, Polyana B. Costa*, Pedro H. C. Vieira*,
João D. S. Almeida*, Cláudio Baptista† Eliana Monteiro‡
*Applied Computing Group (NCA), Federal University of Maranhão (UFMA), São Luís - MA, Brazil
Email: {francyles, polyanacosta, pedrocarvalho, jdallyson}@nca.ufma.br
†Federal University of Campina Grande (UFCG), Campina Grande - PB, Brazil
Email: baptista@dsc.ufcg.edu.br
‡Companhia Energética do Maranhão (CEMAR)
Equatorial Energia, Brazil
Email: eliana.monteiro@cemar-ma.com.br

Abstract—**This paper presents a tool used to solve the Geospatial capacitated clustering problem applied to an energy company scenario. The billing process of an energy distributor in Brazil is connected to the spatially-aware logistics of collecting energy consumption data. Usually, consumer units are grouped into geospatial clusters that will be covered by meter readers. The process of creating those groups, in general, is carried out manually by analysts, which is an exhaustive process and prone to mistakes. In order to automatize this issue, this work presents a system that automatically generates reading groups for the collection of electrical energy consumption. The approach used to solve the capacitated clustering problem was based on a recursive K-Means. The results obtained with the proposed tool are promising.**

Keywords–Geospatial System; Capacitated Clustering Problem; Energy Companies.

I. Introduction

In regards to Brazilian energy companies, the main issues are the management of reading energy consumption and the billing process. The process of reading electrical energy consumption is comprised of two main steps: collecting consumption data from energy metering devices of every spatially distributed consumer unit and delivering the corresponding invoice. Therefore, an energy company must define a reading plan, which is a spatially-aware scheme of reading or collecting the energy consumption of consumer units. This plan changes monthly due to updates in the underlying spatial databases such as including new consumer units or shutting down some of them. In this context, to facilitate and optimize the job of meter readers, it is mandatory to gather consumer units in groups and to define a spatial criterion to create these groups. Groups of geospatial consumer units are called Reading Units (RU), and groups of reading units are called stages.

The requirements for supplying electrical energy in Brazil are regulated by the National Electric Energy Agency (ANEEL). This regulation aims to improve the relationship between utility providers and customers. Among those regulations, ANEEL establishes that the use of geoprocessing is mandatory and an electric power holding company has a certain period to finish the meter reading process [1].

Consequently, energy companies must plan how these readings will be held. The Energy Company of Maranhão (CEMAR) and Power Plants from Pará S.A (CELPA) organize the meter reading task and the delivery of invoices by creating groups of end customers, which can be understood as clusters. Hence, each meter reader must be designated to a group and follow routes to collect consumption data and deliver invoices. In practice, every municipality or region has an individual organization of reading groups and subgroups.

In order to work in this scenario, this paper presents a geographic information system focused on the creation used to optimize the creation of reading plans. This tool focuses on the creation of reading groups in order to reduce costs and optimize the job of meter readers. To achieve this, reading groups must be compact and homogeneous. The result of this work is part of a Research and Development (R&D) project, hired by CEMAR / CELPA (ANEEL PD-00371-0029 / 2016), executed by the Applied Computing Center (NCA) from the Federal University of Maranhão (UFMA).

The compactness of a group refers to its geographical shape and impacts the selection of the consumer units that will be part of each group. Elements of the same group must be close to each other, and the shape of a group should be circular, in order to fully explore a certain area. The homogeneity criterion is used to balance the reading time of the groups. This requirement ensures that the total time required to collect the consumption data from each group will be similar, therefore the workload of meter readers will be balanced. Each group or reading unit must cover the maximum working hours for meter readers, which are 6 hours per day. Therefore, the amount of reading units in a stage corresponds to the number of electrical meters readers required to cover that geographic area.

Alterations in the power network distribution, such as including new customers, or deactivating consumer units require a redefinition of the reading plan. Those changes can happen monthly and in every city in a certain geographic region. Keeping track of changes and updating reading plans is a time-consuming process, and if done manually, is also prone to mistakes. In order to produce more balanced stages and reading units, this paper presents an interactive tool for generating reading plans automatically. In addition, the proposed tool integrates georeferenced data, since each consumer unit is represented by a pair of latitude and longitude coordinates. This geodata is used to map distances between consumer units, which is an essential part in the creation of reading groups.

The remainder of this paper is organized as follows: Section

II describes the capacitated clustering problem and the applicability of the proposed tool. Section III presents recent work done to solve the capacitated clustering problem. Section IV presents the proposed system and its modules, while Section V presents the results obtained with the system and the discussion of the results.

II. Background

This section addresses the main concepts on the capacitated clustering problem and the application scenario used in this research project.

A. Capacitated Clustering Problem

According to França et. al [2], in capacitated clustering problems, a set of N elements must be subdivided into P clusters of limited capacity. Clusters are mutually exclusive, and the clustering model should maximize the homogeneity within a cluster while it maximizes the heterogeneity between clusters [3]. A generalization of this problem, called Capacitated Districting Problem (CDP), aims to group, under some criterion, an initial set of points into P districts, or to redefine an existing set of districts into P districts [4].

In our model, every geospatial point represents a consumer unit of a particular city, and the districts represent a region where a single meter reader will collect consumption data. Each point has a weight associated to it and must belong to a single cluster, while each cluster has a predefined capacity and the sum of the weights associated with them must not be greater than the capacity previously defined. The weight of each point represents the time required to perform the meter reading in the referred consumer unit. The maximum capacity of each cluster is of 6 six hours, the daily workload of a meter reader. The following requirements must be satisfied in the proposed capacitated clustering problem:

- one weight is associated with each element;
- each element must be associated with a single cluster;
- the elements must be divided into p fixed groups or clusters;
- all the elements must belong to a group;
- the sum of weights for each element of a group must not be greater than the previously defined capacity;
- a criterion to determine the proximity/distance between grouped elements is required;

In clustering problems, it is necessary to define a criterion to measure the similarity or dissimilarity between the elements. In this case, the Euclidean distance between two points was used.

B. The System Application Scenario

This section presents important information about the system application scenario, including characteristics and some requirements for the reading plans creation process.

Some criteria should be considered during the creation of a reading plan. One is the geographic shape of a reading group, because it directly impacts the route traversed by the meter readers. These reading groups should also be homogeneous in relation to the meter's work charge in order to minimize operational costs.

Another criterion to be considered is to follow the main rules for electric energy supply in Brazil. They were defined by Brazilian Electricity Regulatory Agency (ANEEL) in the Resolution 414/2010 in order to improve the relationship between power companies and costumers. According to the rules, a power company must perform a read of a consumer unit at 30-day intervals, but it might happen between 27 or 33-day intervals. Moreover, the bill must be delivered to the costumer 5 working days before the bill due date. In the case of first reading of a consumer unit, or changes on the reading calendar, ANEEL also defines, for these cases, intervals of 15 days minimum and a maximum of 47 days. If a company does not follow these rules, it is liable to pay fines.

The creation of reading plans following these requirements should be performed for all cities served by the CEMAR/CELPA power companies every month because of urban transformations and the expansion of their services. However, doing it manually is a slow process, and the delay might cause financial losses. Therefore, a system that creates optimized reading plans automatically is important because it tends to accelerate that process while satisfies those requirements.

III. Related Work

Several works address the capacitated clustering or redistricting problem; some of them are applied to power meter reading, others to the definition of salesman working zones or garbage collecting, etc. This section presents some of those systems and the techniques used to solve the capacitated clustering problem.

A method to group consumer units from an energy company was proposed by Costa et. al [5], with the aim to reduce the execution time of requested services and to properly distribute tasks among groups. Their approach is based on a capacitated P-medians and a genetic algorithm, which produced better results in comparison with the manual grouping performed by the energy company. However, when comparing the results from both approaches, the genetic algorithm produced better solutions to the problem.

Metaheuristics were also used to propose solutions to the capacitated clustering problem applied to power meter reading. De Assis et. al [4] use a greedy randomized adaptive search procedure (GRASP) and multicriteria scalarization techniques to create clusters. Experiments taken on a portion of the city of São Paulo showed the effectiveness of their method.

Capacitated centered clustering was also applied to garbage collecting and definition of salesman working zones, as shown in [6]. The authors present a hybrid data mining heuristic to solve the capacitated centered clustering problem based on a heuristic that combines Clustering Search and Simulated Annealing. The heuristic and the clustering search were used to find the best solutions in the search space, while data mining was used to search for data patterns and improve the searching for newer and better solutions.

In order to collect household water usage data, Smiderle et. al [7] based their approach on operational research techniques in order to find the shortest route between a set of points, leading to a decrease of the time spent by meter readers to collect water consumption data. Their method applied a combination of genetic algorithm and Teitz and Bart algorithm to the P-medians problem, reducing $7,200$ meters in a route that covers a group of 774 houses.

This work presents a system that automatically generates reading plans for collecting electrical energy consumption. The approach used to solve the capacitated clustering problem was based on a recursive K-Means algorithm and a post-processing step was used to improve its results. The reading plan should comply with several restrictions that will be explained in the following sections.

IV. System for Planning of Reading Units

The Consumer Units Reading Planning System uses unsupervised learning to assist the logistic planning creating reading groups, which are organized in Stages (effective reading days) and Reading Units (subdivisions of stages which indicate the necessary amount of power meter readers to perform the reading task).

The system consists of two modules: Manual and Automatic Reading Planning. The first one is responsible for the implementation of the clustering strategy. The second one allows to create or edit reading plans interactively. Figure 1 shows an overview of the system's components.

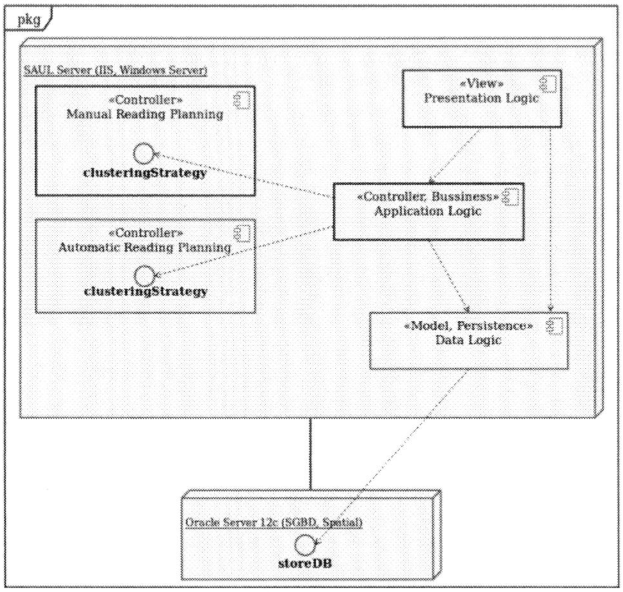

Figure 1. Component diagram of the system.

The main differences between these two approaches are related to internal system performance. In the case of manual approach, the system assists the creation and edition tasks performed by user step by step. On the other hand, in the automatic approach, the user just defines the input parameters for the algorithms.

A. *The Manual Reading Plan Module*

The Manual Reading Planning Module allows the creation of reading plannings interactively. This module uses the metaphor of web maps for consumer units data visualization. The use of maps favors a better comprehension of the location of consumer units and the route that meter readers go through.

In this approach, the definition of stages and reading units is performed manually. The user selects the reading region and the consumer units to be handled on the map. Then, the user must select the option of adding stages to a geographic region or RUs to a stage defined previously. Hence, the manual creation of reading plans is entirely controlled by the user. The application allows to change the order of stages and to swap reading units. Figures 2, 3 and 4 show the steps of manual user interaction to create the reading groups.

Figure 2. Create simulation interface.

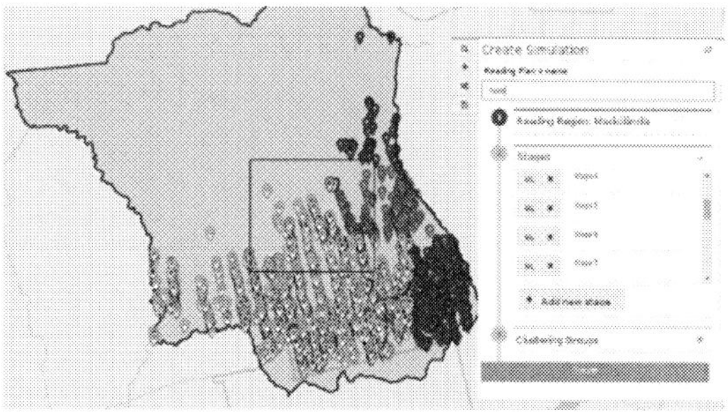

Figure 3. Stages and Reading Units Creation interface.

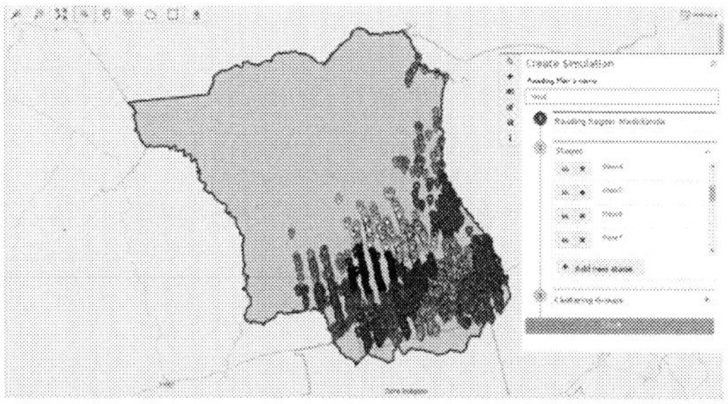

Figure 4. Generated groups in manual planning.

The reading groups contain all the consumer units and the white groups show undefined units. All the consumer units must be in a unique group to enable the calculation of decision-making reports used by the energy company.

Besides the manual interactive possibility, the system enables the automatic creation of those groups and it is possible to propose different approaches in the automatic clustering process.

B. The Automatic Reading Plan Module

In order to minimize costs related to the elaboration of the reading plans, the system proposed in this work has the Automatic Reading Planning Module that generates clusters automatically. This clustering task follows constraints defined by the company in the scenario of the monthly reading planning of the consumer units.

The grouping of consumer units must consider that they should be spatially close, minimizing displacement and maximizing the number of consumer units read by the power meter readers in their working day. According to the described scenario, it is possible to see this required task may be categorized as a capacitated clustering problem in which generated clusters must not exceed a predefined capacity and also respect other constraints. The next section explains the method used in order to solve the clustering problem.

C. Towards Solving the Capacitated Clustering Problem

This section introduces a method that solves the capacitated clustering problem applied in the power companies scenario. Figure 5 shows the five steps of the proposed method.

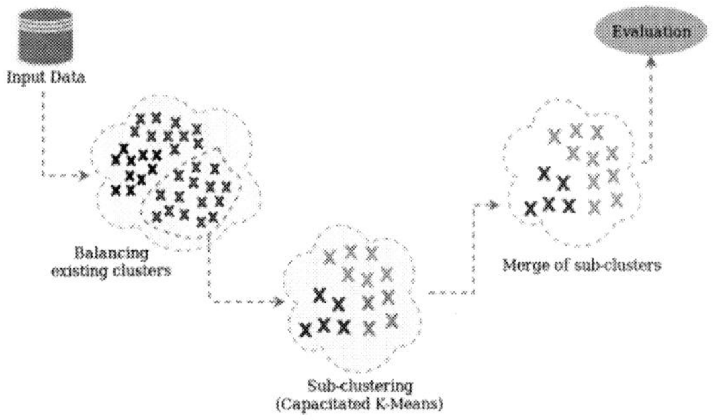

Figure 5. Steps of the proposed method.

Firstly, Latitude and Longitude coordinates, old clustering information and the time of measuring of each consumer unit are collected from the dataset. These data are used as input for the Balancing step and are grouped in order to balance the total time of measuring each group. It is emphasized that the method presented in this work is applied in municipalities that contains a previous reading plan in order to improve it. If a region does not contain reading plan information, consequently there are no measurement time data associated to the consumer units. Thus, in these cases, the automatic creation should consider another set of constraints to be included in this capacitated clustering problem modeling.

After the Balancing step, each balanced group is used as input for the clustering algorithm. In this step, those groups are subdivided into smaller groups. However, some of them contain a small number of points. Hence, these generated clusters are submitted to the merging step, where little clusters are merged based on a proximity criterion. The last step is the evaluation of the generated groups by applying clustering evaluation metrics.

1) Organizing Stages: The dataset contains the reading plans created manually by the company. Geographic coordinates, the reading time of each consumer unit and clusters which they belong to are extracted from the dataset. As described above, these clusters are called Stages. Each stage has a number corresponding to the day when its consumer units will be read by the meter reader.

The balance of clusters step consists of grouping consumer units starting from the previous reading plans in order to balance the sum of the reading times of each Stage, also improving their geographical distribution. Consequently, it also balances the work load of the meter readers. The K-Means algorithm is used in this step.

The K-Means initial cluster centers are the centroids calculated from the previous Stages. The similarity criterion used was the Euclidean distance between the latitude and longitude coordinates.

Another criterion to be considered during the clustering procedure is the minimization of the reading time standard deviation. For this, the average reading time of the new clusters is calculated. These groups are submitted to the clustering procedure until standard deviation reaches the minimum value. Finished the balance of the existing clusters, or Stages, the next step consists of the creation of reading units.

2) Creation of Reading Units using Capacitated K-Means: The Capacitated K-Means is based on the K-Means technique, which is generally used to perform the clustering task. In this one, the data of a set are split into groups according to a similarity criterion. The capacitated version of K-Means, which is used in this work, also includes a capacity constraint for group generation. Figure 6 presents an overview of the clustering method.

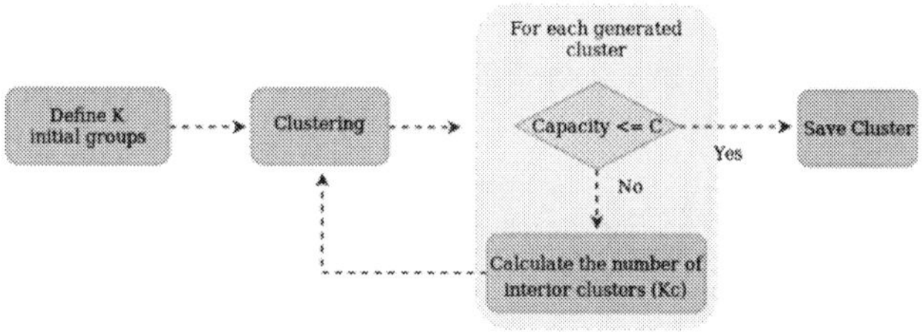

Figure 6. Workflow of Capacitated K-Means algorithm.

The initial number of clusters (K) is defined as 2. Thus, a big cluster is divided into two big parts and it allows these ones to be sub-divided into more parts according to the capacitated clustering strategy. An initial clustering is performed based on the number K. The capacity of each created group is evaluated and, if it exceeds the maximum capacity added to a threshold, the points of a group will be separated for a recursive clustering process. The new generated groups will also be evaluated. The new Kc values are based on the total of points and on the established capacity as seen in 1. The steps of re-clustering, evaluation and group split are repeated recursively until all the generated groups satisfy the constraints. It is important to note that clusters whose capacity satisfies the constraint are preserved.

$$Kc = \frac{N}{C_m} \tag{1}$$

Figure 7. Comparison between results of (a) Current Reading Planning and (b) Automatic Reading Planning.

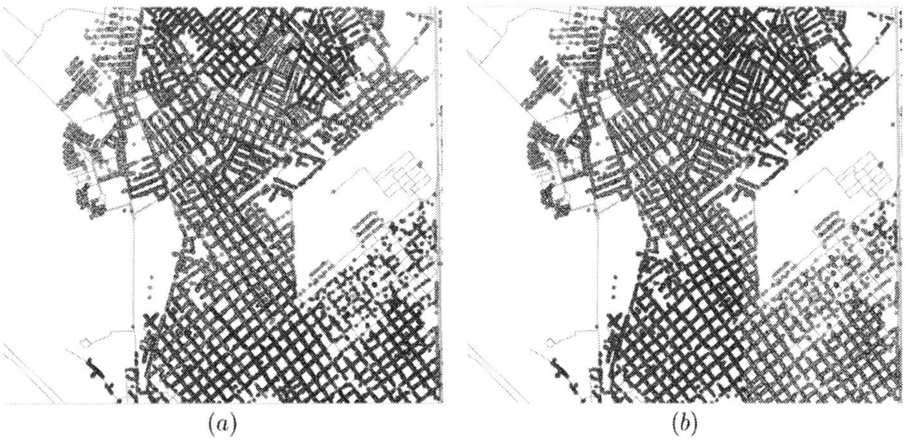

Figure 8. A closer view comparing Stages in (A) Current Reading Planning and (B) Automatic Reading Planning.

In 1, C_m value is the ratio between the defined capacity and the average reading time of consumer units of a sub-group.

There are two guarantees provided by this algorithm: (1) all points belong to a single cluster, and (2) all groups satisfy the desired capacity. To avoid maintaining groups with small capacities, a merge of adjacent clusters is performed in order to ensure the creation of more homogeneous groups.

An under capacity cluster can be merged with other clusters until they reach the maximum capacity, which is of 6 hours per cluster. Besides the capacity, a small cluster must be merged with a close cluster, otherwise the compactness of the group will decrease. In order to merge clusters based on their capacity and proximity, a graph that connects them is created. Each cluster on the graph will be a vertex represented by the cluster's centroid; the edges represent the connection between two centroids, and the weights of the edges are the Euclidean distance between the points. The graph was built based on a Delaunay Triangulation algorithm [8]. After building the graph, a Breadth-First searching algorithm (BFS) [9] was used to search the graph in order to merge adjacent vertices. This post processing step results in less clusters, with more elements in each cluster.

V. Results and Discussion

To analyze the obtained results, the generated stages and reading units must conform to the application's scenario presented in Section II-B. Additionally, the efficiency of the automatic generation of reading plans was evaluated in regards to the homogeneity of the groups, their geographical shape and if they comply with ANEEL's regulation.

Tests were performed based on Imperatriz data, a mildly populated municipality in Maranhão, Brazil. Figure 7 shows the comparison between the manually defined stages and the stages generated by the proposed tool. The image shows that the new groups have become more compact and homogeneous than the manually defined ones. Table I confirms this result and presents the comparison for the mean area of the clusters and the standard deviation of the reading time.

Table I also shows the average Silhouette Coefficient for the entire clustering. The Silhouette Coefficient (SC) is a measure that evaluates a cluster in terms of cohesion and separation [10]. Cohesion quantifies how close the objects within a cluster are, and it expresses the compactness of a group, while separation determines how isolated a cluster is from other clusters. The SC has a range of values that vary from $[-1, 1]$. If the coefficient has a negative value, it means that the clustering is sparse. The closer to 1 the coefficient is, the more compact a cluster is. In a good clustering, all groups should have a positive silhouette coefficient.

TABLE I. RESULTS OF THE CALCULATED METRICS.

	Current State	A. R. Plan
Std. Times	2872.60	2991.09
Average Area (Km^2)	62.38	29.15
Silhouette Coefficient	-0.38	0.26

Manually defined groups tend to be line-shaped, the proposed system, on the other hand, produces circular groups. This happens because of the intricacies of K-means, the algorithm groups the consumer units that are closer to the centroid of each stage. This can be seen in Figure 8, which shows a closer look at a specific region of Imperatriz.

In regards to reading groups, the results of the clustering performed by the capacitated K-Means are similar to ones that the energy company already has, as shown in Figure 9. However, the proposed system assures that the reading groups will have balanced workloads due to the merging clusters step.

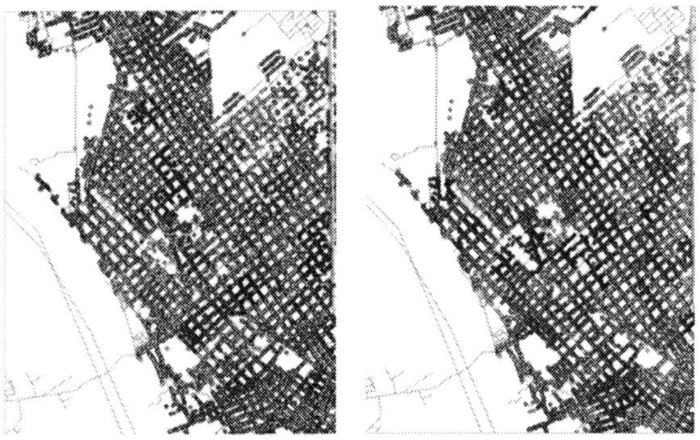

(a) (b)

Figure 9. A closer view comparing Reading Units in (A) Current Reading Planning and (B) Automatic Reading Planning.

Finally, the resulting reading plan is evaluated in relation to compliance with the regulation defined by ANEEL. Figure 10 shows a graph that relates the number of consumer units of the reading plan and the number of days necessary to collect its consumption data. According to the figure, the proposed tool was capable of grouping consumer units in a way that all of them get the invoice within the period of time specified by ANEEL. In comparison with the manually defined reading plan, more consumer units will get the invoices in a period of 30 days, and less of them in a period of 32 days.

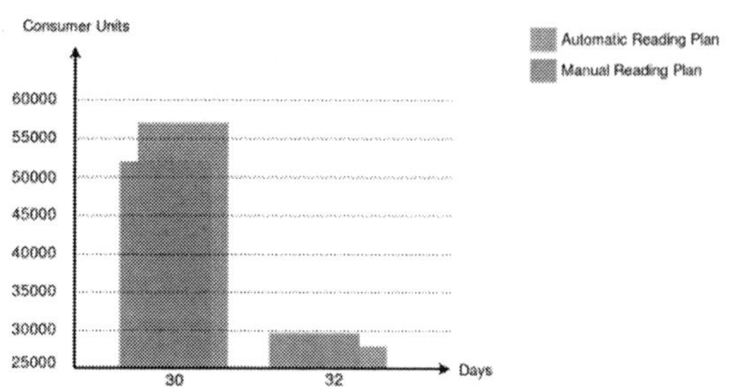

Figure 10. Graph relating the number of consumer units and the number of days necessary to collect their consumption data.

VI. CONCLUSION

This paper presented a geospatial tool for generating automatic reading plans applied to the Brazilian energy companies CEMAR and CELPA. Machine Learning and optimization techniques were used to produce reading groups in an unsupervised way. The generated reading plan should balance the workload of meter readers, completely explore the same region and comply with ANEEL's regulations. The results achieved with the proposed tool were promising, more consumer units were covered within the period of 30 days, the generated reading groups were more compact and homogenous, at the same time, their configuration did not contrast from the manually defined groups. The workload of the groups was balanced and the reading plan complied with the constraints These promising results bring a perception that the proposed method can be applied in domains with analogous constraints, e.g., garbage collection or measurement of water consumption.

For future work, the presented tool should be tested on more cities, especially more populated ones. Along with balancing the workload within reading groups, it is also desirable to balance the workload within the stages of the reading plan.

ACKNOWLEDGEMENTS

The authors would like to thank UFMA, IFMA, FAPEMA, CEMAR/CELPA for making this work possible through the project PD-00371-0031/2017 and CNPq for financial support. This study was financed in part by the Coordenação de Aperfeiçoamento de Pessoal de Nível Superior - Brasil (CAPES) - Finance Code 001.

REFERENCES

[1] ANEEL. Resolução normativa nº 414. [Online]. Available: http://www.aneel.gov.br/documents/656877/14486448/bren2010414.pdf [retrieved: jan, 2019]

[2] P. M. França, N. M. Sosa, and V. Pureza, "An adaptive tabu search algorithm for the capacitated clustering problem," International Transactions in Operational Research, vol. 6, no. 6, 1999, pp. 665–678.

[3] J. M. Mulvey and M. P. Beck, "Solving capacitated clustering problems," European Journal of Operational Research, vol. 18, no. 3, 1984, pp. 339 – 348.

[4] L. S. De Assis, P. M. Franca, and F. L. Usberti, "A redistricting problem applied to meter reading in power distribution networks," Computers & Operations Research, vol. 41, 2014, pp. 65–75.

[5] C. Costa, D. Costa, and A. Góes, "Determinação de setores de atendimento em uma concessionária de energia," Trends in Applied and Computational Mathematics, vol. 8, no. 3, 2007, pp. 381–390.

[6] M. Guerine, M. B. Stockinger, I. Rosseti, and A. Plastino, "Heurística híbrida com mineração de dados para o problema de agrupamento capacitado com centro geométrico," XLIX Simpósio Brasileiro de Pesquisa Operacional, 2017.

[7] A. Smiderle, M. T. A. Steiner, and C. Carnieri, "Problema de cobertura de arcos – um estudo de caso," XXIII Encontro Nacional de Engenharia de Produção, 2003.

[8] D.-T. Lee and B. J. Schachter, "Two algorithms for constructing a delaunay triangulation," International Journal of Computer & Information Sciences, vol. 9, no. 3, 1980, pp. 219–242.

[9] T. H. Cormen, C. E. Leiserson, R. L. Rivest, and C. Stein, Introduction to algorithms. MIT press, 2009.

[10] P.-N. Tan, M. Steinbach, and V. Kumar, Introduction to Data Mining. Boston, MA, USA: Pearson Education India, 2007.

Air Pollution Monitoring and Spatial-Temporal Hotspot Pattern Analysis of Sensors Based on Sensor Grid for the Industrial Parks in Taiwan

Bing-Si Ni
Department of Geography
National Taiwan Normal University
Taipei City, Taiwan (R.O.C)
email: nispc@nispc.tw

Yu-Chieh Huang
Environmental Management Consultant Technologies Inc.
Taipei City, Taiwan (R.O.C)
email: sophia@emct.com.tw

Chun-Ming Huang
Environmental Protection Administration
Taipei City, Taiwan (R.O.C.)
email: chmihuang@epa.gov.tw

***Abstract*—To identify sources of pollution and predict future pollution events, the Environmental Protection Administration of Taiwan has deployed dense sensor networks in industrial districts. In face of overwhelming real-time data collected from the Internet of Things (IoT) applications for smart environmental sensing, no standard procedure based on the space-time statistical methods, such as Getis-Ord G* or Moran's I exist for defining and analyzing pollution events. We used raw data generated from microsensors as the data source, adopted spatial statistics to perform hotspot analysis, then define the event base on the result of statistical hypothesis and grid connectivity. This approach was effective in distinguishing independent pollution events when two or more events occurred concurrently in the same region. Finally, spatial and temporal descriptive statistical analysis was performed on the targeted pollution events, including the identity of pollution events through spatial-temporal hotspot analysis integrated with data visualization.**

Keywords-spatial-temporal patterns analysis; air pollution events; Internet of Things; sensors; industrial parks

I. INTRODUCTION

The media coverage and the government's environmental policies raised environmental awareness among the general population and increased attention to air pollution. Excessive levels of ozone and fine particulate matter which less than 2.5 micrometers in diameter in the air, known as "$PM_{2.5}$", pose a considerable threat to human health. Air quality has become a crucial indicator of people's quality of life, and small-scale air pollution monitoring was seen as increasing demand. In Taiwan, air quality monitoring is typically performed by examining data from the network of national air quality monitor stations. However, the limitations of micro-sensors mean that air quality determined using a single datum cannot be used as evidence for inspection. Therefore, this study organized sensor data into clusters and adopted spatial-temporal statistics to solve problems concerning the processing of microsensor data; in addition, data mining was employed to identify trends in the data clusters. Many industrial districts of various cities in Taiwan have begun to establish microsensor networks embedded in streetlights, which in the future could serve as a source of real-time monitoring for emerging air pollutions or air quality monitoring. Specifically, data regarding local weather dynamics are integrated into microsensor networks, which can be used not only for tracing but also for predicting short-term pollution events to rapidly identify pollution sources.

This paper is organized as follows: Section II introduces the research methods, including statistical methods and the weight matrix we adopted. Section III presents the results. Section IV concludes the paper.

II. RESEARCH METHODS

Studies have reached no consensus on the definitions of pollution clusters or events, and spatial analysis has been a bottleneck in Statistics. Since the 1990s, in addition to national air quality monitoring systems, which are 77 stations in Taiwan, newly deployed microsensors (more 3,000) have monitored $PM_{2.5}$ as an indicator of pollution caused by suspended particulates, volatile organic compounds (VOCs), and black carbons emitted from factories. For various pollutants in the atmosphere, such as the above-mentioned $PM_{2.5}$ and VOCs, there are also nitrogen oxides (NO_x), sulfides (SO_2). These pollutants have different production factors and have different effects on human health. Therefore, the sources of these substances are often discussed in previous researches.

Many studies are discussing the relationship between pollution concentrations and other factors, such as the relationship between different human activities and various pollutant concentrations, the covariation between different pollutants [1], and the relationship between weather factors and various pollutants [2]. In the studies mentioned above, researchers describe the pollution event along the concentration of contaminants, duration, return period, etc. They develop the follow-up study on the characteristics of the above pollutants. Additionally, the EU government also controls the contaminants by the average concentration over a period of time as standards [3]. However, spatial autocorrelation has not been widely used in the above studies. Therefore, there is still a lack of useful indicators for the accumulation of pollutants caused by small-scale human activities in industrial parks, helping researchers to identify the development, concentration, and diffusion of pollution clusters in the study area.

This study performed a hotspot analysis based on spatial statistics approaches. However, a small industrial park in Taiwan is typically 10 – 15 km^2; the occurrence of a severe pollution event easily affects all the devices in the overall industrial park at the same time, so only considering the spatial dimension is insufficient because it will lack relative reference values. Therefore, we must also incorporate the temporal dimension to determine the temporal continuity and trend of the events hotspots. That implies we should conduct a spatial-temporal extended version of spatial autocorrelation instead of pure spatial autocorrelation to prove the assumption [4].

First, data aggregation was conducted to reduce the time complexity involved in data preprocessing. Second, using "Global Moran's I" (1) to confirm whether there is a significant autocorrelation on the concentrations of fine particulate matter through time and space [5]. Third, local spatial statistical techniques such as "Local Getis-Ord Gi*" (2) or "Local Moran's I" were employed to determine the distribution of cold spots and hot spots. [5, 6]

$$I = \frac{\sum_i \sum_j w_{ij} z_i z_j / S_0}{\sum_i z_i^2 / n} \quad (1)$$

$$G_i^* = \frac{\sum_j w_{ij} x_j}{\sum_j x_j} \quad (2)$$

Both global and local spatial autocorrelation methods need to define a weight matrix w_{ij} to point out the degree of dependency between every two elements. Our weight matrix is based on the spatial-temporal neighbors and generated by the three-dimensional "Queen" rule (Fig.1) as in [7]. The identified spatial-temporal hotspots served as the basis for defining pollution events. Finally, the pollution events were analyzed using descriptive statistics, and the results were applied for subsequent analysis of pollution trends and patterns.

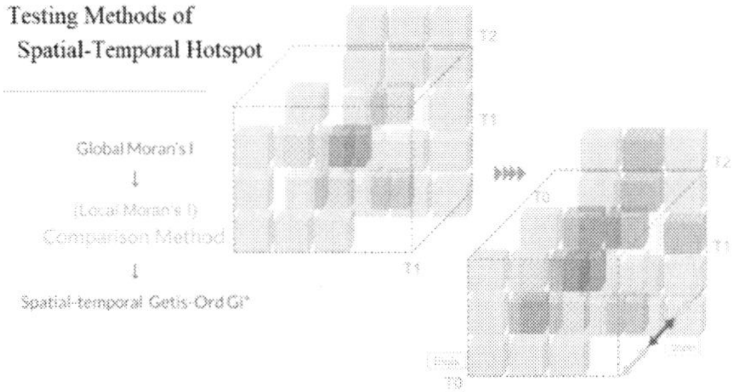

Figure 1. Data processing and testing methods.

III. EMPIRICAL DATA DISCUSSION

The study examined the Dafa Industrial District in Kaohsiung City, a municipality in Taiwan known for its heavy industry. The industrial district is 374 ha with a trapezoid shape. Sensors in the region were deployed every 200 m, with a total of 150 sensors. The Sensors placed in the Dafa Industrial District began operations in September 2018 and encompasses nearly 700 factories that mostly provide services to the light industry and mixed metal-based heavy industry (see Fig. 2).

The raw data were displayed on the leaflet online map which we developed every 5 minutes. During the first month after sensor installation, we found the sensor readings continually increased in the evenings, and the increases were mostly in the southern and northwestern part of the industrial district. From this data, the locations of pollution sources were identified manually according to factory locations and wind directions.

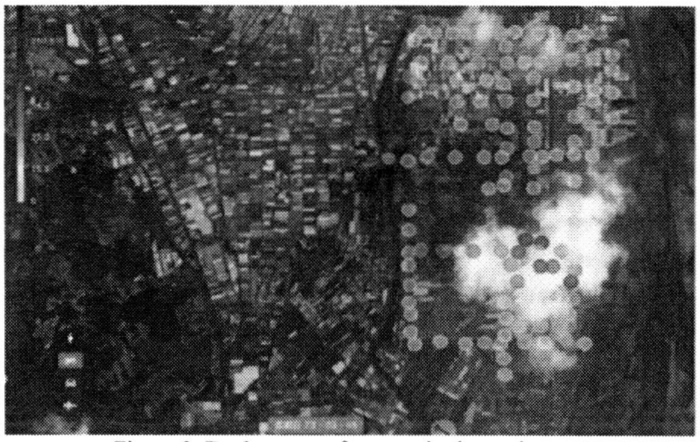

Figure 2. Deployment of sensors in the study area.

In this paper, we further propose an automated hot spot identification program. The implementation details and parameters are set as follows:

First, we number the grids according to the spatial-temporal locations of the sensors, so that we created 200 × 200 meters grids on the XY-plane, with units of time is equal to 10 minutes. Then, we use eight days of sensor data, the temporal dimensions of space-time cubes were divided into 1,110 grids. Therefore, all data be divided into approximately 69,709 data cubes.

Second, we calculate grid neighbors. Some modules of python like GeoPandas, Pandas, and PySal were used to obtain the adjacent 5 × 3 × 3 - 1 spatial-temporal neighbors (excluding the grid itself), and produce a weight matrix based on the spatial-temporal neighbors we calculated above.

Third, Spatial-temporal autocorrelation was calculated using the spatial-temporal weight matrix and sensor data. The "Global Moran's I" is 0.491067 (values of I usually range from −1 to 1). The result indicates there is a positive autocorrelation. In this step, we performed a hypothesis testing using the Monte Carlo method, and the one-tailed p is 0.000; therefore, H_0 (random distribution) was rejected, indicating that significant clustering existed. The result implies that we can use the local autocorrelation to identify when and where the hot spot and cold spot appear and disappear.

Fourth, we conduct local autocorrelation analysis. The cold spots and hot spots were verified using Getis-Ord's Gi*. The Gi* statistics calculated by statistical software are usually converted into Z-scores, which indicates the level of significance and thus could be explained easily.

Finally, we develop a new visualization method combines Z-score statistics, three-dimensional contour plots, and the concept of space-time cubes to present the significance level of local autocorrelation across space and time. With such a tool, let us initially observe whether we proposed is better than the traditional spatial autocorrelation.

TABLE I. COMPARISON OF RESEARCH METHODS

	Experimental group 1*	Experimental group 2	Control group 1	Control group 2
Spatial-temporal interpolation	No	Yes	No	Yes
Definition of neighbors	Spatially and temporally adjacent		Only spatially adjacent	
Calculation results of spatial-temporal Gi*	Non-interpolation	Data pre-interpolation	Non-interpola tion	Data pre-interpola tion
	1. Temporal (continuous) clustering can be detected.		1.Temporal clustering cannot be detected.	
	2. Nonexistent edge hotspots can be estimated through spatial-temporal interpolation.		2. When the polluted area was large, the hotspots area shrank.	

*Research Recommendations

Table 1 shows the comparison between traditional pure spatial autocorrelation which was used as the control group (i.e., the spatial Gi*) and spatial-temporal Gi* which was used as the experimental group.

For the control groups, the results show that although the hotspots mostly exhibited a continuous distribution, they were shaking (see Fig 3. (a)). That is because the Gi* statistics of each time were calculated only according to the values in the corresponding time slice. Moreover, when the raw values of the sensors throughout the study area increase at the same time, the hotspots in the space-time contour plot will become scattered, and each of them will gradually shrink. That is inconsistent with the considerable increase observed in reality.

As for whether we should interpolate the missing values before the hotspot analysis, we found if the grids are located at the perimeter of the study site, the lack of neighbors easily resulted in the appearance of false hotspots at the place. That is because extrapolation is typically less accurate than interpolation.

Compared with control groups, spatial-temporal autocorrelation defines the adjacent space and time as spatial-temporal neighbors. This method was found to generate satisfactory calculation results, and the identified hotspot areas (e.g., Z-Scores > 1.6) continuous changes with the development of the events could also be presented clearly (see Fig 3. (b)). As a result, we chose Experimental group 1 to do the final analysis and discussion.

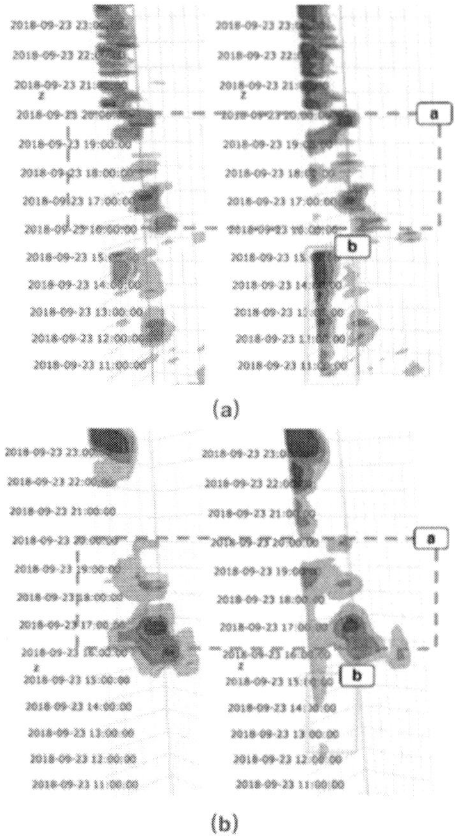

Figure 3. (a) Space-time contour plots for the control groups. (left: non-intepolation; right: intepolation) (b) Space-time contour plots for our work. (left: non-intepolation; right: intepolation)

Hotspot maps were illustrated based on the central points of pollution events and standard distance. Numerous pollution events were observed to be clustered and overlapping in the southeastern region of the study site. This implicated that major pollution sources were located in that region and that therefore further inspection was required (see Fig. 4).

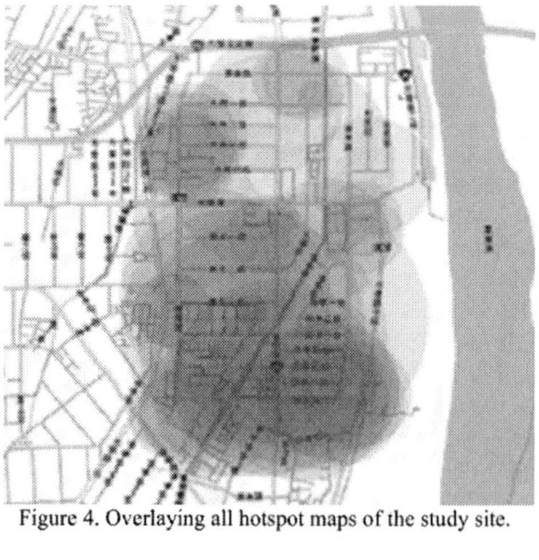

Figure 4. Overlaying all hotspot maps of the study site.

To further demonstrate the potential of using this method to identify events, we first give each event some corresponding descriptive statistics, make simple chart plots, and try to explain the results. In Fig. 5 (a), each point denotes a cluster of individual pollution values. The x-axis indicates the pollution hotspot duration, and the y-axis indicates the standard distance of each pollution events, representing the level of pollution transmission in space. The color of each point indicates the maximum value of the Gi* (Z-score) of the hotspots. In Fig. 5 (b), each point denotes a cluster of individual pollution values. The x-axis indicates the pollution hotspot duration. The y-axis indicates the moving distance, which is the distance between the first geometric center of the statistical unit serving as the hotspot and the last geometric center of the statistical unit that was identified as the hotspot, namely the amount of cluster movement. The color of each point indicates the maximum value of the Gi* (Z-score) of the hotspots.

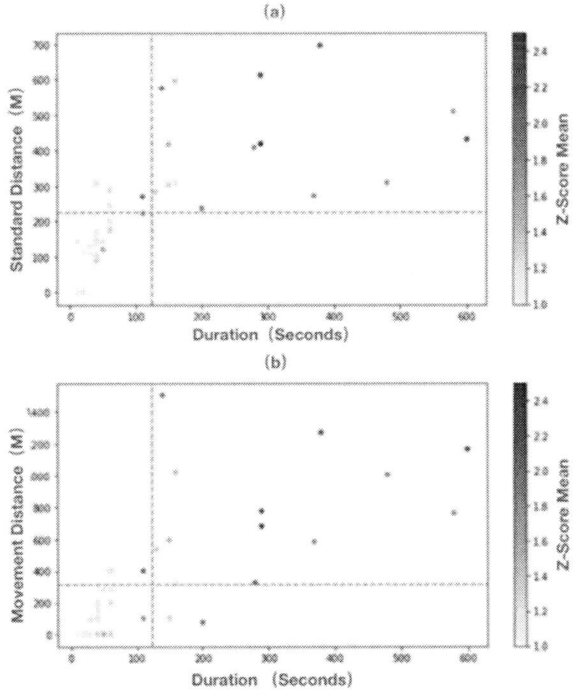

Figure 5. (a) Pollution hotspot duration versus range of the pollution event. (b) Pollution hotspot duration versus cluster movement distance.

In Fig. 5 (a), the data were divided into four quadrants as follows: The first quadrant denotes large-scale pollution events with long durations and large affected areas. Compared with small-scale pollution events, these large-scale pollution events had higher maximal Gi* value; that is, the raw data were highly spatial-temporal autocorrelated. The second quadrant comprises pollution events with short durations but large affected areas. Wind direction and speed were inferred as the causes of pollution transmission within a region. The third quadrant contains local events such as small-scale emission events, which featured short durations and low levels of transmission. The fourth quadrant indicates events featuring long pollution durations but short standard distances. This type of event was not included in our result.

In Fig. 5 (b), the data were divided into four quadrants as follows: The first quadrant represents events featuring long durations and vast moving distances of pollution cluster centers. In this study, this type of event had a relatively high maximum value of Gi* (i.e., the sensor data were highly spatial-temporal autocorrelated). The second quadrant contains pollution events with short durations and large moving distances, which were possibly caused by large wind speeds. The third quadrant denotes instantaneous events featuring short pollution durations and small moving distances, including short-term emissions or equipment failure. The fourth quadrant comprises pollution events with long durations and short moving distances. This type of event had a relatively high Gi* value, representing the continuously accumulating pollution.

IV. CONCLUSION

This study interpolated data points on a 3D plane, and the time dimension was considered to perform raw data interpolation and obtain experimental group 1 (see Fig 6.). When localized pollution became a pollution event for the entire industrial district, spatial-temporal Gi* continued to increase, which is consistent with the distribution of the actual data. Our work demonstrates the feasibility of using spatial-temporal Gi* to examine this type of data. The present study observed spatial Gi* (3D spatial contour plot) and found that the hotspot of each time interval was discontinuous, thus generating the vibration phenomenon, possibly because the statistics for each time section were calculated separately. On the other hand, a 3D spatial-temporal contour plot was drawn to present the results, providing greater continuity to help researchers understand the development of pollution events.

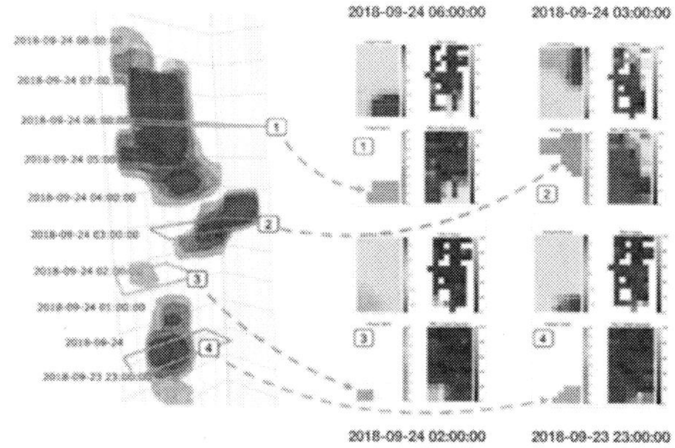

Figure 6. Identification of pollution events through spatial-temporal hotspot analysis integrated with visualized display method.

Moreover, the space-time kernel density was not used because (1) the focus was on clustered sensor data, rather than the number of clustered sensors, and (2) previous studies have often used Gi* to identify hotspots. Therefore, it was most critical to locate the spatial-temporal range.

Continuous transmission of pollutant data in industrial districts requires automatic spatial-temporal monitoring to provide instant warnings regarding excess pollution. In future studies, we will integrate the heterogeneous data of environmental dynamics as the basis for early signs regarding the dispersion of pollutants. Weather dynamics, especially wind-related information, should also be included. Research limitations of the current study included a lack of information about the wind patterns in the industrial district and a lack of building models. Thus, models were fixed by using wind direction and wind speed data from the monitoring station of the Central Weather Bureau to the industrial district.

ACKNOWLEDGMENT

This research has been supported by a grant from the Environmental Protection Administration, Executive Yuan, for the project of Smart Environmental Application Development.

REFERENCES

[1] Battista, G., Pagliaroli, T., Mauri, L., Basilicata, C., and De Lieto Vollaro, R.: 'Assessment of the Air Pollution Level in the City of Rome (Italy)', Sustainability, 2016, 8, (9), pp. 838

[2] Wang, J., and Ogawa, S.: 'Effects of meteorological conditions on PM2. 5 concentrations in Nagasaki, Japan', International Journal of Environmental Research and Public Health, 2015, 12, (8), pp. 9089-9101

[3] 'Directive 2008/50/EC of the European Parliament and of the Council of 21 May 2008 on ambient air quality and cleaner air for Europe', 2008

[4] Shen, C., Li, C., and Si, Y.: 'Spatio-temporal autocorrelation measures for nonstationary series: A new temporally detrended spatio-temporal Moran's index', Physics Letters A, 2016, 380, (1-2), pp. 106-116

[5] Anselin, L.: 'Local indicators of spatial association—LISA', Geographical analysis, 1995, 27, (2), pp. 93-115

[6] Getis, A., and Ord, J.K.: 'The analysis of spatial association by use of distance statistics', Geographical analysis, 1992, 24, (3), pp. 189-206

[7] Gao, S., Zhu, R., and Mai, G.: 'Identifying Local Spatiotemporal Autocorrelation Patterns of Taxi Pick-ups and Dropoffs', in Editor (Ed.)^(Eds.): 'Book Identifying Local Spatiotemporal Autocorrelation Patterns of Taxi Pick-ups and Dropoffs' (2016, edn.), pp. 109-113

Investigating the Impact of Urban Layout Geometry on Urban Flooding

Ahmed Mustafa, Martin Bruwier, Benjamin Dewals, Jacques Teller
Urban and Environmental Engineering department
Liège University
Liège, Belgium
a.mustafa@uliege.be, mbruwier@uliege.be, b.dewals@uliege.be, jacques.teller@uliege.be

Xiao Wei Zhang, Daniel G. Aliaga
Department of Computer Science
Purdue University
West Lafayette, IN, USA
zhan2597@purdue.edu, aliaga@cs.purdue.edu

Abstract— **In this paper, we use a procedural generation system to design urban layouts that passively reduce water depth during urban floods. The tool enables designing cities that passively lower flood depth everywhere or in chosen key areas. Our approach integrates a porosity-based hydraulic model and a parameterized urban generation system with an optimization engine so as to find the least cost modification to an initial urban layout. In order to investigate the relationship between urban layout design parameters and flood inundation depth, correlation coefficient method is used. This paper concludes that the most influential urban layout parameters are average road length and the mean parcel area.**

Keywords- inverse procedural modeling; urban layout design; porosity-based hydraulic model; Pearson correlation; urban flooding.

I. Introduction

Structural flood controls such as levees, dams, and dikes have been widely used to reduce flood impacts. However, these structural measures have been criticized because they interrupt flooding processes by reducing natural water storage capacity and disrupting water flow paths [1] [2]. Currently, there is a shift from hard flood controls towards a more strategic approach characterized by mitigating flood risk and increasing resilience during the urban design process [1] [3]. This study uses a procedural generation system, proposed by [4], that automatically generates 3D urban layouts that consider the influence of geometric urban characteristics (e.g., road width, orientation, curvature, etc.) on water flow properties during urban flooding. Using this system, we explored urban geometric grammars that help reduce flooding, i.e., what urban design rules produce a passive barrier against natural floods?

The procedural generation system [4] consists of three components. First, it represents an urban area by dividing it into cells of 1×1 kilometers. For each cell, the system defines a parameterized procedural model that can generate a wide range of possible urban layout configurations. Second, a porosity-based hydraulic model computes the water flow characteristics of a proposed urban layout cell. Third, the system approximates the relationship between urban layout and flood flow characteristics with a trained neural network. The main contribution of this paper is the measurement of a statistical relationship between urban layout design parameters and water depth during a flood, which, to our knowledge, has not been done before.

The rest of this paper is organized as follows: Section II presents our methodology. Section III presents and discusses our findings. Section IV gives conclusions and as well as suggestions for future study.

II. Methodology

Altogether, our procedural model is controlled by a 10-dimensional parameter vector. These parameters are selected according to a literature survey of common parameters involved in previous studies [5] [6] [7]. In the following, we describe each parameter:

- average road length (P1) -- the distance between two adjacent intersections,
- road orientation (P2) -- orientation of the initial radially-outward road relative to lower-left corner,
- road curvature (P3) -- rotation of a road segment when it passes through an intersection,
- major road width (P4), and
- minor roads width (P5).

Parcels are defined based on a recursive subdivision of oriented bounding boxes (OBB) fit around each city block as in [6]. Parcels are controlled by the following parameters:

- percentage of parcels selected as parks (P6), and
- average parcel area (P7).

Buildings are generated with the following parameters:

- front (P8),
- rear (P9), and
- side (P10) building setbacks.

Our flooding depth simulations are performed by WOLF 2D model [8] [9]. Our hydraulic model focuses on river-based flooding scenarios.

By means of Pearson correlation, we explore the relationship between urban layout design parameters (P1-P10) and inundation depth. The system randomly generated 2000 urban layouts with built-up coverage of 20%, 30%, 40%, and 50% (500 layouts for each built-up coverage).

III. Results and Discussion

Although some urban layouts might not be represented accurately, the proposed urban generation system supports a wide variety of typical urban layouts, which enables us to effectively find the desired layouts from an otherwise huge search space (Figure 1).

Based on several case studies, our findings highlighted that the impact of geometric characteristics of urban patterns (e.g., street width, park ratio, etc.) on flow properties during urban floods is significant. This is especially important for accurate flood/water simulations and for city planners concerned with flooding. Our approach can reduce water depth by proposing layout changes during the design phase of an urban space. Figure 2 (top) demonstrates that our system reduced flood inundation depth by about 6% keeping the same build-up coverage. Moreover, we can increase built-up coverage and keep the same inundation depth (Figure 2-bottom). This is done by only reconfiguring urban layout design without any additional flood controls. The computed water depths are minimum at the downstream faces and maximum at the upstream faces, because of the overall flow resistance induced by the buildings.

Figure 3 shows the Pearson correlation analysis for the relationship between urban layout parameters and flood inundation depth. The Pearson correlation value ranges from -1 for a perfect negative linear relationship to +1 for a perfect positive linear relationship. The value 0 indicates no linear relationship. The results reveal that P1 (average road length) shows the strongest relationship with inundation depth.

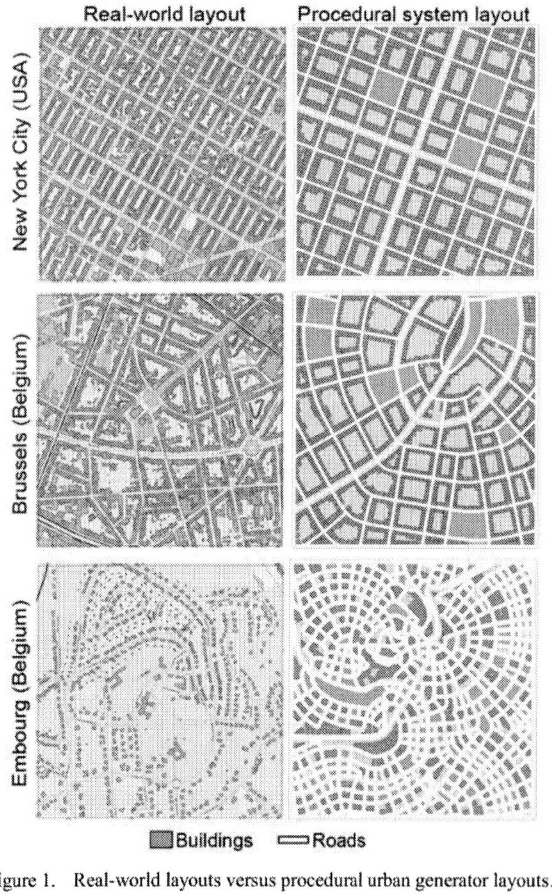

Figure 1. Real-world layouts versus procedural urban generator layouts.

This relation is positive implying that the inundation depth increases by increasing the average road length.

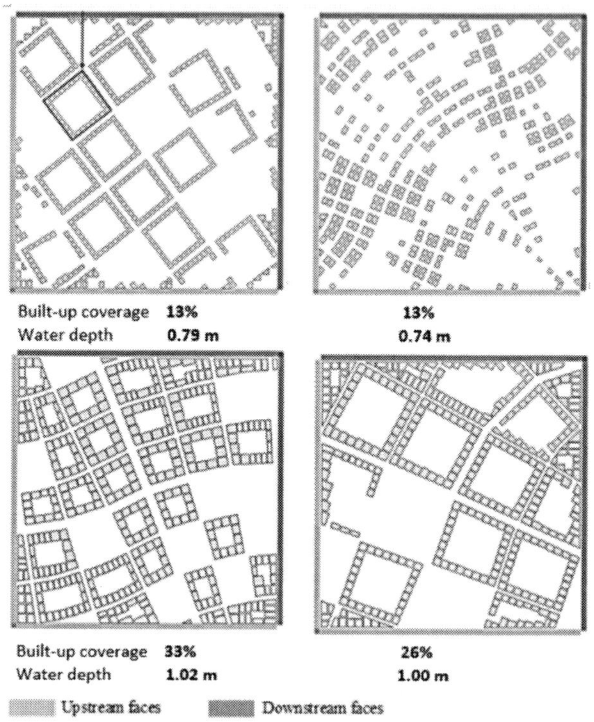

Figure 2. Built-up coverage and flood inundation depth (under the same inundation conditions) in 4 layouts generated by procedural modeling.

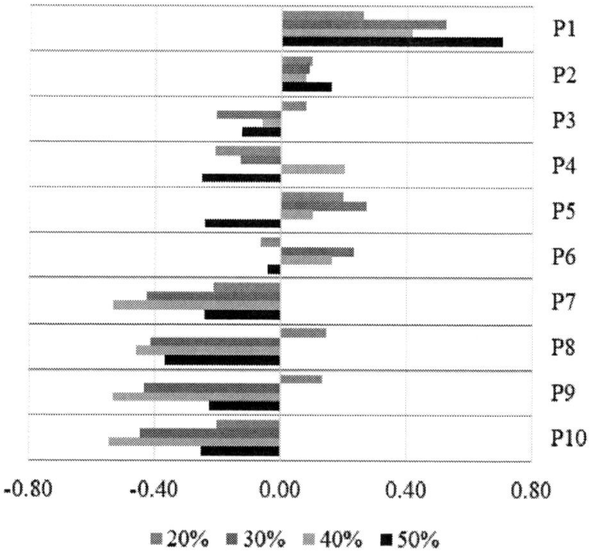

Figure 3. Pearson correlation coefficients that measure the strength and direction of a linear relationship between urban layout design parameter and flood inundation depth considering three built-up coverages (20%, 30%, 40%, and 50%).

P7, P8, P9, and P10 (average parcel area, front, rear, and side building setbacks respectively) have a strong negative relation with inundation depth. The rest of the variables (P2, P3, P4, P5, and P6) show a weak relation with inundation depth. More importantly, the relation between each variable and inundation depth varies based on the built-up coverage.

IV. CONCLUSIONS

This paper used an automatic design approach for urban procedural modeling coupled with a hydraulic model to investigate the relation between urban layout design and flood inundation depth. We systematically explored the inundation flow in quasi-realistic urbanized areas, which links hydraulic modeling results with parameters of direct significance for urban planning. Based on porosity-based hydraulic computations of inundation flow for a set of 2000 different urban layouts, the relative influence of ten urban layout parameters (average street length, street orientation and curvature, major and minor street widths, mean parcel area, rear and side building setbacks and building coverage) on flood inundation depths were assessed. We found that the most influential urban layout parameters were average road length, the mean parcel area, and the building side-setbacks. This work helps with providing guidelines for urban planners to design flood-resilient cities.

An important next step in the research is the analysis of real-world case studies, which would showcase the operationality of our system and therefore increase the impact of this assessment tool for urban planning practice.

ACKNOWLEDGMENT

The research was funded through the ARC grant for Concerted Research Actions for project number 13/17-01 financed by the French Community of Belgium (Wallonia-Brussels Federation), the European Regional Development Fund – FEDER (Wal-e-Cities Project), and NSF CBET 1250232, IIS 1302172, and CHS 1816514.

REFERENCES

[1] M. Lennon, M. Scott, and E. O'Neill, Urban Design and Adapting to Flood Risk: The Role of Green Infrastructure, Journal of Urban Design. 19 (2014) 745–758. doi:10.1080/13574809.2014.944113.

[2] E. O'Neill, Neighbourhood Design Considerations in Flood Risk Management, Planning Theory and Practice. 14 (2013) 129–134. doi:14649357.2012.761904.

[3] I. White, The absorbent city: urban form and flood risk management, Proceedings of the Institution of Civil Engineers - Urban Design and Planning. 161 (2008) 151–161. doi:10.1680/udap.2008.161.4.151.

[4] A. Mustafa, X. Wei Zhang, D.G. Aliaga, M. Bruwier, G. Nishida, B. Dewals, S. Erpicum, P. Archambeau, M. Pirotton, and J. Teller, Procedural generation of flood-sensitive urban layouts, Environment and Planning B: Urban Analytics and City Science. 0 (2018) 1–23. doi:10.1177/2399808318812458.

[5] D.G. Aliaga, C. Vanegas, M. Lei, and D. Niyogi, Visualization-Based Decision Tool for Urban Meteorological Modeling, Environ Plann B Plann Des. 40 (2013) 271–288. doi:10.1068/b38084.

[6] C.A. Vanegas, I. Garcia-Dorado, D.G. Aliaga, B. Benes, and P. Waddell, Inverse Design of Urban Procedural Models, ACM Trans. Graph. 31 (2012) 168:1–168:11. doi:10.1145/2366145.2366187.

[7] J.J. Sarralde, D.J. Quinn, D. Wiesmann, and K. Steemers, Solar energy and urban morphology: Scenarios for increasing the renewable energy potential of neighbourhoods in London, Renewable Energy. 73 (2015) 10–17. doi:10.1016/j.renene.2014.06.028.

[8] S. Erpicum, B.J. Dewals, P. Archambeau, and M. Pirotton, Dam break flow computation based on an efficient flux vector splitting, Journal of Computational and Applied Mathematics. 234 (2010) 2143–2151. doi:10.1016/j.cam.2009.08.110.

[9] M. Bruwier, A. Mustafa, D.G. Aliaga, P. Archambeau, S. Erpicum, G. Nishida, X. Zhang, M. Pirotton, J. Teller, and B. Dewals, Influence of urban pattern on inundation flow in floodplains of lowland rivers, Science of The Total Environment. 622–623 (2018) 446–458. doi:10.1016/j.scitotenv.2017.11.325.

Flexible Access to a Harmonised Multi-resolution Raster Geodata Storage in the Cloud

Lassi Lehto, Jaakko Kähkönen, Juha Oksanen and Tapani Sarjakoski
Finnish Geospatial Research Institute (FGI)
National Land Survey of Finland
Masala, Finland
e-mail: lassi.lehto@nls.fi, jaakko.kahkonen@nls.fi, juha.oksanen@nls.fi, tapani.sarjakoski@nls.fi

***Abstract*—A viable approach for tackling the challenges of integration and analysis of geospatial raster data is to pre-process datasets into a common framework and store them into a cloud repository, accessible through a set of well-defined access protocols. This paper describes an initiative called GeoCubes Finland, where the aim is to provide a number of country-wide raster geodatasets in a common schema. In addition to more traditional access methods, a custom Application Programming Interface (API) has been designed for supporting the various tasks related to retrieval, use, visualisation and analysis of the contained raster datasets.**

Keywords—raster data; multi-resolution; harmonisation; cloud service; RESTful access.

I. Introduction

Geospatial datasets are increasingly being managed in cloud service platforms. Improved performance of wired and mobile networks has made it a viable approach to centralise data maintenance procedures. At the same time, one can recognize a steady shift from simple data file downloads to the use of flexible content access APIs. Similarly, a gradual shift can be noticed from data analysis run on a local computer to the use of centralised computing resources, possibly allowing access to High-Performance Computing (HPC) platforms with extensive parallel computing capabilities.

Raster-formatted geospatial datasets have qualities that ease the integration and analysis tasks considerably. Raster data is usually simple to manage and store. Effective parallelisation of the analysis problem is usually relatively straightforward for local and neighbourhood functions. Visualisation of raster-formatted content is effective.

A few challenges remain though. In many cases raster datasets are stored in individual spatial reference systems and in differing resolutions. It is often difficult to find out the explanation for the coded cell values, as there are no standardised mechanisms available for presenting this information to the user. In visualisation, it is often a challenging task to produce reliable and visually pleasing representations for small scales. In analysis processes, it might be difficult to achieve consistent results across a range of resolution levels.

One possible approach for tackling the challenges related to the integration, analysis and visualisation of geospatial raster data is to pre-process the datasets into a common harmonised framework and store the resulting representations into a cloud platform, accessible through a set of well-defined access protocols. A development aimed at building this kind of raster cloud storage is described in this paper. The initiative is called GeoCubes Finland and is carried out by a consortium of Finnish Universities and governmental research institutions [1]. The predominant goal of the initiative is to facilitate the use of raster-formatted geospatial datasets in academic research.

The paper is organized as follows. In Section II the existing approaches comparable with the proposes access API are described. In Sections III and IV harmonization aspects and implementation details of the data storage are discussed. Section V deals with access methods generally and Section VI details the developed custom API. In Section VII the applications of the proposed multi-resolution approach are discussed and Section VIII concludes the paper.

II. Existing Approaches

The predominant standardised access mechanism for raster datasets in network service-based architecture is the Web Coverage Service (WCS) interface specification of the Open Geospatial Consortium (OGC) [2]. A WCS is supposed to provide access to raster datasets via its GetCoverage operation. This operation allows the calling application to indicate the requested coverage by name, limit the requested area by a bounding box, and optionally ask the service to produce the result in certain resolution by setting the SCALEFACTOR query parameter. For performance reasons, in many WCS implementations the maximum allowed size of the requested dataset is set to a rather low value.

III. Storage - Harmonisation, Multi-resolution

In the GeoCubes Finland raster data storage, the individual content layers are pre-processed during the ingestion process into the common spatial reference grid (the national standard grid). GeoCubes Finland is inherently a multi-resolution data storage. A fixed set of resolution levels (10 values) has been selected and all ingested datasets are pre-processed into those resolutions. Individual, dataset-specific generalisation procedures, suggested by the original data provider, are applied in the process. This way the best possible consistency among the resolution levels can be achieved.

IV. Implementation in Cloud-Optimized GeoTIFF

GeoCubes Finland data storage is implemented in the form of Cloud-Optimized GeoTIFF (COG) files (TIFF: Tagged Image File Format), each representing a 100 km * 100 km block [3]. The area of the country is divided into 60 such blocks. The resolution levels are stored both as internal GeoTIFF overview layers and as individual resolution-specific GeoTIFF files. The set of 60 blocks is aggregated into a single content representation by using the GDAL's (Geospatial Data Abstraction Library) Virtual format (VRT) mechanism [4]. VRT files also combine together the files on individual resolution levels. GDAL's Python API is extensively used in the data ingestion and data provision procedures. Parallelisation of the computing processes is done applying Python's subprocess mechanisms.

V. Access methods - HTTP GET Range, VRT, REST

A set of different access methods are supported in the GeoCubes Finland's raster data repository. The traditional standardised methods for raster data access and visualisation are supported. These include OGC-specified interfaces WCS, Web Map Service (WMS) and Web Map Tile Service (WMTS). Individual block-wise GeoTIFF files can be accessed using a standardised URL (Uniform Resource Locator) scheme and the conventional HTTP (Hypertext Transfer Protocol) based data transfer. In addition to that, a HTTP GET Range request can be applied for partial file downloads. This process is efficient, because of the optimised organisation of the contents in the COG files.

The GDAL Virtual format (VRT) mechanism is used to combine together the 60 blocks covering the country. VRT is a light-weight XML (Extensible Markup Language) formatted text file describing the parts that belong to the merged dataset. Data transmission is optimised, as only the actually needed part of the raster data content - on the requested resolution level - is transferred over the network.

A Django-based service platform has been developed to facilitate flexible access to the GeoCubes content. A RESTful API (REST: Representational State Transfer) supports the various tasks related to the retrieval, use, visualisation and analysis of the contained raster datasets.

VI. RESTful access API

The designed RESTful API is based on the following general semantic structure of the path components:

```
/ what to do / on which resolution level
/ with which content layer / where / how
```

The API contains operations for accessing basic metadata of the contained raster layers. Based on the provided information, the client application can find out the names of the theme layers in the storage and form the URLs needed for accessing the individual files.

The API contains operations for efficient and flexible retrieval of raster content. The area of interest can be selected by a bounding box, a set of block identifiers, and by a list of codes or names of administrative units of the country (three administrative levels supported). The layer contents can be downloaded either as GeoTIFF content or as a VRT file. When using the VRT alternative, the user can determine, if only the requested resolution level should be returned or if all the coarser levels have also to be included.

Once retrieved, one of the first tasks in using a raster dataset is to understand the meaning of the cell values. In some cases, it is rather straightforward to interpret the values, for instance, if data represents a continuous variable. However, for categorical data, it is often difficult to find meaning for the values. In the GeoCubes API, there is an operation for finding the explanation for a given code value. It is also possible to ask for the category description by layer name, resolution level and a coordinate point. This enables dynamic lookup of category information by moving the cursor on top of a visualised map.

The API also contains demonstrative examples of analysis functions performed on server side, using GeoCubes content layers as input data. Examples include value distribution calculations by administrative unit, change detection between two epochs of datasets with time series, and aggregation between theme layers.

VII. Applications of multi-resolution storage

There are some recognised use cases, where the multi-resolution approach of the GeoCubes Finland repository can be utilised. Sometimes an analysis process has to be carried out on certain resolution level, because another input data set is only available on that resolution. In addition, there are long-standing conventions for analysing certain phenomenon on a specific resolution level. Furthermore, while developing an analysis procedure, it is often useful to first test the analysis on coarser levels of resolution, before launching the real long-running procedure on a fine-grained resolution level.

An interesting application of multi-resolution raster data storage is a geospatial analysis task, where results are explored visually in the form of a map. When the user explores the resulting visualisation in various zoom levels, the background analysis can always be interactively run, utilising data from the corresponding resolution level in the data storage. This way the analysis can be run in roughly constant time over the whole range of the visualisation scale. This approach makes it also possible to configure a visualisation of an analysis result as a new content layer for the data storage.

VIII. Conclusion

GeoCubes Finland is a new initiative to provide academic sector users with an easy-to-use raster geodata repository in the cloud, with a set of flexible content access methods and support for server-side analysis procedures. Modern raster data management techniques, like Cloud-Optimized GeoTIFF, HTTP GET Range protocol and GDAL Virtual Format, are applied in the data access process. A new RESTful API has been designed for facilitating data retrieval, interpretation and analysis. The data repository is currently under construction. First user tests will be carried out in the next coming months.

Acknowledgment

The work described in this paper has been carried out in the context of the project 'Open Geospatial Information Infrastructure for Research' (oGIIR, urn:nbn:fi:research-infras-2016072513), a part of Finland's Roadmap for Research Infrastructures. The project is funded by the Academy of Finland, grant number 306536. The computing infrastructure used in the work is funded by the Academy of Finland through 'Finnish Grid and Cloud Infrastructure', urn:nbn:fi:research-infras-2016072533, grant number 283818.

References

[1] oGIIR, Open Geospatial Information Infrastructure. http://ogiir.fi [retrieved: Jan, 2018]

[2] OGC, Web Coverage Service. http://www.opengeospatial.org /standards/wcs [retrieved: Jan, 2018]

[3] GeoTIFF, GeoTIFF home page. http://trac.osgeo.org/geotiff/ [retrieved: Jan, 2018]

[4] GDAL, Geospatial Data Abstraction Library. http://gdal.org [retrieved: Jan, 2018]

WhizPS: An Architecture for Well-conditioned, Scalable Geoprocessing Services Based on the WPS Standard

Marius Laska, Stefan Herle and Jörg Blankenbach

Geodetic Institute and Chair for Computing in Civil Engineering & Geo Information Systems, RWTH Aachen University 52074 Aachen, Germany
Email: marius.laska@gia.rwth-aachen.de

Eric Fichter and Jérôme Frisch

Institute of Energy Efficiency and Sustainable Building, RWTH Aachen University 52074 Aachen, Germany
Email: fichter@e3d.rwth-aachen.de

***Abstract*—Spatial simulations and models are often expert tools which solve a specific spatial problem or model a spatial process. Exposing theses analysis capabilities as a web service is a huge benefit to users of web-based Geographic Information Systems (GISs). The Web Processing Service (WPS) standard was developed to realize these services. In the Geothermal Information System for Potential Studies in Subsurface Soil Layers (GeTIS) project, several complex analysis tools should be exposed as a WPS service and, simultaneously, follow the concept of well-conditioned, scalable services. In this paper, we describe our implemented backend, which can be used to bind expert tools and facade them with the WPS interface. The architecture rests on different communication mechanisms such as Remote Procedure Calls (RPCs) and message queuing as well as geospatial services such as Web Map Service (WMS).**

***Index Terms*—Geoprocessing; Web service; Web Processing Service; Scalability; Geothermal Simulation**

I. Introduction

The Web Processing Service (WPS) interface was introduced in 2007 by the Open Geospatial Consortium (OGC) for accessing geospatial processing capabilities by HTTP methods. Unlike other important and already established services in the geospatial world, such as Web Map Service (WMS) or Web Feature Service (WFS), the new standard should not just give access to data but enabled processes and models to be requested. But still, the WPS is not heavily used basically because of required advanced knowledge to develop an application as a compliant service and some drawbacks of the underlying protocols.

However, in the Geothermal Information System for Potential Studies in Subsurface Soil Layers (GeTIS) project the WPS interface is a central component of the architecture. The goal of the project is the development of a web-based information system that provides all required data for the regulatory approval and planning of geothermal systems [1]. Currently, these information has to be requested explicitly by the approval authority from different governmental agencies (e.g., geological service, environmental agency, cadastral agency), which is not trivial and inhibits a faster diffusion of geothermal systems. In order to have a single access point, different data sources have to be integrated by standardized service interfaces in such an information system. Apart from that also simulation processes (e.g., for simulating the extent of the temperature plume) are connected to the web portal. However, these simulation tools are developed as expert desktop applications and are not supposed to be deployed as web services. For exposing them as standardized web services, a sophisticated architecture relying on the WPS standard was designed. Based on the following requirements, we implemented a distributed WPS architecture:

- The effort of the service provider for making software accessible and ensure interoperability at the same time should be minimized.
- The system should be loosely coupled, which means that service providers can freely choose on which operating system the task is executed. Furthermore, service providers have the capabilities to run their software in a distributed environment or on their local server. This allows for minimal deployment effort as well as scalable execution of resource dependent tasks.
- The architecture should be built based on open source software and reuse existing and well-known solutions.

This paper describes the distributed architecture developed in the GeTIS project. It starts in Section II with a research about the state-of-the-art of distributed services and especially other WPS-based solutions. After introducing the basic concepts of the WPS interface in Section III, we describe our architectural approach (see Section IV) with the conceptual design and our implementation. Then in Section V, the GeTIS Online Simulation (GOS) as a use case and its integration in our distributed WPS architecture is presented. Finally, we summarize the insights of the implemented system and discuss further developments.

II. State of the Art

A WPS interface is used in the geospatial community to provide geospatial analysis algorithms as a service to users. Often, these processes, such as simulations or predictions are very time consuming, which makes it important to run these on appropriate hardware to speed up processing time. Additionally, the implemented algorithms are often expert tools, which are developed by scientist for running on a single machine and are not supposed to be provided as a service. The WPS facades the expert software to facilitate execution and to provide interoperability. The important factor in merging expert tools with a service interface is to implement the WPS with respect to requirements of well-conditioned services.

A *well-conditioned service* is defined as a simple pipeline, which depth is determined by the path through the network and the processing stages of the service [2]. Thus, increasing load also increases the delivered throughput proportionally until the pipeline is full and the throughput saturates. In other words, the service is not allowed to overcommit its resources, otherwise all clients would suffer. The key property of well-conditioned services is *graceful degradation*, which implies that the service maintains a high throughput without a dramatic increase in response time. In concurrent server designs, multiple requests can be accepted and processed at once. The *threaded server design* uses a dispatcher to distribute each incoming request to a separate thread. Each thread processes its request and returns a result to the client. Challenges with long-lasting processes may occur in this setup. With many clients connecting simultaneously, many threads may be active at the same time and context switching may consume large memory and CPU resources. Limiting the number of concurrent clients e.g. by thread pools can tackle this problem. Another approach is the *event-driven server design*. It does not follow the thread-per-connection model, but uses an event loop in a single thread to consume events from an event queue. This main thread processes incoming events and drives the execution of many finite state machines (FSM) with so-called event handlers. Each FSM represents a single request but the complexity is the event scheduler which controls the execution of each FSM [2]. Both architectural models can be used to build highly scalable servers [3], however, the highest scalability and load adaptability can only be accomplished with a distributed approach, since it can easily expand the resource pool.

In the literature, some approaches can be found for distributing WPS request between multiple processing units. In [4] a WPS mediation is implemented to process geospatial data on different computing backends. The job submission software Ganga [5] is used to provide distributed computing in a grid or on a cluster. Performance and scalability were improved successfully. Similarly, other approaches use different distributed computing infrastructure, such as Unicore [6] [7] or forward the WPS request to a Hadoop Cluster [8]. In these solutions, the processes are invoked by sending the input data and the executable of the application to the grid utilizing the job submission tool. The implementations improve calculation performance and service availability enormously. In [9], a spatial computing node based on WPS is designed. In their approach, the utilized spatial data libraries, such as Geotools or GDAL are deployed in distributed machines to process spatial data concurrently and effectively. The single instance uses an appropriate middleware to communicate. Data processing velocity was improved for common spatial processing tasks. In [10] a RabbitMQ queue is used to communicate with a high performance cluster to calculate flooded tiles. The request is computed on the cluster while the result handling is done by the WPS server. They conclude that exploiting supercomputing infrastructures provides scalability and performant processing. Other approaches use middleware software to distribute the requests directly to multiple machines. The WPS remote community module of the GeoServer [11] allows to run requests on one or more remote machines by exposing processes with the WPS protocol. For realizing this, some RPC methods, such as run, progress, complete or kill are implemented utilizing the Extensible Messaging and Presence Protocol (XMPP) protocol for remote commands. Additionally, a remote balancer is included to distribute incoming request based on occupancy of the servers.

III. Web Processing Service (WPS)

Standardized geo web services are used in modern Spatial Data Infrastructures (SDIs) to ensure interoperability. With the OGC WPS version 1.0, a standard for accessing and initiating geospatial processing was introduced in 2007 [12]. The main characteristics of the standard are the introduced rules to define in- and outputs of deployed processes and the different request methods of the service.

The Hypertext Transport Protocol (HTTP)-based WPS follows the request/response messaging pattern and has three core operations: The *GetCapabilities* operation can be used by requesting clients to receive meta-information about the server and its services. The response includes descriptions and the identifier about each process. Detailed information about in- and outputs of each process can be requested by the *DescribeProcess* operation given the process identifier. Finally, the *Execute* operation invokes the process. The user submits the request by posting necessary input parameters to the server. The inputs and outputs can have different data types, such as literals or references to other geo web services.

Processes can be executed in *synchronous* or *asynchronous* mode. In synchronous mode, the server parses the requesting XML, executes the process with respect to the inputs, waits until all calculations are performed and returns the resulting *ProcessExecuted* XML response to the client. In asynchronous mode, after receiving and accepting the request, the server sends a *ProcessAccepted* response immediately to the client. The response contains an URL with can be requested to check the process status while the process runs in the background. When the process finishes successfully, the server creates a final response and stores this document at the specified URL.

The client fetches the result when it requests the given URL the next time.

Since WPS version 1.0 has some drawbacks, the version 2.0 was released in 2014. The introduced features cover for instance improvements in the process descriptions or a *Dismiss* operation to cancel a process.

IV. Architectural Approach

A. Conceptual approach of the architecture

Research projects in the GIS domain, such as the GeTIS project often involve the development of expert tools and processes. While rapid prototyping displays a major demand, the deployment of theses processes and accessibility remains a challenge. Implemented processes should be discoverable and exposed as a service via web technologies. This requires that they are accessible using a uniform interface and that their inputs and outputs are clearly formulated. The WPS specification aims at solving this demand. However, existing implementations, such as the PyWPS [13] server lack the ability to bind services and initiate processes remotely. It requires central development and deployment of the processes, which has two major drawbacks: First, development of processes is slowed down since the exposure as a service usually requires adaption and deployment on a web server and, thus, cannot be directly offered on the developer's machine. Second, horizontal scaling is not possible if the WPS server simultaneously represents the single computing back-end. Processing large-scale data or long-lasting processes would influence the responsiveness of the server, which contradicts the well-conditioned service paradigm.

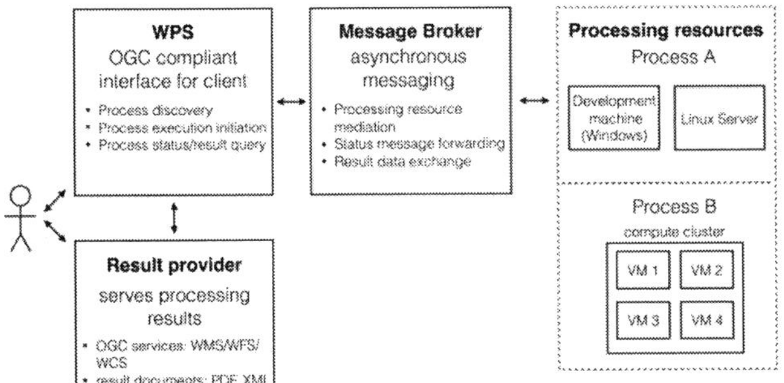

Fig. 1. High level view of main components of the distributed WPS architecture.

An architecture to meet the requirements of exposing expert tools and to handle the described drawbacks in WPS servers is illustrated in Figure 1. Providing an OGC compliant WPS interface for the client is reasonable to allow for process discovery and initiation in a standardized way. Thereby, the possibly multi-layered back-end and expert processes are masked by the WPS interface. Furthermore, instead of directly processing the requested task on the WPS web server, mediating the request to available computing resources constitutes a much more sophisticated way to process the request. Enabling physical separation between the WPS interface and the processing resources requires some orchestration via asynchronous message exchange. A message broker mediates the task to one of the available processing resources and forwards status messages as well as the final result data to the WPS interface. In order to make both, the status messages and the results, accessible for the client, a result provider is required. Depending on the result data format, it should offer the client direct access to documents, such as PDF or XML files, or provide a OGC compliant service for discovering and accessing spatially referenced data.

B. Applied tools

A PyWPS server (version 4.0.0) builds the foundation for constructing the WPS compliant interface in our architecture. PyWPS is an implementation of the WPS standard from the OGC written in Python. It enables integration, publishing and execution of Python processes via the WPS standard [13]. PyWPS can be deployed with integrated Flask [14] web server, or with an Apache web server. Currently, only the WPS specification 1.0.0 is supported but adaption of the new version 2.0.0 is planned. Geospatial processes can be implemented by extending the *Process* class, which contains a handler and a list of input and output according to the WPS specification. Whenever the PyWPS server receives a new WPS Execute request, it creates a new thread and executes the defined handling method. This limits the ability to distribute processing load over multiple processing machines, since all processes run on the same machine where the PyWPS server is deployed. In order to employ remote processing resources, they have to be addressed via patterns like RPC, which requires asynchronous messaging. In our architecture, a RabbitMQ server is chosen for tackling this issue.

RabbitMQ is the most widely deployed open source message broker. It is lightweight and easy to deploy on premise or in distributed cloud settings and supports multiple messaging protocols. Producers send messages to *exchanges* from which they are forwarded to queues that consumers bind to the specific exchange. This allows for realizing patterns like a worker queue, where multiple consumers listen for messages on the same queue. Furthermore, publish/subscribe patterns can be implemented by using an exchange with *fan-out* characteristics, such that each consumer that wants to receive the messages can bind its own queue to that exchange. In the proposed architecture a RPC like pattern is implemented. Each PyWPS process has its own worker queue. Processing resources for that PyWPS process listen for tasks on that queue. Upon entering the worker queue, an incoming task is fairly dispatched to one of the available resources. In order to allow communication between the PyWPS process and the processing resource, the PyWPS process creates a temporary response queue that the processing resource utilizes for exchanging status message and result data.

In order to use the described RPC pattern, a threaded python implementation using the Pika BlockingConnection [15] has been realized, which will be referred to in the following as PyRPCproducer and PyRPCconsumer. Each PyWPS process has its dedicated PyRPCprocuder. Furthermore, each processing resource operates its own PyRPCconsumer, which can be configured to listen to a specific worker queue and starts a specifiable script. The PyRPCconsumer listens for the console output and forwards messages that contain a specific logging keyword back via the temporary response queue. After having successfully executed the script, all data of a specifiable output folder is encoded and sent back using the temporary response queue. In order to configure a new processing resource, solely the PyRPCconsumer has to be installed and configured, which minimizes the deployment overhead.

C. Workflow

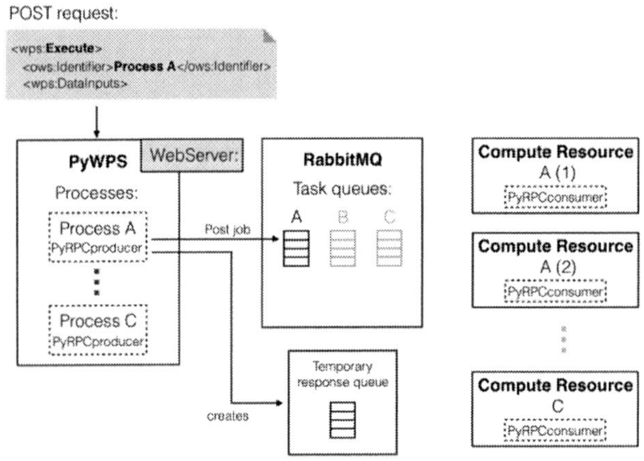

Fig. 2. Workflow after client requests new processing task at the PyWPS server with focus on setup required for task mediation and communication.

The PyWPS server offers multiple processes (according to WPS formulation), which can be discovered and described according to the WPS specifications using the *GetCapabilities* and *DescribeProcess* operations. A process can be started using the *Execute* operation, while specifying the process identifier as well as supplying the process with the specified input data. This request is illustrated by Figure 2. Each of the processes deployed in the PyWPS server uses a dedicated instance of the PyRPCproducer implementation, which was introduced before. The process encodes the input data in JSON format and sends it to the corresponding task queue. In Figure 2, an execute operation for process A is sent to the PyWPS server, such that its PyRPCproducer posts the job to task queue A. Simultaneously, it instantiates a temporary response queue, which will be used by the assigned working machine of the service provider to transmit status messages and the final results of the process. The service provider of process A might be offering multiple physical machines for handling incoming tasks in order to handle increasing processing load. This facilitates horizontal scaling.

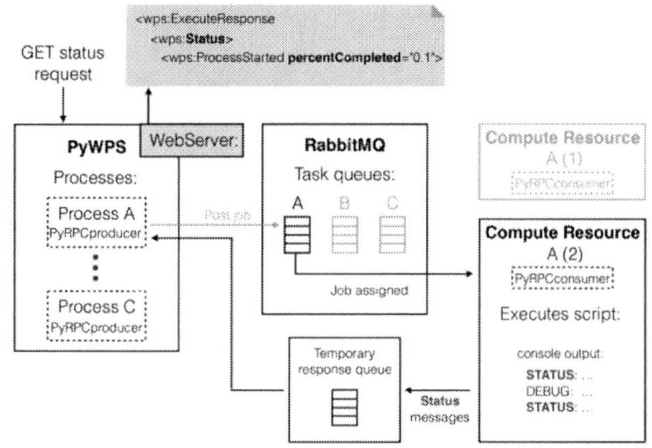

Fig. 3. Workflow after remote processing machine is assigned with emphasis on communication between PyWPS, the computing resource and the requesting client.

Each working machine of a process provider is subscribed to one or multiple task queues, depending on which processes it should handle. Given that computing resources are available, processing requests that arrive at the RabbitMQ broker are immediately forwarded to one of the subscribed clients. This process is illustrated by Figure 3. Worker resource A (2) is assigned to handle the task and starts the processing software. The process' RPC client listens for the console output and forwards messages, which contain specific keywords, such that status updates can be communicated back to the PyWPS server. The messages containing the keyword (e.g., *STATUS*, green in Figure 3), are forwarded via the temporary response queue.

After successful completion of the script, all result documents that are present in a specific folder (*output folder*, green in Figure 4) are encoded and returned via the same temporary response queue.

During the whole processing of a request, the initiator of the *Execute* operation is able to access the status messages of the processes by requesting a resource at PyWPS server. All status messages as well as the results and input files of the processes are served by an integrated Flask web server. PyWPS can also run as WSGI application on an Apache HTTP server. Finally, the results of the process are served back to the process' initiator, either as direct data, or as references to the location where the data can be requested (illustrated by Figure 4).

D. Result handling by PyWPS extension

The implemented PyWPS extension offers various result handling solutions, which are conform to the WPS standard. They are basically divided into direct responses containing the result in plain text, such as an XML document, or responses that contain a reference to a resource combined with its format specification. Typically, geo processes deliver spatially referenced data as result, such as GeoTIFFs (raster data)

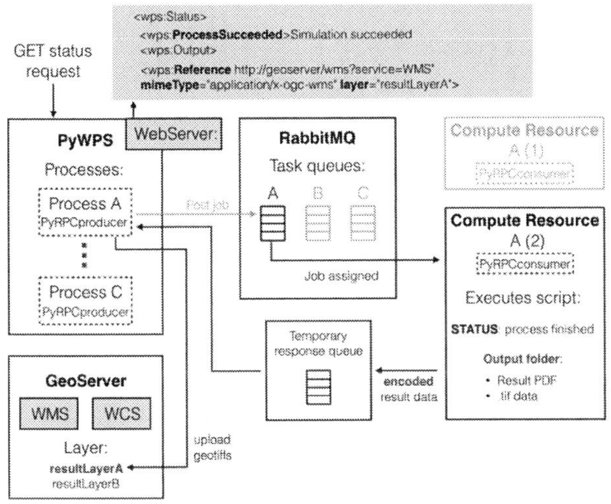

Fig. 4. Workflow of result data provisioning with emphasis on handling spatially referenced data.

or shapefiles (vector data format of ESRI). For convenience reasons, it is beneficial to offer access to these results via a dedicated service. The OGC defines several standards for services and encodings. The WMS is a so-called portrayal service, which delivers georeferenced data as styled images for visualization purposes. Raw georeferenced raster data is accessible by the Web Coverage Service (WCS), while vector data can be provided by the WFS standard. Several implementations of these services exist, among other the GeoServer [16], which is a widely used implementation of an open source server for sharing geospatial data. It provides OGC compliant implementation of the mentioned standards WMS, WFS and WCS. Spatial data, such as GeoTIFFs can be uploaded and function as data source for any of the services.

In our proposed solution, the PyWPS process uploads the spatially referenced result data of the remote process to a GeoServer instance via its REST interface [17]. When a client requests the status of a finished process, the output section of the result XML file links to the WMS *GetCapabilities* request, but also includes the name of the corresponding layer. This enables the client to specifically discover information on how to access the WMS layer that has been generated as result of the process.

Non-spatial data, such as a resulting PDF file are served by the internal web server of the PyWPS instance and are also linked in the outputs section of the status response.

Additionally, for long-lasting processes it might be inappropriate to constantly poll status updates from the web server. Therefore, we implemented a notification mechanism that sends out an email to the initiator of the process as soon as the results of the process are available. It requires a specified email address in WPS execute request. Other notifications mechanisms are conceivable, which could include sending an SMS or a message via any other messaging protocol like XMPP [18].

V. Use Case - Online Geothermal Process

For demonstrating our architecture in a real usage scenario, an example process is described below that was developed within the scope of the GeTIS project.

The GeTIS Online Simulation (GOS) [19] is a transient three-dimensional subsurface simulation that allows to plan geothermal borehole heat exchangers. Using a finite volume approach, it considers heat conduction in the rock as well as convectional heat transport caused by ground water flow. For this purpose, spatial, physical and geological properties of the subsurface are needed. The GOS requires these input data encoded in an XML file. Therefore, the WPS server facades the corresponding process with a single input field for the XML input file and transfers it via the messaging broker to the computing machine on which the GOS runs. The structured and parsed information is allocated to the setup functions building the three-dimensional simulation grid. While solving the mathematical equations for the simulated time span of 50 years, the remaining processing time is communicated to the WPS. The results of the GOS are processed textually and graphically to inform the user. Information about simulation and subsurface conditions as well as plots for time series and spatial field data, e.g., to visualize volume fluxes and performances, are copied into a single PDF. Horizontal section views showing temperature data are processed to GeoTiff files. All result documents are transferred back to the WPS server via the messaging broker. The georeferenced files are uploaded to the GeoServer using the REST interface such that a WMS service can be offered to demonstrate the influence of the heat extraction caused by the borehole heat exchangers on neighboring properties. Among the request parameters of the WMS specification is a so-called elevation dimension, which enables the presentation of geospatial information at different elevations. In the context of the GOS, the elevation dimension is used to allow the requester to browse through the different subsurface levels. The resulting PDF file is stored on a web server and can be accessed by a request specific URL.

Like the GOS simulation, the GeTIS project involves two other processes, which can be invoked by the WPS interface and computed in our architecture. This includes an analytical subsurface model and a building simulator (see [19]).

VI. Conclusion

We proposed the implementation of an architecture to expose geospatial processes as web services. Since a wide range of developed spatial simulations and models can be classified as expert tools, we formulated specific requirements. The architecture facilitates deploying implemented tools with minimal effort, it is loosely coupled with the actual expert tools allowing for hardware independent deployment and, furthermore, it is based on existing open source components. In detail, we implemented an OGC compliant WPS interface based on the PyWPS server with respect to the stated requirements. The RabbitMQ middleware is used to distribute WPS requests based on occupancy to available processing resources. For this, we developed a PyRPCconsumer script that serves as the sole interface for software providers to connect their expert tools such that they can be invoked with standardized WPS request. The WPS implementation is able to handle spatial as well as non-spatial result data by generating standardized geospatial portrayal and data services (e.g., WMS) provided by a GeoServer or by serving documents through a simple web server. The applicability of the proposed architecture has been demonstrated by utilizing it in the GeTIS project to expose several complex analysis tools. For demonstration purposes, the GOS has been described, which simulates the subsurface allowing to plan borehole heat exchangers.

Currently, each WPS request facades a single expert tool, however in the future the architecture could be easily extended so that requests can be split up into sub-tasks, which could be run concurrently on multiple machines to decrease processing time. Furthermore, it is not possible to cancel running processes at the moment, since the underlying PyWPS implementation is based on the WPS 1.0 specification, which lacks of the *Dismiss* operation that has been first introduced in version 2.0. However, our architecture does already support the abortion of processes by sending broadcast messages to all computing resources. If the request is already accepted and invoked, it is cancelled directly. Otherwise, the en-queued and pending request is ignored by the computing machines. As soon as the PyWPS implementation has been upgraded to support WPS 2.0, the abortion of running processes can be effortlessly integrated.

ACKNOWLEDGMENT

The work and implementations described in this paper are conducted in the GeTIS project which is funded by the German Federal Ministry for Economic Affairs and Energy (BMWi).

REFERENCES

[1] S. Weck-Ponten, R. Becker, S. Herle, J. Blankenbach, J. Frisch, and C. van Treeck, "Automatisierte Datenaggregation zur Einbindung einer dynamischen Gebäudesimulation in ein Geoinformationssystem," in *Tagungsband der 7. Deutsch-Österreichischen IBPSA-Konferenz BauSIM 2018*, Karlsruhe, 2018, pp. 516–523.

[2] M. Welsh, D. Culler, and E. Brewer, "Seda: An architecture for well-conditioned, scalable internet services," in *Proceedings of the Eighteenth ACM Symposium on Operating Systems Principles*, ser. SOSP '01. New York, NY, USA: ACM, 2001, pp. 230–243. [Online]. Available: http://doi.acm.org/10.1145/502034.502057

[3] D. Pariag, T. Brecht, A. Harji, P. Buhr, A. Shukla, and D. R. Cheriton, "Comparing the performance of web server architectures," in *Proceedings of the 2Nd ACM SIGOPS/EuroSys European Conference on Computer Systems 2007*, ser. EuroSys '07. New York, NY, USA: ACM, 2007, pp. 231–243. [Online]. Available: http://doi.acm.org/10.1145/1272996.1273021

[4] G. Giuliani, S. Nativi, A. Lehmann, and N. Ray, "WPS mediation: An approach to process geospatial data on different computing backends," *Computers and Geosciences*, vol. 47, pp. 20–33, 2012. [Online]. Available: http://dx.doi.org/10.1016/j.cageo.2011.10.009

[5] "Ganga," URL: https://ganga.readthedocs.io/en/latest/ [accessed: 2018-12-13].

[6] "Unicore," URL: http://www.somewebpage.org/ [accessed: 2018-12-13].

[7] B. Baranski, "Grid computing enabled web processing service," in *GI-Days, Münster*, 2008, pp. 1–12.

[8] Z. Chen, N. Chen, C. Yang, and L. Di, "Cloud computing enabled web processing service for earth observation data processing," *IEEE Journal of Selected Topics in Applied Earth Observations and Remote Sensing*, vol. 5, no. 6, pp. 1637–1649, Dec 2012.

[9] L. Liu, G. Li, and J. Xie, "Design & implementation of distributed spatial computing node based on WPS," in *IOP Conference Series: Earth and Environmental Science*, ser. IOP Conference Series: Earth and Environmental Science, vol. 17, 2014, pp. 1–8.

[10] A. Tellez-Arenas, R. Quique, F. Boulahya, G. Le Cozannet, F. Paris, S. Le Roy, F. Dupros, and F. Robida, *Scalable Interactive Platform for Geographic Evaluation of Sea-Level Rise Impact Combining High-Performance Computing and WebGIS Client*. Cham: Springer International Publishing, 2018, pp. 163–175. [Online]. Available: https://doi.org/10.1007/978-3-319-74669-2_12

[11] Open Source Geospatial Foundation, "GeoServer WPS Remote community module," 2018. [Online]. Available: http://docs.geoserver.org/stable/en/user/community/remote-wps/index.html

[12] P. Schut, "OpenGIS Web Processing Service 1.0.0 [OGC 05-007r7]," Open Geospatial Consortium, Tech. Rep., 2007.

[13] PyWPS Development Team, "Python Web Processing Service (PyWPS)," 2009, URL: http://pywps.org [accessed: 2018-12-13].

[14] "Flask," URL: http://flask.pocoo.org/ [accessed: 2018-12-13].

[15] "Pika Blocking Connection," URL: https://pika.readthedocs.io/en/0.10.0/modules/adapters/blocking.html [accessed: 2018-12-13].

[16] "GeoServer," URL: http://geoserver.org/ [accessed: 2018-12-13].

[17] "GeoServer REST Interface." [Online]. Available: https://docs.geoserver.org/stable/en/user/rest/index.html

[18] "Extensible Messaging and Presence Protocol (XMPP)," URL: https://xmpp.org/ [accessed: 2018-12-13].

[19] E. Fichter, S. Weck, R. Becker, J. Derksen, S. Düber, J. Frisch, D. Koppmann, R. Löhring, J. Blankenbach, C. van Treeck, and M. Ziegler, "Geothermal Information System for Potential Studies in Subsurface Soil Layers," in *Proceedings of Building Simulation: 15th Conference of IBPSA*, San Francisco, CA, USA, 2017, pp. 662–671.

Automated Construction of Road Networks from GPS Tracks

Weiping Yang
Analysis and Geoprocessing, Esri, Inc.
380 New York St. Redlands, USA
email: wyang@esri.com

Abstract--**This paper describes a framework for automating road networks using GPS (Global Positioning Systems) track measurements. Through observation and experiments on the data, it is decided that automating road networks is done in a two-step process. The first step is to identify intersections of roads, following an intersection model that also identifies and holds tracking groups leading to the first legs of incident roads. The second step, road segments incident to intersection nodes will be iteratively discovered by moving probe lines perpendicular to the heading directions of the generated roads. Initial intersections are assessed through analysing turns of vehicle trajectories and characteristics pertinent to where roads meet. Statistical techniques are used on tracks in relation to probe lines to exclude outliers and to locate median positions as vertices of roads. The method described in this paper exploits topological and geometric measures about neighbourhood of roads and applies machine learning techniques that iteratively compute optimized results for these measures.**

Keywords – vehicle GPS data tracking; automated road extraction; road network analysis; geospatial data mining and knowledge discovery; machine learning.

I. INTRODUCTION

The availability of ever increasing amount of GPS data has given rise to the needs for capabilities of processing large quantities of data and of discovering knowledge, patterns, or actionable information. One practical need is to find roads from GPS tracks representing trip trajectories of vehicles moving on roads or parking areas. The roads can serve as base maps for mapmaking, trip planning, guiding navigations, or as updates to existing map databases. Compared to traditional methods of collecting transportation data through field surveying or remotely sensed images, GPS tracks provide an inexpensive, significantly massive, and timely data sources for conventional and emerging applications requiring road networks. This paper proposes an algorithm that generates roads from GPS tracks which are chronological records, for example, of Uber vehicle trips. No prior knowledge of existing road databases is assumed. Fig. 1 illustrates a study area which contains a dataset of Uber GPS points captured around San Francisco area (left). The tracks formed by chronologically connecting GPS points belonging to same vehicle trips are shown at the right.

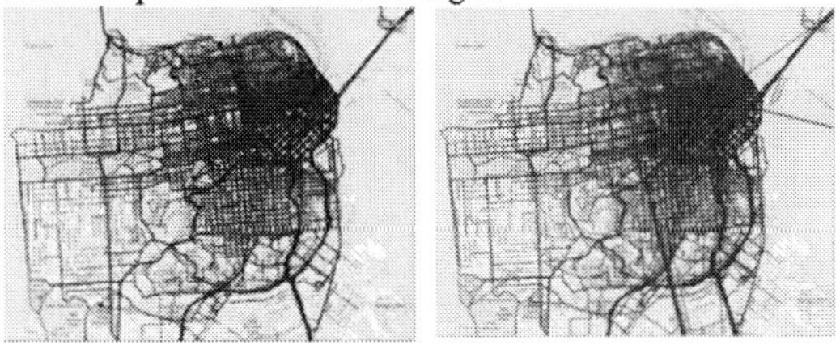

Figure 1. Uber GPS points and tracks.

As evident from the above figures, GPS points or connected tracks form clusters largely in linear shapes along roads in background images. Comparing the left and right maps in Fig. 1, one can see that "discrepancies" of data become a norm as arbitrary lines can be observed crossing the map. These lines are indeed caused by errors in GPS data. In addition, there are GPS tracks or sections of which that appear ambiguous on which roads they are supposed to adhere to. These ambiguities are noises among the largely clustered data. Furthermore, in the highly built-up downtown area where GPS location estimation becomes widely inaccurate, large number of spurious points have severely blurred street patterns. The errors and noises in GPS data collection presents additional challenges for devising a robust automated method of extracting roads.

Problems of extracting roads from GPS tracks have been tackled ever since GPS became a popular addition to vehicles. The diversity of published methods reflects usages of the extracted road structures. One type of the objectives, refining and enriching existing maps for advanced trip planning and navigation, requires accurate road geometries, better connectivity, multi-lanes, and intersection structures [1][2]. The algorithms to this end usually depend on existing road networks; and have a prerequisite for a map matching [3][4] algorithm to find correspondence between GPS tracks and existing roads. Another type of goals is more general. It does not require the existence of road maps but attempts to extract roads from scratch on GPS tracks only [5]-[9]. This type of algorithms usually applies statistical and machine learning techniques, such as least squares, k-means or density-based spatial clustering of applications with noise (DBSCAN), to discover road network patterns. The result roads can be served as base maps for new development areas or as timely updates to existing databases. Biagioni and Eriksson [10] made a comprehensive survey on earlier methods of map generation and pointed out the issue of lacking automated procedures for verifying and evaluating results. Ahmed et al [11] followed up with a book summarizing the published major algorithms on map construction and highlighted three types of algorithms, namely point clustering, incremental track insertion, and intersection linking.

The method proposed in this paper constructs road networks, as planar graphs, by discovering linear and connectivity patterns from GPS tracking points. Upon observations and experiments on data, it is decided that the first step is to identify intersections of roads, based on an intersection model. In the second step, road segments incident to each intersection node will be iteratively discovered by progressively moving probe lines perpendicular to the heading directions of the trailing road segments. Statistical techniques are used on tracks in relation to probe lines to exclude outlier tracks and to locate median positions as vertices of roads. The output is a dataset of road features with an average speed and a count indicating the number of vehicles travelling on each road. The method that determines intersection first is in line with the approach taken by Fathi and Krumm [12]. Unlike training a shape descriptor and time-exhaustively moving it around to detect intersections [12], the intersections in this paper are discovered by evaluating and clustering turns of trajectories, so the intersections are found analytically and are more likely corresponding to real world road junctions with stop signs. Furthermore, the validation process designed in this paper, in addition to determining final positions of intersections, accomplishes a discovery of similar tracks belonging to same roads incident to intersection nodes.

Testing and evaluating the goodness of generated road networks faces a challenge to producing automated qualitative and quantitative assessment. Fortunately, recent development in feature matching [13] and the commercially available Detect Feature Changes ArcGIS® geoprocessing tool [14] can provide comprehensive comparisons with existing roads in databases.

Section II will be devoted to identifying intersections. It is followed by Section III, analyzing track orientations bearing on which incident roads starts or ends. In Section IV, road segments, starting from an intersection will be extracted in a progressive fashion. Preliminary results of road networks will be presented in Section V and evaluated in Section VI. Discussion and future work will conclude the paper.

II. IDENTIFY INTERSECTIONS

In a prime [15] planar graph, intersections are nodes at which road segments meet as edges. Real world roads projected on a plane can be viewed as crossing each other, not all of the crossing points are intersections, i.e., there are no stop signs or roads not crossing at the same elevation level. Computing all intersections between two tracks is not only expensive, as there are too many of them, but also inconclusive. The results have to be screened considering elevations and other factors. On the other hand, real world intersections can be identified through a number of statistically significant indications. For example, 1) vehicles must stop at the stop signs or red lights; 2) vehicles are able to turn left or right; 3) the degrees of turning angles formed by adjacent roads cannot be arbitrary; and 4) the number of incident roads unlikely exceeds 6. Considering these indications and performance effectiveness, it is decided in this research that road intersections will be sought after first. Apparently, the first indication is of temporal: it can be revealed by observing longer time laps between two consecutive points around an intersection. This indication can help determining intersections with no turning tracks. Establishing a reliable tolerance for the laps, however, needs to be further investigated. The other indications can be captured through metric measures. In this paper, intersections are primarily identified by traffic turns.

A. Determine Turns at Intersections

Turns in a trajectory, from one road to another, can be captured by turning angles. It is assumed most roads intersect by an angle near 90 degrees. If two legs of a trajectory before and after a turn form an angle, say 90 ± δ, where δ is a tolerance threshold, a turn point could be located. In the experiment taken by this research, we calculate turn points considering three turning cases shown in Fig. 2.

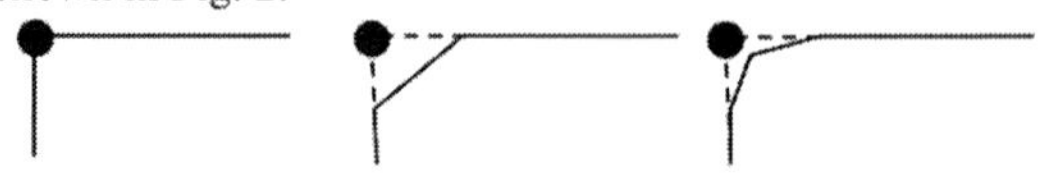

Figure 2. Three cases determining turns.

Additional screening processes are needed, however, to disqualify turns in parking lots, which are characterized by multiple turns within an area with short legs. It is desirable to identify the trajectory sections roaming around parking lots, and to exclude these GPS points from participating in extraction of roads. The accumulation of these GPS points may help to outline parking areas. Observation shows most of the parking lot GPS points are occurred at the beginning or end of trips.

B. Find Clusters of Turns

Intuitively, turns at the same intersections should be located near a real intersection center, which form a cluster. Finding these clusters, using a DBSCAN, involves building a spatial index to facilitate searches and expanding neighboring turns from any seeds. The prime criteria for stopping expanding a cluster is the distance between any two neighboring turn points. Additional criteria may consider the shapes of clusters which, ideally, are round and limited in sizes. Compact clusters, round and gathered with large numbers of turns, are excellent candidates for computing intersection centers.

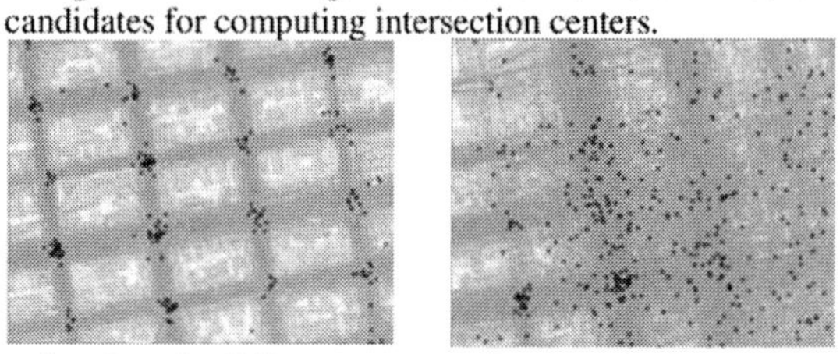

a. Turn clusters in grid-like street area b. Turn clusters in urban core area

Figure 3. Clusters of turn points.

Fig. 3a illustrates a distribution of turn points (black dots) within a regular grid street area. Referred to the background map image, most intersections are superimposed with densely clustered turn points. At the low traffic volume areas, only one or two turns can be identified near intersections. The clusters with one or two turn point will also be considered for the reason that we don't wish to miss an intersection. This needed relaxation brings in a lot of dubious clusters. As shown in Fig. 3b, there is a large number of loosely distributed turn points in the urban core area where GPS points are scattered, mostly due to the street canyon effect. Verification is a must to exclude false clusters.

III. VALIDATE CLUSTERS AND COMPUTE INTERSECTIONS

Turn point clusters are intended for computing centers of road intersections. Validating turn clusters will largely rely on this purpose, by examining all nearby tracks passing through or turning at a cluster center. This process will also identify and group tracks that are statistically appropriate to form coherent clusters for roads which are, regardless outgoing or incoming, incident to the cluster center, i.e., the intersect. Fig. 4 illustrates turns that might or might not lead to intersections.

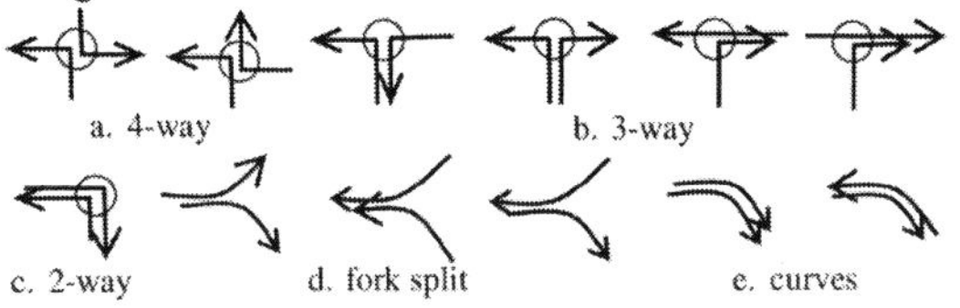

Figure 4. Intersection model.

When trajectories of multiple tracks form one of the configurations in cases a, b, and c, an intersection will be validated. Cases in d will not be assessed as intersections at this time but will be recognized as fork-like splits later in extracting roads. Fork-like splits will be dynamically treated as intersection nodes. The 2-way intersection in case c qualifies only when it constitutes a near 90-degree turn. Otherwise it is just like a curve as one in cases e.

A. *Collect Tracks Involved Around an Intersect*

Validating a cluster uses a square box centered at its mass center to clip all tracks intersecting the box. The size of the box, say 60x60 m^2, is experimented to cover the entire intersection area. The clipped lines, mostly straight some with a vertex within the box, will be served as the basis for the analysis (Fig. 5), as described below.

For each clipped straight or near straight line, a projection from the box center is made. If the foot is in the box, the line will be split into two oppositely directed lines, as shown in the left box. For a non-straight line, there must be a turning point and the turning angle is near 90 degrees. The turning point will be used to extend the two sections from both ends to meet the box border. The two thus formed straight lines will start from the extended border points, shown in the middle box. The extension will be needed later for computing intersections. As is shown in the right box, without the extension, (dashed parts), some tracks will be missed for intersecting and the initial mass center cannot be accurately located.

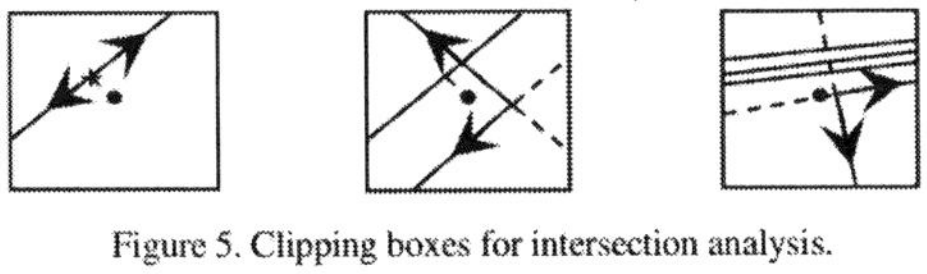

Figure 5. Clipping boxes for intersection analysis.

B. *Group Tracks by Orientation*

Orientations of straight lines obtained from above will be classified for grouping similar tracks. We use an 8-sector circle to classify track clips (Fig. 6), i.e., an 8-means clustering. The east axis is on degree 0 and angles increases anticlockwise. Each sector has a range of 45 degrees to hold orientations falling in. For example, the first group is the shaded sector. It holds orientations from -22.5 to 22.5 degrees, as (-22.5, 22.5]. Orientation values in the range of (22.5, 45] will fall into the second group, and so forth.

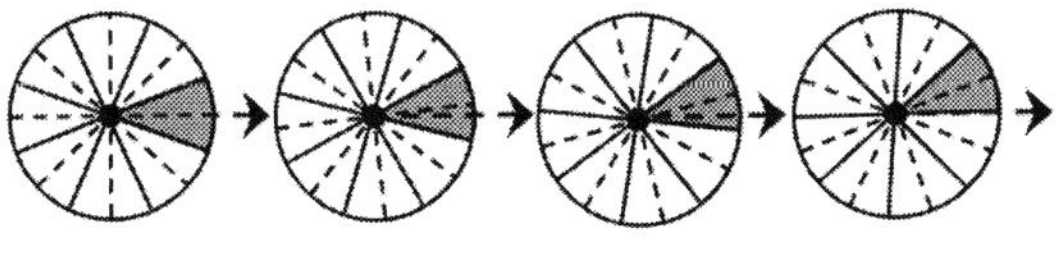

Figure 6. An 8-sector circle for clustering orientations.

After assigning clipped tracks into sectors based on their orientations, some groups may have large number of occurrence and some may end up empty. Empty groups will be removed. Mean values and squared errors of each group orientations are calculated. The template circle will then be rotated an interval of 7.5 degrees anticlockwise from its initial sector division, up to 3 times, which brings the first group ranges to be (-15.0, 30.0], (-7.5, 37.5], and (0, 45.0], respectively. After each rotation, clipped tracks will be re-assigned and the mean and squared errors re-calculated. The new error values will be compared with the previously saved ones. If they are not better, the rotation is stopped. Experiment shows that the optimized results are obtained after 1 or 2 iterations.

C. *Remove Unlikely Incident Tracks*

Track clusters with three or more groups will be further validated. False track groups, that would lead to plausible incident roads, need to be eliminated. Given the fact that we use an 8-means clustering method, at most 8 cluster groups may be initially produced. Fig. 7 shows 8 initially grouped tracks by orientation (left) and the final groups remained after removal of false groups (right). One distinguished characteristic about intersections is that most of the times, there is at least one pair of track groups (like Groups 1 and 6) would lead to through traffic roads before and after the intersection. Furthermore, straight-through tracks usually form larger groups. This observation is useful in eliminating smaller groups that are slant to through-pairs. The analysis and reasoning below illustrate the removal of plausible groups.

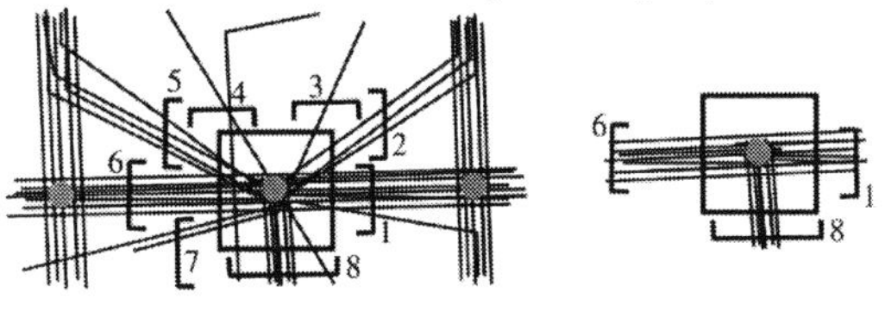

Figure 7. Eliminating false track groups.

Group 3 can be immediately removed due to lacking confidence for a determination of an incident road from a single track. Groups 2 and 5, slanting to a through-pair, are removed because they are likely the shortcut tracks missing a GPS point near the neighboring intersections. This hint can be verified by looking at the rightness of the sum of the turning angles at both ends of a slanting track segment. Group 4 is removed for it does not have an agreeable orientation. Group 7 will be removed because it slants to the through-pair with an angle smaller than 30 degrees. Of the remaining groups, the lowest track in Group 1 will be removed because its orientation is an outlier compared with the group mean. The left track in Group 8 is removed because its intersect position on the square box is an outlier. The right track in Group 8 is excluded because both its orientation and intersect position are outliers to respective means of the group.

The clustering that ends up with only two groups will not result in an intersection, if the difference of their mean orientations is not an anger near 90 degrees. Two track clusters forming a shallow angle are likely trajectories that traverse through a circular curve. They will not be considered further.

D. *Adjust Intersection Centre with Validated Tracks*

After removing plausible track groups, intersections are left with mostly 3-way and 4-way traffic routes. Some 5-way intersections exist, but 6-way intersections are rare the relationship of whose traffic routes usually need to be sorted out by additional analysis and reasoning. The final intersection point will be computed with the validated tracks. Fig. 8 shows the final intersections (red dots) on top of turn points (black dots).

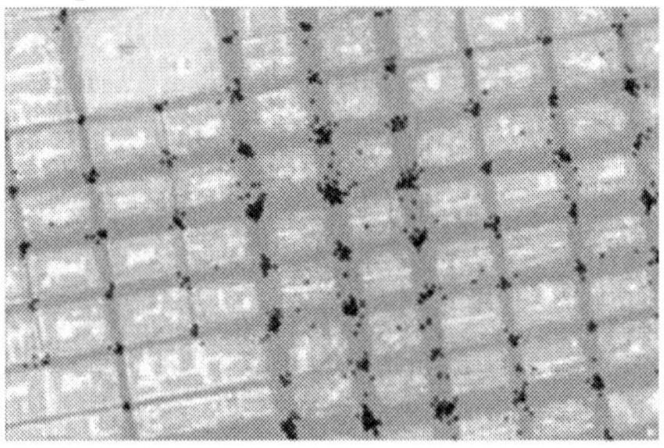

Figure 8. Verified intersections shown as red dots.

IV. EXTRACT ROADS

With a successful establishment of road intersections, extracting roads becomes relatively easier and controlled. Recall that associated with each intersection node are emitting orientations of incident roads which indicate the directions where the roads extend. All extraction will do is to use probe lines perpendicular to a road orientation and to progressively discover concentrations of tracks likely traversing on the road. Once a concentration is located, calculating and analyzing intersections of the tracks on the probe line, eliminating tracks unlikely traversing the road, and then taking the mean intersection point as the next vertex. New probe lines will be progressively moving ahead based on what has been discovered previously. A road will be terminated once another intersection node is discovered or no proper tracks can be found by the last probe line. This section describes what need to be considered in each step.

A. *Sort Road Initial Segments by Track Frequencies*

Firstly, the result from Section III.C, which are all intersection nodes and track groups organized together by similar orientations, will be sorted in descending order by the number of tracks in each group. Utilizing a priority queue holding the sorted track groups, each element of the queue contains the node ID, intersection point, the orientation to extend the first segment of a road, and the count of tracks in the group. The reason for earlier extracting roads from more heavily concentrated tracks is, the more tracks found traversing on a road, likely the more accurately the road can be extracted. The earlier accurate knowledge can be discovered, the easier successive analysis on insufficient data can be made. Since heavily traveled roads likely represent major roads or freeways, early extraction of them can help to control quality of a hierarchical road network.

B. *Probe and Compute Road Vertices*

Iteratively popping the top element from the priority queue, we will have the node location as the first vertex of a working road, the initial orientation bearing on which the first road segment will be proposed, and a list of track IDs passing the intersection. The initially proposed second vertex is a polar point whose coordinates are determined by an offset distance from the first vertex and the bearing orientation. To finally determine the first road segment, a probe line will be utilized. The probe line is centered at the polar point, has the length of a specified road width, and is perpendicular to the bearing orientation of the proposed road segment (Fig. 9). Intersections of the probe line with the known tracks associated with the node will be computed. From the intersections, the second vertex is obtained by an k-means clustering. The previous and the current vertices forms a road segment, which provides an updated orientation for the next probe line. Retained for a new probing are the track IDs and their intersection points with the previous probe line. Fig. 9 illustrates the terms of entities used in this section, and their relationships.

Unlike the initial probing where the tracks are already known to a road branch associated with the intersection node, spatial searches will be needed for the second probe line and onwards to find intersecting tracks. It is obvious that there could be tracks involved in previous probing will no longer be found (fading away) and tracks not seen previously be discovered (emerging). It is also easy to understand that not all intersected tracks should be used for computing a new vertex. Erroneous tracks should be identified and be eliminated. This research uses the following clues to identify erroneous tracks:

- Firstly, most of the intersected tracks should be known and are continuous from the previous probing. For each known track, computing its moving orientation from previously retained and current intersections, and comparing it with the extended orientation of the previously extracted road segment, if the orientation difference is too big, say greater than 60 degrees, the track will not be used.
- Secondly, newly found tracks will be more carefully inspected for use, considering their orientations and occurrence frequencies. If an emerging track does not satisfy orientation requirement but its intersection falls in the probe intersect point range, its occurrence frequency will be increased so it might be admitted for use in next probing.

This iterative process continues until an intersection node is found on the way, or a probing line catches no or just one track. In the case that an intersection is met, the road will be terminated there. In the other case, the road may end dangling, or additional analysis is needed for detecting possible turns that are missed in Section II, to be described next.

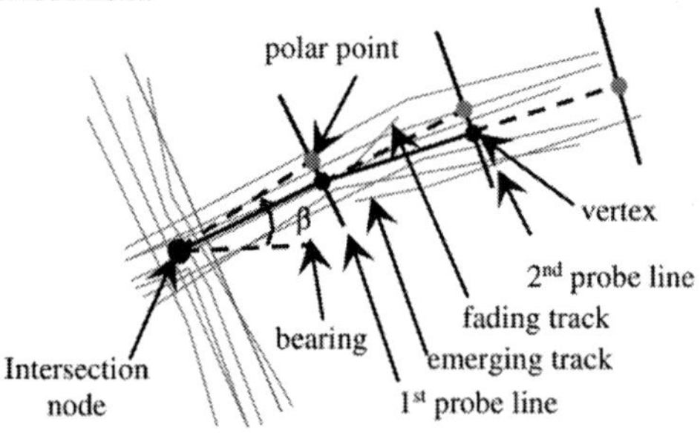

Figure 9. Terms and concept involved in probe lines.

C. Detect Turns

In the case that a probe line does not find any proper intersections, it is possible that the tracks have sharp turns, like what is shown in Fig. 10a. The task here is to find a turning point and an updated moving orientation after the turn, like what is shown in Fig. 10b. The turning point can be found by examining one or two vertices of a track near the last probe line intersection, and two segments prior to and after the vertices. If the angle formed by the two segments is near 90 degrees, a turn and changing orientation are computed. Doing so for all tracks retained in the last probing and taking the means of both the turning points and the post-turn orientations.

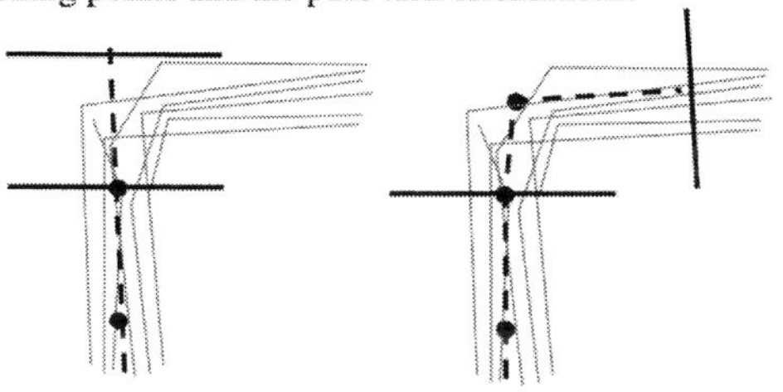

a. A new probe line intersects no tracks   b. Detect turning point and determine new orientation

Figure 10. Finding a turn and modifying probing orientation.

D. Reach an Intersection Node

Every time when a new polar point is obtained to start a probing, a search in the vicinity of the point will be made to check whether there is a proper intersection node to snap onto. For each node found, a verification process will be carried out to make sure the bearing orientation of the incoming road matches the orientation of a track group associated with the node. If no such a match can be found, a decision needs to be made whether to keep or discard the generated road. In the experiment of the paper, the number of tracks contributed to the last road segment will be the key factor for the decision. If the number is greater than 20, the road will snap onto the node; if less than 10, the road will be discarded; otherwise, the road will end and dangle at the last vertex. The verification has been proven especially useful in areas where GPS tracks are messed up to avoid erratically generated lines.

Once a snapping node is determined, the node ID and the orientation corresponding to the track group will be marked as processed, so the same road will be not be extracted again from the other end.

E. Split or Merge

As probe lines move forward, a fork-like split might be encountered (Fig. 11) when the range of intersections on the probe line becomes wider (left), or some of the track IDs suddenly missed from intersecting (right). Recall in Section III that fork-like shallow turns do not produce an intersection node, which will be created here. To find the split node, the probe line can be extended long enough to intersect the missing tracks. It is followed by finding two intersection clusters and their median positions on the probe line. With the knowledge of two track groups, a mean orientation for each group can be obtained. Two lines each passing a cluster center and bearing respective orientation can be used to find the intersection node. A final adjustment might be needed to make sure the node is on the heading direction of the last segment of the road extracted so far. After this, the current road will be terminated at the new node, which will be associated with the two splitting track groups and added to the priority queue of tracking groups.

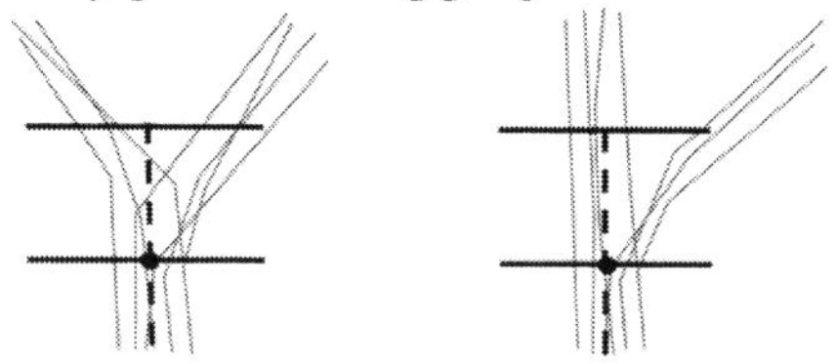

Figure 11. Detect splits by checking changes on probe.

Similarly, a merge node could be discovered when a range of intersection point on a probe line is shifted with new tracks appeared. The new IDs represent the other group of tracks involved in the merge. To find the intersection node, shallow turning vertices between the current and the previous probe lines can be found from which the merge intersection can be determined.

V. EXPERIMENT RESULT

Based on the algorithm, a geoprocessing tool to generate road networks from GPS tracking points has been prototyped using the ArcGIS® Pro platform. Applying the prototype tool, experiment on Uber GPS tracking data in San Francisco and surrounding suburb has been carried out. The dataset contains over 1 million GPS points covering urban core area with high rise buildings, streets of regular grids, and sparsely travelled country roads. It took about 30 minutes running on a desktop PC to create a road network with identified intersections. The result is displayed on top of a background image, shown in Fig. 12 where input tracks are in gray, the generated roads in purple, and the intersection nodes in red.

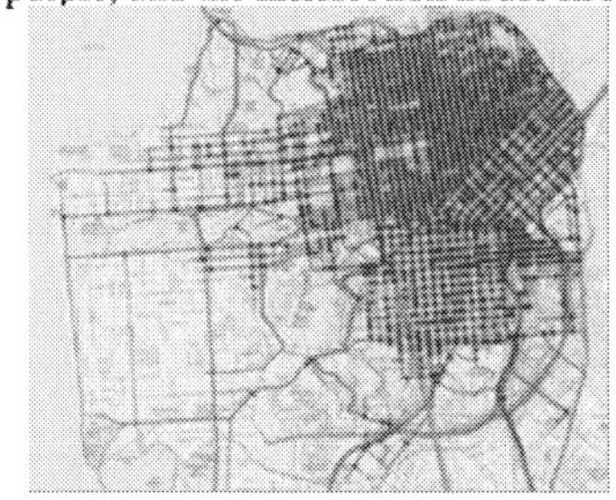

Figure 12. Road Network of SF area from GPS Points.

Fig. 13-15 illustrate zoomed-in images of the generated roads and intersections in grid-street, irregular road, and urban core areas.

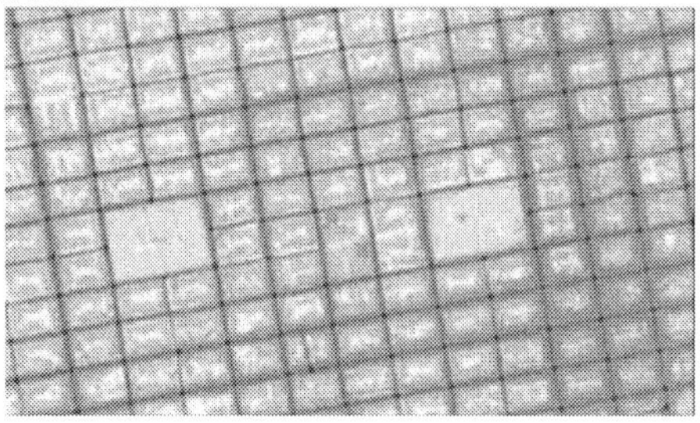

Figure 13. Generated roads of regular grids.

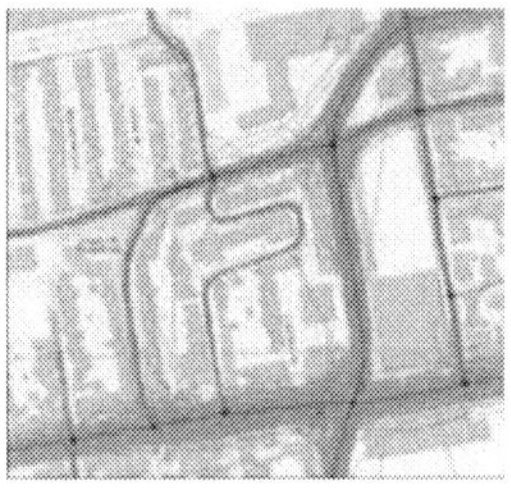

Figure 14. Generated irregular roads.

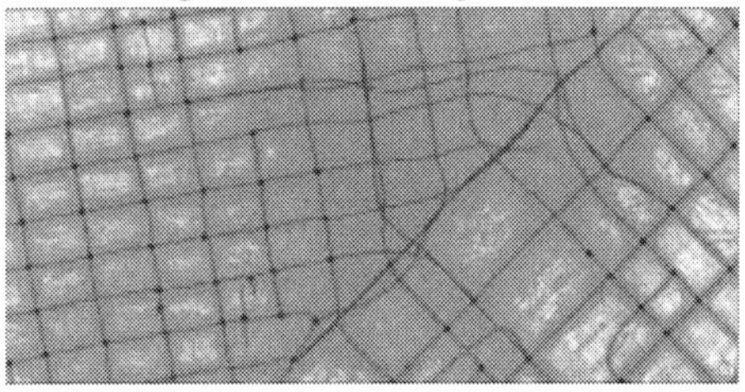

Figure 15. Generated roads around urban core.

It is easy to see that the proposed method works better when input tracks present clear linear threads and poor when there are no obvious patterns.

VI. THE EVALUATION METHOD

Evaluating the goodness of roads generated from GPS tracks, quantitatively, is challenging in that there has been no standard automated workflows to carry out the task. The challenge is aggravated due to the fact that tracking data is simply a snapshot of all possible travel patterns. Less travelled roads may not have any tracking records in the snapshot. In this paper, we explore a framework of evaluation and database updates by considering temporal aspects of GPS datasets. The commercially available GIS tool, Detect Feature Changes (DFC), in ArcGIS® Pro is utilized as a start for the framework. Based on a feature matching algorithm, the DFC tool takes in an existing road map as the base, a new road map as the update, a search distance and a change tolerance. The goal is: for each road in update dataset, find the correspondent road in base. If there is a match and the update road is within the tolerance buffer of the base road, the change type of the update will be NC – no change. If not within the buffer, or there is a 1:m / m:1 relationship, the change type would be S – spatial change. If an update finds no match, the type would be N – new. Any base roads with no matches in update would have the change type D – to delete. Let's use a map section (Fig. 16) to illustrate the evaluation process.

Figure 16. Existing streets (brown) on topographic image (gray).

Fig. 16 shows the existing road map in brown, on top of a topographical image (gray) for visual reference. The new roads (black) and the intersections (red dots) generated by the method presented in this paper are displayed in Fig. 17. Also displayed in Fig. 17 are GPS tracks (gray) and the brown base map for comparison.

Figure 17. Automated roads and intersections.

Now running the DFC tool with the new and base, giving 10 meters and 5 meters for search distance and change tolerance, respectively. The result is a feature layer symbolized with change types (Fig. 18).

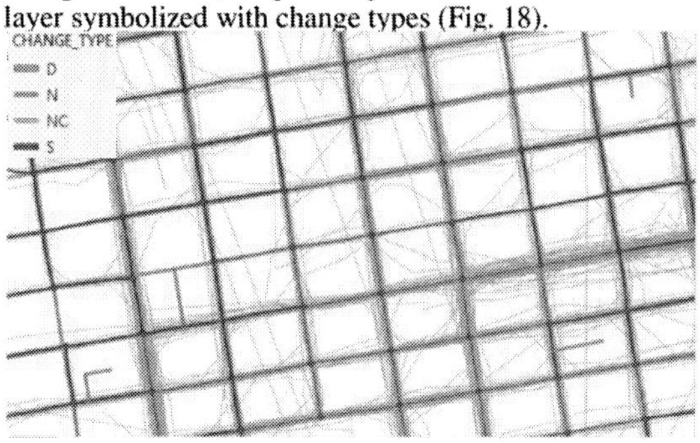

Figure 18. Symbolized DFC output layer.

The records holding the DFC output features are shown in Tab. 1. The table and the layer map provide interactive ways to inspect DFC result.

TABLE I. DFC OUTPUT, TOPOLOGICAL CHANGES HIGHLIGHTED

OBJECTID	SHAPE	UPDATE_FID	BASE_FID	CHANGE_TYPE	LEN_PCT	LEN_ABS	SHAPE_Length
135	Polyline	-1	33601	D	-1	-1	0.00085
136	Polyline	-1	33602	D	-1	-1	0.001653
74	Polyline	1115	31561	S	0	0	0.001912
76	Polyline	1153	33396	S	0	0	0.000999
80	Polyline	1212	31559	S	0	0	0.000888
83	Polyline	1338	31835	S	0	0	0.003342
87	Polyline	1445	32124	S	0	0	0.00191
96	Polyline	1601	33317	S	0	0	0.001655
105	Polyline	1842	31456	S	0	0	0.001641
99	Polyline	1718	32556	S	0.002827	0	0.000978
98	Polyline	1716	32947	S	0.002906	0	0.000904
101	Polyline	1751	32847	S	0.00291	0	0.001677
108	Polyline	2220	33155	S	0.030578	0.000001	0.00169
67	Polyline	495	32770	S	0.15369	-0.000001	0.00093
69	Polyline	582	32182	S	0.247986	-0.000004	0.001626

For example, one can highlight features with change type S and 0s under LEN_PCT, meaning 0 percent geometry change. the highlighted features will be displayed in the map (Fig. 19). By looking at the map result, it becomes obvious that these highlighted new roads match 2 or 3 features in base. The reason for the 1:m relationship is that there are no intersections identified with the tracks. At this time, the inspector could modify the change type to NC. Similarly, the inspector can examine the features with D type (brown roads in Fig. 19) and would find that there are no GPS tracks recorded on those roads during the time. Upon verification, they would not be counted as errors.

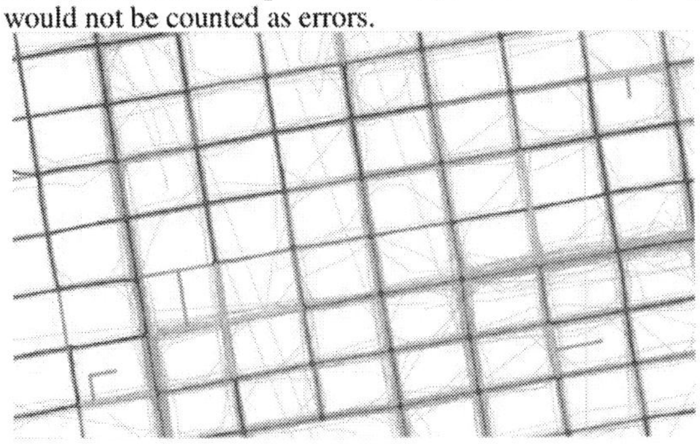

Figure 19. Features with topological changes.

After all suspected features are inspected, we can summarize the quality assessment for the map section: Of the 125 roads generated, all match corresponding ones in base. Furthermore, 71 roads are within 5 meters similar to their base peers, and all, except one, features with the S type are within 7 meters of their peers. The finding is encouraging for areas with clear patterns.

Other areas can be inspected based on the DFC result. It can be expected that there would be a lot of D type features that do not have roads generated from this snapshot. They might be available with additional tracking data taking from various other time periods. Automation could be enhanced to reduce manual inspection. For example, for each DFC feature with D change type, a proximity search can be made to verify that there are indeed no tracking data for the missing roads.

VII. CONCLUSION AND FUTURE WORK

The proposed method constructed road networks from scratch on input GPS tracking points by paying premier attention to analyzing road intersection nodes. The quality of nodes and roads produced is largely dependent on the quality of GPS tracks. The method identifies and excludes erroneous or outlier tracks by analyzing temporal gaps and excessive turns within a limited area, and by combining the use of spatial reasoning, statistical, and machine learning techniques.

Future work includes the following considerations:

- Paying attention to implementation details to learn and refine parameter values for better result;
- Adding algorithms to generate ramps, possibly with supervised ramp patterns and learning;
- Refining k-means clustering on the intersecting points along probe lines to identify and generate multiple lanes;
- Researching on quantitative and qualitative assessment methodology using feature matching tools and considering dynamic and real-time updates; and
- Developing a post processing tool to detect and if possible, to correct errors in the output road networks to prepare them ready for use in routing and network analysis.

ACKNOWLEDGMENTS

The Uber data used in this paper is obtained from: https://github.com/dima42/uber-gps-analysis/tree/master/gpsdata

The author appreciates the support from members in Esri Geoprocessing and GeoAnalytics teams.

This paper discussed an ongoing research. The author is solely responsible for any errors. The content should not be interpreted as any commitment by Esri to provide specific capabilities in future software releases.

REFERENCES

[1] S. Schroedl, K. Wagstaff, S. Rogers, P. Langley, and C. Wilson, "Mining GPS Traces for Map Refinement," Data Mining and Knowledge Discovery, vol. 9, no. 1, July 2004, pp. 59-87.

[2] S. Rogers, P. Langley, and C. Wilson, "Mining GPS Data to Augment Road Models," 5th ACM SIGKDD Int. Conf. Knowledge Discovery and Data Mining, 1999, pp. 104-113.

[3] P. Newson and J. Krumm, "Hidden Markov Map Matching Through Noise and Sparseness," 17th ACM SIGSPATIAL Int. Conf. Adv. in GIS, 2009, pp. 336–343.

[4] S. Brakatsoulas, D. Pfoser, R. Salas, and C. Wenk, "On Map-Matching Vehicle Tracking Data," 31st VLDB Conf., Trondheim, Norway, 2005, pp. 853 – 864.

[5] S. Edelkamp and S. Schrödl, "Route Planning and Map Inference with Global Positioning Traces," In Computer Science in Perspective (R. Klein, H.-W. Six, and L. Wegner, eds.), LNCS 2598, Springer, Berlin, 2003, pp. 128–151.

[6] S. Karagiorgou and D. Pfoser, "On vehicle tracking data-based road network generation," ACM SIGSPATIAL GIS, 2012, pages 89–98.

[7] J. J. Davies, A.R. Beresford, and A. Hopper, "Scalable, Distributed, Real-Time Map Generation," IEEE Pervasive Computing, vol. 5, no. 4, Oct. 2006, pp. 47-54.

[8] M. Ahmed and C. Wenk, "Constructing Street Networks from GPS Trajectories," In: Epstein L., Ferragina P. (eds) Algorithms – ESA 2012. LNCS 7501. Springer, Berlin, Heidelberg.

[9] L. Cao and J. Krumm, "From GPS Traces to a Routable Road Map," 17th ACM SIGSPATIAL Int. Conf. on Advances in GIS, 2009, pp. 3-12.

[10] J. Biagioni and J. Eriksson, "Inferring Road Maps from Global Positioning System Traces," Transportation Research Record: J. Transportation Research Board, No. 2291, Washington, D.C., 2012, pp. 61–71.

[11] M. Ahmed, S. Karagiorgou, D. Pfoser, and C. Wenk, "Map Construction Algorithms," Springer International Publishing Switzerland 2015, ISBN 978-3-319-25164-6.

[12] A. Fathi and J. Krumm, "Detecting Road Intersections from GPS Traces," In S.I. Fabrikant et al. (Eds.): GIScience, LNCS 6292, 2010, pp. 56–69.

[13] W. Yang, D. Lee, and N. Ahmed, "Pattern Based Feature Matching for Geospatial Data Conflation," GeoProcessing 2014: 6th Int. Conf. Advanced GIS, Applications, and Services, Barcelona, Spain. March 2014, pp. 64-69.

[14] D. Lee, W. Yang, and N. Ahmed, "Conflation in Geoprocessing Framework-Case Studies," GeoProcessing 2014: 6th Int. Conf. Advanced GIS, Applications, and Services, Barcelona, Spain. March 2014, pp. 58-63.

[15] S. Porta, P. Crucitti, and V. Latora, "The Network Analysis of Urban Streets: A Primal Approach," Environment and Planning B: Planning and Design, vol. 33, 2006, pp. 705-725.

A Universal Large-Scale Trajectory Indexing for Cloud-Based Moving Object Applications

Omar Alqahtani
Department of Computer Science and Engineering
University of Colorado Denver
Denver, USA
e-mail: omar.alqahtani@ucdenver.edu

Tom Altman
Department of Computer Science and Engineering
University of Colorado Denver
Denver, USA
e-mail: tom.altman@ucdenver.edu

Abstract—**The tremendous upsurge in low-cost geospatial chipsets brings out huge volumes of moving object trajectories, which catalyze a wide range of trajectory-driven applications (e.g., sustainable cities, smart transportation, green routing, intelligent homeland security, etc.). Consequently, there has been an emergence of more divergent queries and increased processing complexity. Instead of developing a query-specific approach for limited applications, we propose a Universal Moving Object Index, a flexible index that is capable of fine-tuning based on the application needs, without any structural modification. Also, we introduce a Light-Weight Hybrid Index for heavily-loaded memory. Besides the ability to support trajectory-driven applications universally, both approaches are designed to be easily adopted by cloud-compatible MapReduce platforms. An extensive empirical study is conducted to validate our approaches and to highlight some critical challenges.**

Keywords–big data; moving objects; distribution algorithms; spatial indexing; Apache Spark.

I. Introduction

The evolution of Global Positioning System (GPS) with the growth of embedded systems and electronic gadgets generate massive numbers of moving object trajectories. Most of our daily devices (e.g., smartphones, wearable devices, navigation systems, tablets, etc.) are capable of recording our movements. Also, the rise in modern transportation services (e.g., ridesharing, electric-bike renting, car sharing, etc.) has increased the number of these trajectories. Moving object trajectories are used in many applications over a wide range of domains. Transportation services and smart navigation heavily depend on both historical and near-future trajectories, e.g., analyzing a hotspot area and routing based on specific preferences, such as green routing. Historical trajectory is also playing a significant role in planning smart cities by analyzing many trajectory-driven factors related to environmental or economic issues.

Consequently, advanced techniques and large-scale computing platforms have become a necessity to cope with storing and processing vast volumes of big spatial data [1]. MapReduce is an exemplary solution that provides an effective distributed computation framework used by many large-scale data processing platforms, such as Apache Spark [2]. Spark is a general-purpose in-memory computing platform, which is supported by most of the cloud computing systems (e.g., Amazon AWS, Google Cloud Engine, IBM Cloud, Microsoft Azure, Cloudera, etc.).

However, the diversity of applications and the adoption of distributed computation platforms raises new challenges in trajectory processing. One of the natural characteristics of trajectory, and spatial data in general, is spatial skewness, which leads to an imbalance in distribution and computation. Although imbalance distribution can be unfolded by using one of the state-of-the-art indexes, which offer a balanced distribution [3]–[5], the skewness will arise again in the intermediate result of a multistage query. Another skewness form is computation skewness, which occurs because the selective queries are most often related to self-skewed space or trajectory. In most cases, computation skewness affects performance by reducing cluster utilization, i.e., creating hotspots within each cluster. Moreover, a space-splitting distribution works fine for simple space-based queries. However, the communication cost for object-based or sophisticated (multistage) space-based queries represents a performance bottleneck. One of the critical challenges is how to take advantage of the spatial and object localities.

To overcome the aforementioned challenges, we propose a Universal Moving Object index (*UMOi*) for in-memory processing of large-scale historical trajectories. *UMOi* is a universal approach that is capable of leveraging two different thoughts of trajectory partitioning (i.e., space-based and object-based partitioning) to preserve spatial and object localities together. The goal of *UMOi* is to satisfy various query types by providing a variable locality mechanism, which boosts *UMOi*'s flexibility to be suitable for a wide range of applications. This advantage makes it more appealing for cloud platforms. Also, we introduce a Light-Weight Hybrid index (*LWHi*), which focuses on object-locality more than spatial-locality during partitioning. *LWHi* provides an ideal computation distribution and guarantees a full *trajectory-preservation* without losing the advantages of spatial pruning. *LWHi* provides a significant performance in heavily-loaded memory situations, i.e., the main memory is saturated with data, which helps reduce the overall cloud cost. The main contributions of this paper are as follows:

- We introduce *UMOi* that is able to control both spatial and object localities.
- We also introduce *LWHi*, which guarantees a full *trajectory-preservation*.
- We formalize and analyze different queries, including continuous spatial queries, and select a representative query for each query type. Next, we develop efficient algorithms for query processing.
- We evaluate our work by conducting extensive per-

formance experiments comparing varies space-based indexing schemes and reveal the implications of computation skewness, intermediate results skewness, and communication.

The rest of the paper is organized as follows: the related work is highlighted in Section II. The structure of the proposed algorithms is discussed in Section III. The query processing approaches are detailed in Section IV. An extensive experimental study is presented in Section V, and a conclusion in Section VI.

II. Related Work

The development and improvement of computing platforms and the demands of new applications create opportunities to adopt new techniques and methods for managing and processing moving object trajectories. From the computing platforms perspective, we classify the prior work into three groups: centralized systems, parallel databases, and MapReduce-based systems. However, we first review some of the access methods and index structures used in most of the related work.

A. Access Methods

R-tree [3] and its variants (e.g., R*-tree [6], R+-tree [7], etc.) are among the most popular access methods which work in a hierarchical manner to group objects in a minimum bounding rectangle. Other types of indexes focus on space-splitting instead of grouping the objects, such as simple grid, k-d-tree [4] and its variants (e.g., k-d-B-Tree [8] and Quad tree [9]). Many versions of the previous structures were adapted for moving object trajectories, which can be grouped into augmented multi-dimensional indexes and multi-version structure indexes. Augmented multi-dimensional indexes can be built using any of the previous indexes, mostly R-trees, with augmentation on the temporal dimension, e.g., spatiotemporal R-tree and Trajectory-Bundle tree (TB-tree) [5]. Spatiotemporal R-tree keeps segments of a trajectory close to each other, while TB-tree ensures that the leaf node only contains segments belong to the same trajectory, i.e., the whole trajectory can be retrieved by linking those leaf nodes together. On the other hand, multi-version indexes, such as Historical R-tree (HR-tree) [10], use, mostly, R-trees to index each timestamp frame. Then, the resulting R-trees are also indexed by using a 1-d index, such as a B-tree. Unchanged nodes from time frame to time frame do not need to be indexed again. Instead, they will be linked to the next R-tree.

B. Centralized Systems and Parallel Database

Reference [11] uses centralized architecture to process a top-k query on activity trajectories, where the points of the trajectory represent some events such as tweeting or posting on Facebook. They use a simple grid to partition the space and some auxiliary indexes to process the events and trajectories. Also, [12] implements a parallel spatial-temporal database to manage both network transportation and trajectory and to support spatiotemporal SQL queries. They use a space-based index that partitions the data based on a space-splitting technique. Any trajectory that crosses a partition boundary is going to be split into sub-trajectories, while any sector of the transportation network that crosses a partition boundary is going to be replicated in all of the crossed partitions.

C. MapReduce-Based Contributions

SpatialHadoop [13] is an extension of Hadoop designed to support spatial data (Point, Line, and Polygon) by including global and local spatial indexes to speed up spatial query processing as range query, k-Nearest Neighbors (k-NN), spatial join, and geometry query [14]. MD-HBase [15] is an extension of HBase; a non-relational Key-Value database that runs on top of Hadoop, which only focuses on spatial point types. The main idea of MD-HBase is to use any multidimensional index and then linearize it to a single dimensional index via the Z-order space-filling technique. Hadoop-GIS [16] extends Hive, a warehouse Hadoop-based database, to process spatial data by using a grid-based global index and an on-demand local index. [17] only focuses on processing the nearest neighbor queries by using a Voronoi-based index. However, none of the previous systems support trajectories directly. PRADASE [18] concentrates on processing trajectories, however, it only covers range queries and trajectory-based queries. It partitions space and time by using a multilevel grid hash index as a global index where no segment cross the partition boundary. Another index is used to hash all segments on all the partitions belonging to a single trajectory to speed up the object retrieving query. Nevertheless, all Hadoop-based contributions inherit the continuous disk access drawback.

GeoSpark [19] is implemented on-top of Spark, and it is identical to SpatialHadoop in terms of indexing and querying. LoctionSpark [20] reduces the impacts of query skewness and network communication overhead. It tracks query frequencies to reveal cluster hotspots and cracks them by re-partitioning. Network communication overhead is reduced by embedded bloom filter technique in the global index, which helps avoid unnecessary communication. SpatialLocation [21] is aimed to process the spatial join through the Spark broadcasting technique and grid index. However, the trajectories are not directly supported by the previous contributions. [22] implements trajectory searching query by using an R-tree as a local and global index. Also, [23] processes top-k similarity query (a trajectory-based query) by using a Voronoi-based index for spatial dimension, where each cell is statically indexed on temporal dimension. Any trajectory that crosses a partition boundary is going to be split, and all segments belong to a trajectory are traced with Trajectory Track Table. SharkDB [24] indexes trajectory only based on time frames in a column-oriented architecture to process range query and k-NN.

Generally, most of the prior work focused on static spatial data (Point, Polygon, and Line), which does not fit moving object trajectories. On the other hand, the works focusing on trajectory rely on spatial or temporal distribution, i.e., data distribution depends on partitioning space and time dimensions. Most often, the resulting distribution would partially preserve spatial and object localities.

Locality represents a key performance, and it might affect the whole system attainments. The nature of a trajectory (i.e., as consecutive time-stamped spatial points) creates contradictory domains, which can be seen in spatial locality and object locality. As a result, some of the previous contributions optimize their systems to contain this contradiction by focusing on spatial locality and spatial queries (e.g., range query, k-NN, etc.) with an object-based auxiliary index, or by narrowing it down to a particular operator and building an ad-hoc index for that purpose only. To the best of our knowledge, there is

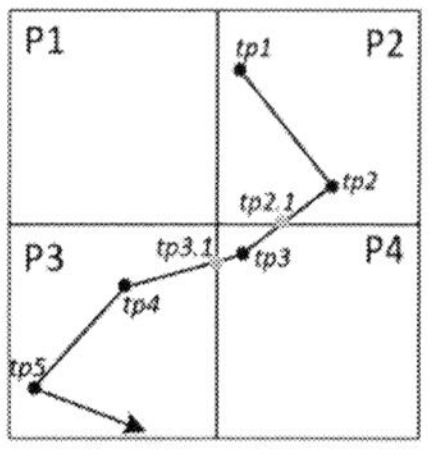

Figure 1. Space-based partitioning.

no work that has been conducted on a distributed computation that would balance the losses and gains of both localities and cover a large variety of queries.

III. TRAJECTORY INDEXING OVERVIEW

In this section, we present our proposed approaches for historical trajectories processing. Before that, we will overview the traditional Space-Based Index (SPI), since it is intensively used by the related works and represents the baseline in our experiments. Based on [25], three phases: Partitioning, Global Index, and Local Index are the most general steps used, but with some differences. In the partitioning phase, a master node partitions the space based on flat or hierarchical indexes. Each partition is assigned to a worker node. When a segment crosses more than one partition, it is divided into several segments as illustrated in Figure 1. As shown, $Seg{<}tp1, tp2{>}$ will be placed in partition 2. However, $Seg{<}tp2, tp3{>}$ needs to be split into two segments where $Seg{<}tp2, tp2.1{>}$ is assigned to partition 2 and $Seg{<}tp2.1, tp3{>}$ is assigned to partition 4.

The global index is also built by the master node based on the partitions that are distributed over the worker nodes. The idea is to speed up query execution by only targeting the partitions that contain the required trajectories instead of searching the whole data. A local index is built and managed by each worker node for each partition to speed up the process of refinements. Similar to the global index, flat or hierarchical indexes might be used for the local index. Some related work, such as [19], use a cost-based model to see if building a local index is worth it.

There are some drawbacks related to space-based partitioning, which increases the performance by pruning the searching space on some types of queries on centralized systems. However, applying the same methodology on a distributed system would result in pruning the searching space, but it would reduce the cluster utilization (i.e., some cluster nodes will be idle), especially when using coarse-grained partitioning. Moreover, since the partitioning is only based on the spatial and temporal dimensions, processing advanced multistage queries (e.g., continuous geo-fencing query) will increase network communication overhead. For example, consider the Continuous Range Query (CRQ) in Figure 2, which we formally define in Section IV-B. It consists of three range queries. The final result should contain all trajectories passing all three ranges. Assuming each cluster node has one partition, $P1$, $P2$, and $P7$ will be idle. The rest will return Trajectory ids ($Tids$) of any segment crossing any of the three ranges to the master node. The master node needs to process them to find the trajectories pass all the ranges. Processing such a query results in higher communication, or even worse if it exceeds the master memory limit. Another side effect is the

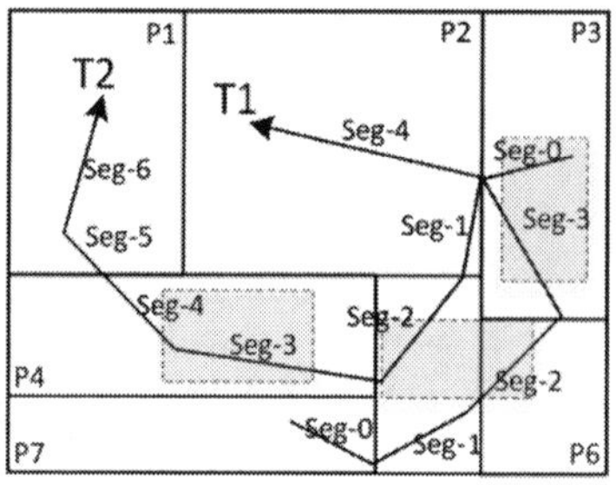

Figure 2. Continuous range query with three shaded regions.

reduction in cluster utilization, where some cluster nodes sit idle. This can be improved by using batch queries technique. However, that results in more complicated queries and needs more refinement processing steps to get the final answer, which negatively influences the response time.

A. LWHi Index

LWHi is a light-weight, efficient trajectory index which fuses object-based distribution with spatial index to get the most benefit of them and reduces the impacts of their drawbacks if they were deployed alone. The key performance of *LWHi* is to focus on moving objects instead of spatial properties in the partitioning phase, as illustrated in Figure 3, which forces each trajectory to be located on a single partition. It distributes trajectories based on the $Tids$. So, $T1$ and $T3$ are settled in partition 1, and $T2$ and $T4$ are settled in partition 2. As a result, *LWHi* ensures full *trajectory-preservation* which results in increasing the moving object's locality while still keeping the advantage of pruning the searching space by employing a local spatial index.

Building LWHi Index: It starts by reading the trajectory dataset as segments of trajectories, where each segment carries its own Segment id (Sid) and Tid. Next, *LWHi* launches a *GroupBy* transformation, which will get all the worker nodes engaged, to group all the segments of one trajectory to reside on one partition. The grouping is based on a hash function on the $Tids$, which is implemented using a Spark *Partitioner*. The *Partitioner* is responsible for returning the *Partition_Id* through a modular hashing when a Tid and the required number of partitions are given. At this point, all the trajectories are distributed among the clusters through the partitions of the Spark RDD. After that, by launching a *MapPartitions* transformation, each worker node will create a local spatial index, using a Sort-Tile-Recursive packed R-tree (*STR-tree*) [26], for its own partitions.

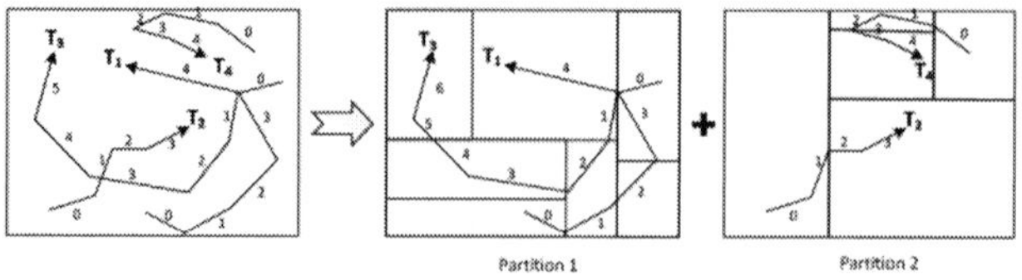

Figure 3. Partitioning and local index of *LWHi*.

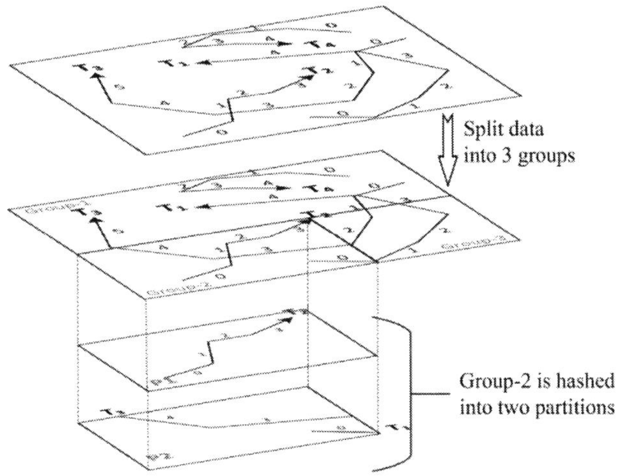

Figure 4. Partitioning phase in *UMOi* with $pd = 2$ and $tpn = 6$.

B. *UMOi Index*

The idea of *UMOi* is to have a flexible index which merges space-based and object-based partitioning techniques together. It is capable of balancing both spatial and object localities by providing a locality preservation mechanism, which gives the flexibility to satisfy different applications' demands. The required preservation degree (pd) can be given as an input. The range of pd is $< 1, 2, \cdots, tpn >$, where tpn is the target partitions number (i.e., the required number of partitions to be distributed on the cluster). Consider the trajectory set in Figure 4 with $pd = 2$ and $tpn = 6$. *UMOi* will start by splitting the global space into three spatial groups because $tpn \div pd$ gives the required number of spatial groups. Then, each group will be hashed into two partitions to generate the required six partitions as given. The result is a combination of spatial and object partitioning which cannot provide spatial locality like SPI, or object locality like *LWHi*, but it can instead provide a balance of both localities simultaneously with a pivot that can be adjusted without changing the index structure.

Both SPI and *LWHi* are special cases of *UMOi*. When pd is set to the maximum value (i.e., $pd = tpn$), *UMOi* does not have a space-split step. This is because the required number of spatial groups is $tpn \div pd = 1$, which is the global space itself. So, *UMOi* continues in building the index in the same manner as *LWHi*. On the other hand, when $pd = 1$, *UMOi* needs to split the space into tpn spatial groups. Those groups represent the final partitions, just like SPI. As a result, *UMOi* is capable of universally supporting trajectory-driven applications that depend on space-based or trajectory-based queries by adjusting pd.

Building UMOi Index: the partitioning phase in *UMOi* consists of two steps: space splitting and hashing. Given a trajectory dataset T on space S, *UMOi* starts by generating $ST \subset T$ as a sample set which can fit the master node's memory. Then, on the master node, it builds a binary skeleton tree (*sk-tree*) on ST. This new *sk-tree* is similar to a k-d-B-tree in the way it is constructed, but it is only used to represent the required sub-regions (i.e., the required groups). Even though it would be sufficient to stop building the *sk-tree* after having $tpn - pd$ leaf nodes, *UMOi* continues until we have tpn leaf nodes. We will discuss the reason for this later. After that, *UMOi* merges the regions of pd leaf nodes to form one group. Next, each segment $\in T$ is inserted in the *sk-tree* to be tagged by the correct leaf's code. In case of having a segment that does not fit in a leaf's region, the segment is split into two segments and then reinserted again. Each segment's tag, denoted as Seg_Tag, contains on the leaf's code and its Tid. Finishing partitioning phase, *UMOi* constructs a *Partitioner*, where it is used through *GroupBy* transformation to place each segment to its target partition. *Partitioner* is essential in distribution and query processing. Given a Seg_Tag, *Partitioner* first locates the proper spatial group. Then, using a hashing function on Tid based on pd and a particular group, it returns the required $Partition\_Id$.

UMOi continues building the *sk-tree* to the end, i.e., without stopping at $tpn - pp$ leaf nodes, for two reasons. *UMOi* essentially is used as a proof-of-concept and needs to be dynamic for changing pd without reconstructing the *sk-tree*. More importantly, during the experimental process, it is critical to have a consistent space-split among SPI and *UMOi*s, where *UMOi*s refer to different *UMOi* versions based on the pd values. The different statistical readings of the empirical study require consistency to isolate the impact of the dissimilarity in space-splitting, so they only show the influences of different pd values.

Tracking trajectory has been addressed in the literature, such as [18] [23] [27]. *UMOi* follows the same notion by building a Trajectory Tracking Table (TTT) as a hash table. Each entry in TTT consists of a Tid, as a key, and a list of $Partition\_Ids$. It is mainly used when there is a need to retrieve a trajectory (i.e., Lookup query). After tagging the segments, *UMOi* can build TTT by launching a *Job* to locally reduce segments on their Tid for each partition and to combine it with the corresponding $Partition\_Id$. Then, the result is globally reduced on Tid to create a list of different $Partition\_Ids$ for each trajectory.

TABLE I. QUERY TYPES

Category	Query Type	Signature
Space-Based Query	Simple	Trajectory × Spatial → Trajectory
		Trajectory × Spatial → Spatial
	Continuous	Trajectory × Spatial → Trajectory
	Constraint	Trajectory × Spatial → Trajectory
		Trajectory × Spatial → Spatial
Trajectory-Based Query	Similarity	Trajectory × Trajectory → Trajectory
		Trajectory × Trajectory → Boolean
	Aggregation	Trajectory × Trajectory → Trajectory
		Trajectory × Trajectory → Real
	Lookup	Trajectory → Trajectory

IV. QUERY PROCESSING

In this section, we first discuss different query types. After that, we explain how *LWHi* and *UMOi* process different queries.

Our focus is on a query that is formed to ask about the interaction or the relationship between a trajectory and a defined place in the space or between a trajectory and other trajectories. We can classify the query into two categories: space-based query and trajectory-based query, as seen in Table I. For simplicity, we do not include temporal queries at this early stage because we only need to focus on space and object (with their related quires, localities, and partitioning) without increasing complexity by adding time.

Space-based query can be classified into: Simple, Continuous and Constraint query. Simple spatial query emphasizes the interaction or relationship between a trajectory and a defined spatial type such as region, point or line. The best example of a simple spatial query is the range query, which has been discussed in most previous studies. Continuous spatial query represents a sequence of simple queries. It comes as a result of the nature of a trajectory and the demands of modern applications by requiring queries that identify certain trajectories based on their movements. For example, agencies might be interested to know who might have been in three suspected areas which can be directly addressed by a continuous range query, as seen in Figure 2. Another example involving continuous spatial query would be a query that is used to understand traffic flow by showing long-distance commuters, short-distance commuters, and visitors in one query. The third group in space-based query, called constraint query, represents the spatial queries that are constrained by a defined function (e.g., Euclidean distance, Counting, Maximum, etc.), such as k-NN or top-k.

The second category, trajectory-based query, concentrates on the interaction and relationship between and among trajectories. We divide this group, based on the nature of the queries, into three types: Similarity, Aggregation and Lookup queries as seen in Table I. The first query type, similarity query, depends on a well-defined similarity function, which is mostly used in trajectory data mining, as in [28]–[30]. Aggregation query employs aggregation functions to provide statistical information about trajectories (e.g., longest trajectory) or their different properties (e.g., average speed). Lookup query is the simplest, but it is still an essential query that basically retrieves a particular trajectory by giving its *Tid*.

In our framework, we concentrate on both space-based and trajectory-based queries to reveal the compliance level of the proposed approaches in different scenarios. A representative query is selected from each query type, except similarity and constraint, since they are structurally similar to the other types. The selected queries are as follows: Range Query, Continuous Range Query, Longest Trajectory, and Lookup Query. Next, we discuss each selected query and how it is processed by *UMOi* and *LWHi*.

A. Range Query

Given a range query $RQ =< P_{bl}, P_{ur} >$, where P_{bl} is the bottom left point of the spatial range and P_{ur} is the upper right point, *UMOi* first determines the involved *Partition_Ids*. It traverses the *sk-tree* to find the required groups that spatially overlap with RQ space and then returns all the engaged groups' partitions. Next, a Spark *Job* is initialized that targets only the required partitions (Spark RDD partitions) based on a given hash set of *Partition_Ids*. During the *Job* execution, the engaged worker node traverses a partition's local index tree (*STR-tree*) based on RQ space. SPI follows the same steps, with a minor difference when traversing *sk-tree*. It returns the engaged *Partition_Ids* directly, since it does not have the groups and their hashed partitions concept. Alternatively, *LWHi* starts a Spark *Job* directly on all *Partition_Ids*. Each worker node traverses its partitions' *STR-trees* based on the given RQ space. The result of all the approaches comes as a new RDD, which only contains the segments covered by RQ.

Algorithm 1: *UMOi*: Processing *k-CRQ*

```
   Input: k-CRQ
   Output: RDD < Tid >
1  Pid[k]{} <- φ
2  for i <- 1 to k do
3  |  Pid[i] <- SK-Tree.traverse(RQ_i.space)
4  Transformation MapPartitions(k-CRQ, Pid)
5  |  R[k][ ] <- φ
6  |  for i <- 1 to k do
7  |  |  if i ∈ Pid[i] then
8  |  |  |  R[i] <- STR-Tree.intersect(RQ_i.space)
   |  |  |  /* It returns all Tids intersect
   |  |  |     with RQ_i space                      */
9  |  return R as list of 2-tuple < i, Tid >
   /* By now, all participated worker nodes
      finished MapPartitions and returned R
      lists will be collected in
      RDD < RQ_id, Tid >                            */
10 Transformation GroupBy(RDD < RQ_id, Tid >)
11 |  return Tid as Key
   /* The result is formed as a
      PairRDD < Tid, [RQ_ids] >                     */
12 Transformation Filter(k, PairRDD < Tid, [RQ_ids] >)
   |  /* Eliminate duplication [RQ_ids]             */
13 |  Set U <- [RQ_ids]
14 |  if U.size == k then
15 |  |  return True
16 |  else
17 |  |  return False
18 return RDD < Tid >
```

B. Continuous Range Query

When receiving a k-$CRQ =< RQ_1, RQ_2, \cdots, RQ_k >$ on a trajectory set T, the algorithm needs to return any $Traj \in T$ *s.t.* $Traj_{space} \cap RQ_{space}$ $\forall$ $RQ \in CRQ$. From Algorithm 1, *UMOi* traverses the *sk-tree* for each RQ_i, where $1 \leq i \leq k$, to determine the required *Partition_Ids*. It returns: an overall set and an array of sets. The overall set contains all the *Partition_Ids* required for all RQs of CRQ. It is used when initializing the Spark *Job*. The second returned item, an array of sets, contains the required *Partition_Ids* as an individual set for each RQ_i. It is used to refine unnecessary *STR-tree* traversal, as shown in line 7. In line 4, *UMOi* identifies any trajectory that intersects with any RQ by using a transformation *MapPartitions*, which is running in parallel by the worker nodes on the given RDD partitions, known as map phase. An array of lists is used by each engaged worker node for each RDD partition to collect the *Tid*s intersect with a RQ and the corresponding *RQ_id*. The results, coming as lists of 2-tuple of *RQ_id* and *Tid*, are then reduced in a new RDD, known as the reduce phase. The new RDD, called RDD_{map}, includes any trajectory overlap with at least one RQ_i. Next, we group all the elements in RDD_{map} by the *Tid*s, as shown in

Algorithm 2: *LWHi*: Processing *k-CRQ*

```
   Input: k-CRQ
   Output: RDD < Tid >
1  Transformation MapPartitions(k-CRQ)
2      L[ ] ← φ
3      R[k]{ } ← φ
4      for i ← 1 to k do
5          R[i] ← STR-Tree.intersect(RQ_i.space)
           /* It returns all Tids intersect
              with RQ_i space                    */
6      foreach Tid ∈ R[1] do
7          Flag ← True
8          for i ← 2 to k do
9              if Tid ∉ R[i] then
10                 Flag ← False
11                 Break
12         if Flag = True then
13             L ← push(Tid)
14     return L
   /* The result is formed as a RDD < Tid >
      from returned Ls                           */
15 return RDD < Tid >
```

line 10. After that, it filters any Tid that does not intersect with all $RQ \in CRQ$. SPI, again, follows the same steps exactly except in the *sk-tree* as mentioned before.

Algorithm 2 shows how *LWHi* processes $k\text{-}CRQ$. The master node runs a transformation *MapPartitions* directly on all the worker nodes for all partitions. Through *MapPartitons*, each worker node traverses its local *STR-tree*, for every $RQ \in CRQ$. The result is an array of hash sets that contains overlapped $Tids$, as shown in line 5. It uses a hash set to eliminate duplication among trajectories of a particular RQ_i and to speed up the searching in the next step. Then, to find all $Tids$ that overlap with $k\text{-}CRQ$, each Tid from the first set (i.e., $Tids \cap RQ_1.space$) is checked for whether it belongs to the other sets. If it does not belong to at least one set, the process on this Tid is stopped and cannot be included in the final result. The returned lists are then formed in an RDD.

In *LWHi*, all intermediate processing is carried out in parallel by the worker nodes locally, without the need to process them globally by launching another *Job* and causing a costly *shuffle*. This is because *LWHi* guarantees full trajectory preservation. On the other hand, *UMOi* and SPI need to conduct a global refinement on the intermediate results (i.e., *GroupBy* and *Filter* in Algorithm 1, lines 10 and 12) which affects the overall performance in many respects, such as communication, cluster utilization, and GC scan. The communication between nodes is obviously going to increase, especially during *GroupBy*. Also, the distribution of RDD partitions after executing *GroupBy* transformation is skewed because of the keys' original places ($Tids$), which were collected based on $k\text{-}CRQ$. The degree varies based on the number of involved partitions in solving $k\text{-}CRQ$, so SPI would have the worst case. The intermediate result skewness affects any further computations (e.g., *Filter*, *Count*, etc.) and, therefore, reduces the cluster utilization. In some cases, the skewness with the previous consecutive computation on certain worker nodes could cause cumulative stress and a GC's full scan at the end.

Algorithm 3: *UMOi*: Processing *LTQ*

```
   Input: LTQ
   Output: Tid_LT
1  Transformation MapPartitions(LTQ)
2      D{ , } ← φ                      /* Dictionary */
3      forall Tid ∈ Parition do
4          Tid_Length ← Compute.Length(Tid)
5          if D contains Tid then
6              D ← push(Tid, OldValue + Tid_length)
7          else
8              D ← push(Tid, Tid_length)
9      return D as a list of 2-tuple
   /* Result is pairRDD < Tid, Tid_length >         */
10 Define Sum(Tid_length 1, Tid_length 2)
11     return Tid_length 1 + Tid_length 2
12 Transformation Aggregate(pairRDD < Tid, Tid_length >)
13     apply(Sum) /* Apply Sum function on
         elements have the same key Tid             */
14
15 return Max( pairRDD < Tid, Tid_length > )
```

Algorithm 4: *LWHi*: Processing *LTQ*

```
   Input: LTQ
   Output: Tid_LT
1  Transformation MapPartitions(LTQ)
2      D{ , } ← φ                      /* Dictionary */
3      forall Tid ∈ Parition do
4          Tid_Length ← Compute.Length(Tid)
5          if D contains Tid then
6              D ← push(Tid, OldValue + Tid_length)
7          else
8              D ← push(Tid, Tid_length)
9      return D as a list of 2-tuple
   /* Result is pairRDD < Tid, Tid_length >         */
10 return Max( pairRDD < Tid, Tid_length > )
```

However, the overall influence fluctuates based on the different pd values, which reflect the trajectory's preservation degree.

C. Longest Trajectory Query

This query belongs to the aggregation query type, which depends on a well-defined aggregation function. Given a longest trajectory query LTQ on T, it needs a Tid s.t. $Tid_{length} \geq \forall\ Tid_{length} \in T$. Algorithm 3 shows how *UMOi* processes LTQ. It first executes a local reduction, lines 1–8, and then global reduction by using *Aggregation* transformation, line 11. *Aggregation* transformation reduces the elements of pairRDD on their Tid keys by using an aggregation function, as in line 9, and causes a data shuffle. The element with the maximum value is then returned as the longest trajectory. The same steps are used in SPI. *LWHi*, as shown in Algorithm 4, does not require a global reduction since the whole trajectory resides in one partition.

Aggregation transformation actually does a local aggregation on partitions and then a global aggregation on the results. However, in our case, we need to compute the length of different sub-trajectories, and our partitions are built in a way that is hard for a passed function to deal with. So, we implement the first part in both algorithms to compute the

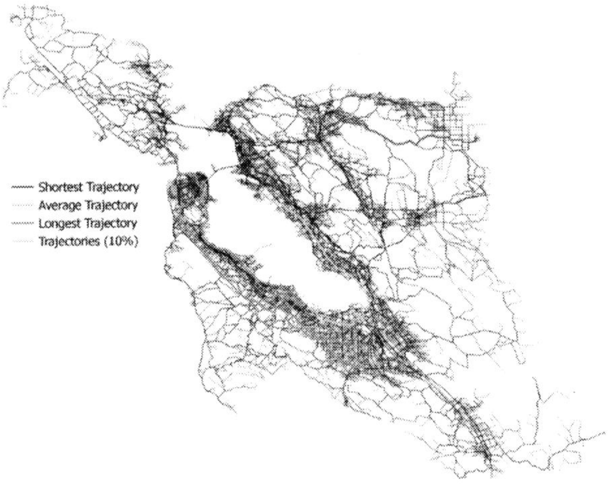

Figure 5. Trajectory dataset.

length of the trajectory and process the local aggregation at the same time.

D. Lookup Query

UMOi uses TTT to identify the required partitions. Then, it uses a *MapPartitions* transformation to retrieve segments of the given *Tid*. The same procedure is followed in SPI. In *LWHi*, identifying the required partition is fairly simple. It uses the same hash function used by the *Partitioner* to find the required *Partition_Id*. Then, similar to *UMOi*, it retrieves the segments of the given *Tid* from the required partition.

V. Experimental Study

In this section, we discuss the evaluation of our proposed approaches *LWHi* and *UMOi* and compare them with SPI. We present an assessment for trajectory skewness and its impact on spatial and object localities. From the performance perspective, we conduct extensive experiments to evaluate different query types.

A. Experiment Setting

Our implementation uses Apache Spark 2.2.0 with Java 1.8. We adopt Java *ParallelOldGC* as a garbage collector and *Kryo* for serialization. The experiments are conducted on AWS EMR 5.9.0. We use six m3.xlarge instances, where each instance provides 4 vCPU (Intel Xeon E5-2670) and 15 GB of RAM with high network performance. From Spark perspective, the master node (driver) is using one instance with 8 threads (cores) and 10.22 GB. The worker nodes (executors) are using 5 instances, each of which is using 6 threads (cores) and 10.22 GB. Thus, the total worker threads are 30, and they are distributed over 5 instances.

From the data side, we use the well-known moving object generator [31]. The trajectory set consists of more than 119 million trajectory segments (140,000 trajectories) over San Francisco, as seen in Figure 5. Since we are only focusing on in-memory computation, the data is always cached to the main memory during experiments.

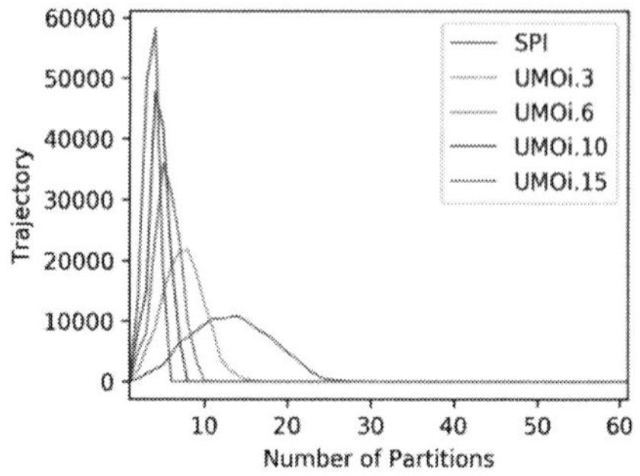

Figure 6. Trajectories settling frequency.

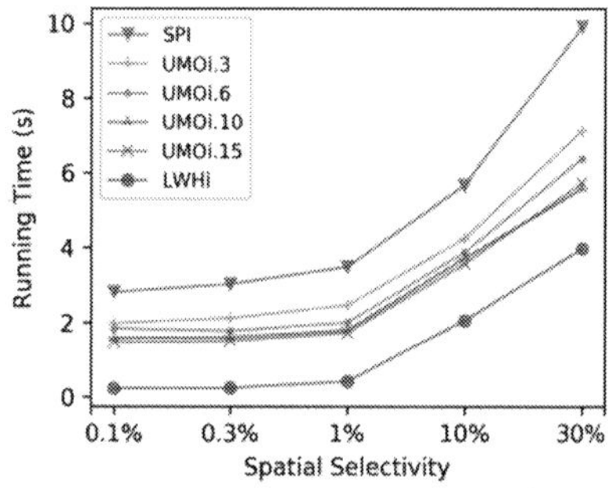

Figure 7. Running time for range query.

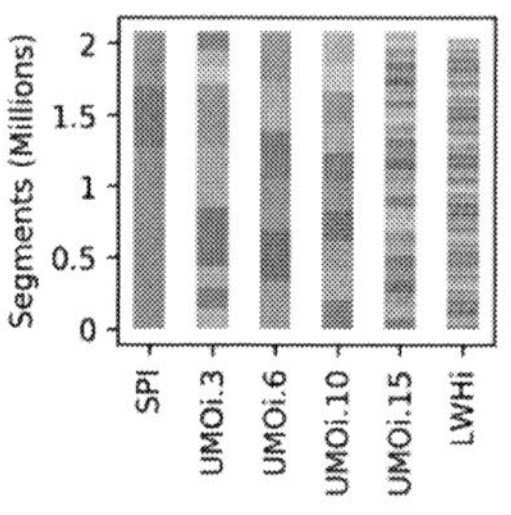

(a) 0.1% Selectivity

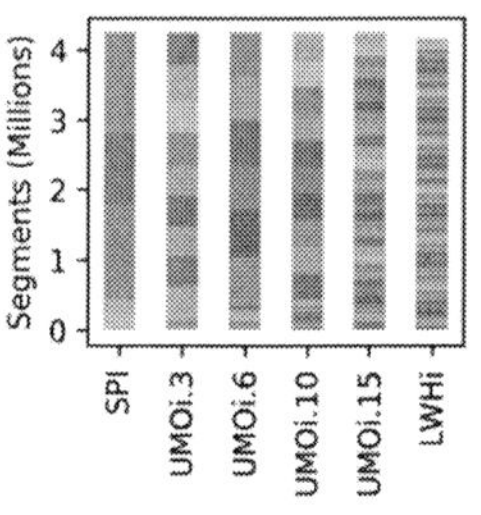

(b) 0.3% Selectivity

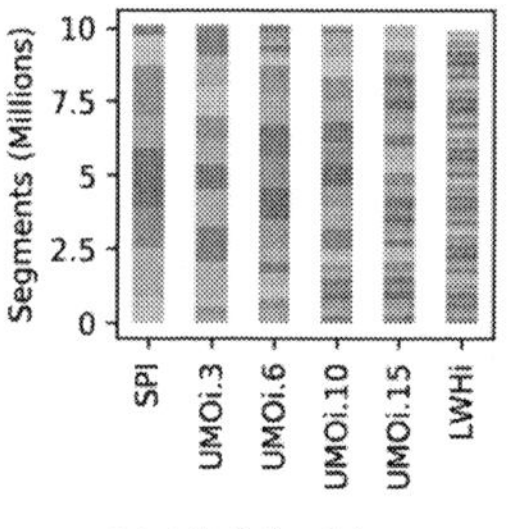

(c) 1% Selectivity

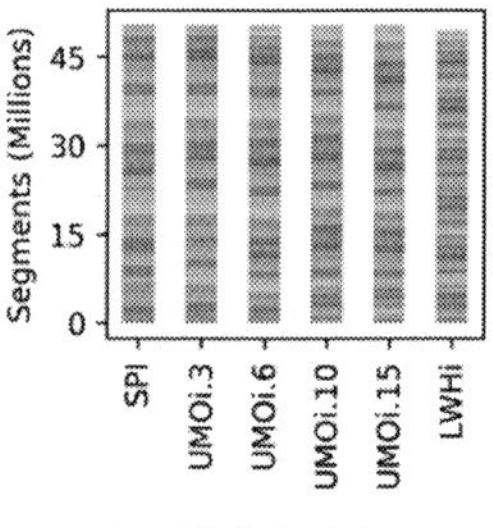

(d) 10% Selectivity

Figure 8. Engaged partitions for a particular range query with different spatial selectivity.

B. Skewness

We are more interested in analyzing the effects of eradicating the skewness rather than the skewness itself. Figure 6 shows trajectory occupancy on 60 partitions, i.e., the frequency

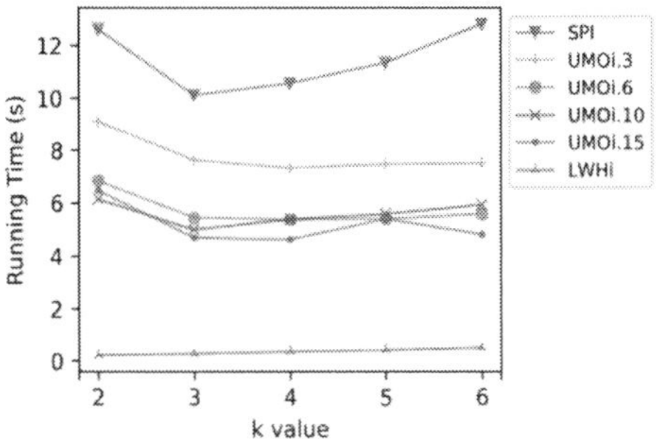

(a) 0.3% Spatial Selectivity

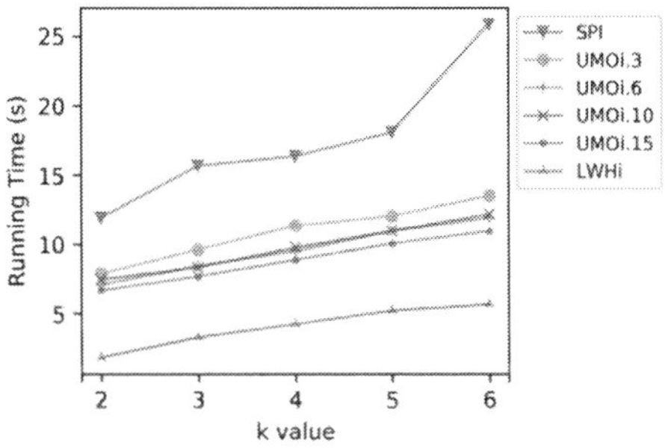

(b) 10% Spatial Selectivity

Figure 9. Running time for continuous range query.

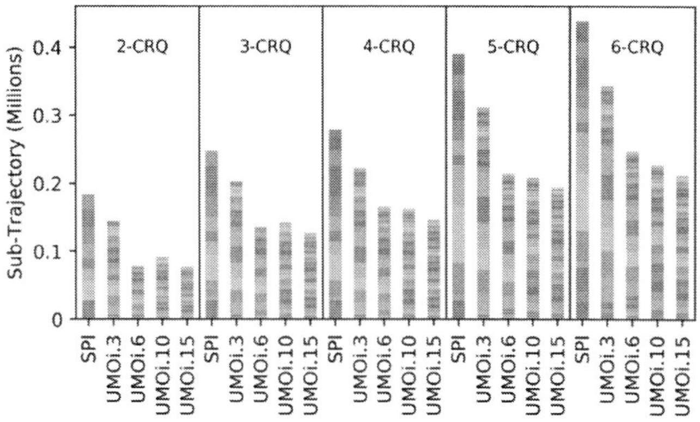

Figure 10. Engaged partitions for a particular CRQ with different k values.

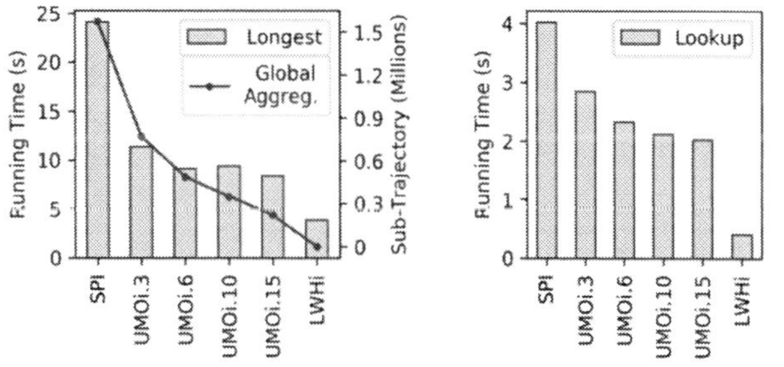

(a) Longest Query (b) Lookup Query

Figure 11. Running time for longest and lookup queries.

of required partitions to hold a particular trajectory, and also reflects the trajectory preservation for each method. *UMOi.x* means *UMOi* with $pd = x$. We do not include *LWHi*, since it only shows that all trajectories need one partition. The big impact is on SPI, where most trajectories need from 5 to 20 partitions. With increasing pd in *UMOi*, the required partitions numbers decrease which means more trajectory preservation. However, the decrease slows down after *UMOi.3*. The influences of trajectory segmentation on each query type are discussed further in the next section.

C. Construction of the Indexes

The average time to construct *UMOi* is 223.6 seconds, while it only takes 75.1 seconds for *LWHi* and 205 seconds for SPI. It is expected that *UMOi* takes longer since it needs to conduct space-based and object-based distributions. However, *UMOi* merges both distributions into one Spark *Job*, just like SPI, and this is why the difference is not significant.

D. Performance Evaluation

We test *LWHi* and *UMOi* and compare them with SPI on the following quires: Range Query, Continuous Range Query, Longest Trajectory (aggregation query), and Lookup Query. We set tpn to 60 and pd to $3, 6, 10$, and 15.

Starting with range query, Figure 7 shows the average running time of 100 random range queries. The running times of all methods increase with larger spatial selectivity. *LWHi* is better than all other algorithms, while *UMOi.3* outperforms SPI by a factor 1.4x on average. *UMOi.6* and *UMOi.10* outperform SPI only by a factor of 1.6x and 1.7x, respectively. Figure 8 shows the required partitions for only one range query, where each involved partition is uniquely colored, and the size of the colored partition reflects the amount of processed segments. The best case is when we have a significant number of engaged partitions, each of which participates equally while processing the same amount of segments. One of the performance factors is the GC's full-scan, which might be triggered when a big chunk of processed segments is settled on one node. Another observation is that increasing pd value does not necessarily mean more involved partitions, as we see in Figure 8a and 8b, where *UMOi.3* has more involved partitions than *UMOi.6*.

For continuous range query, we run 100 random queries with $k = 2, 3, 4, 5$, and 6, and we use two spatial selectivity (0.3% and 10%) as seen in Figure 9. In general, *LWHi* shows a significant speedup, especially with small spatial selectivity, and that is so because it only needs one Spark *Job* to execute the query locally, without any communication overhead. With small selectivity, *LWHi* outperforms SPI by a factor of 33x on average, and by a factor of 4.3x with 10% selectivity. *UMOi*s (*UMOi.3*, *UMOi.6*, etc.) gain a speedup range from 1.5x to 2.1x. Figure 10 gives an important glance at many factors during a particular k-CRQ's execution with different k values. The length of the bars represents the sub-trajectories after the first Spark *Job*, which is responsible for the local computation. They also reveal the remaining amount of global execution. If we take only one k-CRQ, we can see the difference in communication needed by the *GroupBy Job*. In 2-CRQ and 3-CRQ, *UMOi.6* needs less global reduction than *UMOi.10* because of the query location. The second *Job* performance depends on the location, size, and number of the partitions resulting from the first *Job*, which are uniquely colored in Figure 10. In this case, *UMOi*s have better situations than SPI which leads to more parallelism with a reasonable partition size. More importantly, with fewer resulting partitions, a cluster tends to constrain computation on fewer nodes, which affects cluster utilization and causes a GC's full-scan.

Figure 11a shows the average running time to find the longest trajectory. *LWHi* outperforms SPI by a factor 6.2x. The speedup factors for *UMOi*s range from 2.1x to 2.9x compared to SPI. It also shows the amount of sub-trajectories after the local aggregation that need to be processed globally. It reveals the tremendous difference between SPI and *UMOi.3* in trajectory preservation and how it slows down with higher *pd*, which reflects in the performance of each index. Also, Figure 11b shows the average running time of lookup query. *LWHi* gives the highest speedup by a factor of 10x, since it does not need a secondary index, such as TTT, and it only has to process one partition.

All the experimental results show that *LWHi* outperforms *UMOi*. However, *UMOi* is more useful in some cases when spatial locality is required. For example, consider applications that require special datasets such that the trajectories are mixed with static spatial data (e.g., buildings, road-network, etc.). With *LWHi*, all the partitions share the same global space. So, all the static spatial data need to be copied to all the partitions of *LWHi*, which results in full redundancy. SPI depends on space-based partitioning which is also suitable for static spatial data, similar to [12], and will have the lowest redundancy. With *UMOi*, the redundancy depends on the value of *pd*. So, the application user will be able to control the trade-off between performance and redundancy.

E. Limitations

Even though *UMOi* and *LWHi* show a significant performance improvement over traditional techniques, both have some limitations. The first challenge is how to select the optimal *pd* for a particular application. The optimal value for a *pd* depends on the nature of the application's queries, the characteristics of the trajectories, and the cluster settings. *UMOi* could be extended to contain a small simulation engine to give the best value for a *pd* based on a sample from the queries and trajectories. However, that will reflect on the construction time which is already higher than SPI and *LWHi*.

Moreover, both *UMOi* and *LWHi* are designed for in-memory usage. However, Spark also supports partially in-memory computation, which is useful when the data exceeds the main memory limits (i.e., usually 30% of the data reside on the disk). In this case, *LWHi* will always suffer from disk I/O for space-based queries, while it depends on the location of the engaged partitions for SPI and *UMOi*.

VI. Conclusion and Outlook

The huge volumes of moving object trajectories catalyze more trajectory-driven applications with more space-based and trajectory-based queries. As a result, cloud computing platforms are the typical solution to cope with the large-scale data and applications' demands. Spark has been adopted by most of the cloud platforms, and it offers an in-memory distributed computation platform. However, the large-scale trajectories and the adoption of a distributed platform raise the following challenges: communication cost, computation skewness, intermediate results skewness, and GC scan.

Therefore, our goal is to develop a large-scale historical trajectory index to support in-memory processing for both space-based and trajectory-based query types. Also, it needs to overcome all the previous challenges. As a result, we propose *UMOi* as a universal index that is capable of representing different partitioning techniques (i.e., space-based partitioning and object-based partitioning). It provides a flexible preservation degree (*pd*) parameter to control both spatial and object localities making it suitable to accommodate divergent trajectory-driven applications. With the lowest *pd* value, *UMOi* will act just like the traditional space-based index. However, with the highest *pd* value, it will act as our second index, *LWHi*. We distinguish *LWHi* as a standalone index because it guarantees a full *trajectory-preservation*, which allows optimizations to take place on both index construction and query processing.

We also conduct extensive experiments to validate our approaches. The results show a significant performance improvement (on both space-based and trajectory-based query types) compared to space-based indexing. The significant speedup is a result of reducing the communication cost and increasing the cluster utilization. Also, we present an analysis for heavy-loaded memory to show the far-reaching implications, such as GC scan and intermediate results skewness.

For future work, several optimizations and extensions could be considered. Both approaches could be extended to include partially in-memory data processing, which is also provided by Spark. Also, the space-splitting could be enhanced to maximize trajectory preservation by adopting an object-aware spatial partitioning. Finally, it is important to consider nested queries, i.e., queries that consist of different query types, and to analyze how they would benefit from different preservation degrees.

References

[1] D. Abadi et al., "The beckman report on database research," Commun. ACM, vol. 59, no. 2, Jan. 2016, pp. 92–99. [Online]. Available: http://doi.acm.org/10.1145/2845915

[2] https://spark.apache.org/, [retrieved: January, 2019].

[3] A. Guttman, "R-trees: A dynamic index structure for spatial searching," SIGMOD Rec., vol. 14, no. 2, Jun. 1984, pp. 47–57. [Online]. Available: http://doi.acm.org/10.1145/971697.602266

[4] J. L. Bentley, "Multidimensional binary search trees in database applications," IEEE Transactions on Software Engineering, vol. SE-5, no. 4, July 1979, pp. 333–340.

[5] D. Pfoser, C. S. Jensen, and Y. Theodoridis, "Novel approaches to the indexing of moving object trajectories," in Proceedings of 26th International Conference on Very Large Data Bases, ser. VLDB 2000, Sep. 2000, pp. 395–406.

[6] N. Beckmann, H.-P. Kriegel, R. Schneider, and B. Seeger, "The R*-tree: An efficient and robust access method for points and rectangles," SIGMOD Rec., vol. 19, no. 2, May 1990, pp. 322–331. [Online]. Available: http://doi.acm.org/10.1145/93605.98741

[7] T. K. Sellis, N. Roussopoulos, and C. Faloutsos, "The R+-tree: A dynamic index for multi-dimensional objects," in Proceedings of the 13th International Conference on Very Large Data Bases, ser. VLDB '87, 1987, pp. 507–518.

[8] J. T. Robinson, "The k-d-b-tree: A search structure for large multidimensional dynamic indexes," in Proceedings of the 1981 ACM SIGMOD International Conference on Management of Data, ser. SIGMOD '81. ACM, 1981, pp. 10–18. [Online]. Available: http://doi.acm.org/10.1145/582318.582321

[9] R. A. Finkel and J. L. Bentley, "Quad trees: A data structure for retrieval on composite keys," Acta Informatica, vol. 4, no. 1, Mar. 1974, pp. 1–9.

[10] M. A. Nascimento and J. R. O. Silva, "Towards historical R-trees," in Proceedings of the 1998 ACM Symposium on Applied Computing, ser. SAC '98. ACM, 1998, pp. 235–240. [Online]. Available: http://doi.acm.org/10.1145/330560.330692

[11] K. Zheng, S. Shang, N. J. Yuan, and Y. Yang, "Towards efficient search for activity trajectories," in 2013 IEEE 29th International Conference on Data Engineering (ICDE), April 2013, pp. 230–241.

[12] Z. Ding, B. Yang, Y. Chi, and L. Guo, "Enabling smart transportation systems: A parallel spatio-temporal database approach," IEEE Transactions on Computers, vol. 65, no. 5, May 2016, pp. 1377–1391.

[13] A. Eldawy and M. F. Mokbel, "Spatialhadoop: A mapreduce framework for spatial data," in 2015 IEEE 31st International Conference on Data Engineering, April 2015, pp. 1352–1363.

[14] A. Eldawy, Y. Li, M. F. Mokbel, and R. Janardan, "CG_hadoop: Computational geometry in mapreduce," in Proceedings of the 21st ACM SIGSPATIAL International Conference on Advances in Geographic Information Systems, ser. SIGSPATIAL'13. ACM, 2013, pp. 294–303. [Online]. Available: http://doi.acm.org/10.1145/2525314.2525349

[15] S. Nishimura, S. Das, D. Agrawal, and A. E. Abbadi, "Md-hbase: A scalable multi-dimensional data infrastructure for location aware services," in 2011 IEEE 12th International Conference on Mobile Data Management, June 2011, pp. 7–16.

[16] A. Aji et al., "Hadoop gis: A high performance spatial data warehousing system over mapreduce," Proc. VLDB Endow., vol. 6, no. 11, Aug. 2013, pp. 1009–1020. [Online]. Available: http://dx.doi.org/10.14778/2536222.2536227

[17] A. Akdogan, U. Demiryurek, F. Banaci-Kashani, and C. Shahabi, "Voronoi-based geospatial query processing with mapreduce," in 2010 IEEE Second International Conference on Cloud Computing Technology and Science, Nov. 2010, pp. 9–16.

[18] Q. Ma, B. Yang, W. Qian, and A. Zhou, "Query processing of massive trajectory data based on mapreduce," in Proceedings of the First International Workshop on Cloud Data Management, ser. CloudDB '09. ACM, 2009, pp. 9–16. [Online]. Available: http://doi.acm.org/10.1145/1651263.1651266

[19] J. Yu, J. Wu, and M. Sarwat, "Geospark: A cluster computing framework for processing large-scale spatial data," in Proceedings of the 23rd SIGSPATIAL International Conference on Advances in Geographic Information Systems, ser. SIGSPATIAL '15. ACM, 2015, pp. 70:1–70:4. [Online]. Available: http://doi.acm.org/10.1145/2820783.2820860

[20] M. Tang, Y. Yu, Q. M. Malluhi, M. Ouzzani, and W. G. Aref, "Locationspark: A distributed in-memory data management system for big spatial data," Proc. VLDB Endow., vol. 9, no. 13, Sep. 2016, pp. 1565–1568. [Online]. Available: https://doi.org/10.14778/3007263.3007310

[21] S. You, J. Zhang, and L. Gruenwald, "Large-scale spatial join query processing in cloud," in 2015 31st IEEE International Conference on Data Engineering Workshops (ICDEW), April 2015, pp. 34–41. [Online]. Available: doi.ieeecomputersociety.org/10.1109/ICDEW.2015.7129541

[22] H. Wang and A. Belhassena, "Parallel trajectory search based on distributed index," Information Sciences, vol. 388-389, 2017, pp. 62 – 83. [Online]. Available: https://doi.org/10.1016/j.ins.2017.01.016

[23] D. A. Peixoto and N. Q. V. Hung, "Scalable and fast top-k most similar trajectories search using mapreduce in-memory," in Databases Theory and Applications. Springer International Publishing, 2016, pp. 228–241.

[24] H. Wang et al., "Sharkdb: An in-memory column-oriented trajectory storage," in Proceedings of the 23rd ACM International Conference on Information and Knowledge Management, ser. CIKM '14. ACM, 2014, pp. 1409–1418. [Online]. Available: http://doi.acm.org/10.1145/2661829.2661878

[25] A. Eldawy and M. F. Mokbel, "The era of big spatial data: A survey," Information and Media Technologies, vol. 10, no. 2, 2015, pp. 305–316.

[26] S. T. Leutenegger, M. A. Lopez, and J. Edgington, "STR: A simple and efficient algorithm for R-tree packing," in Proceedings 13th International Conference on Data Engineering, April 1997, pp. 497–506.

[27] F. Chang et al., "Bigtable: A distributed storage system for structured data," ACM Trans. Comput. Syst., vol. 26, no. 2, Jun. 2008, pp. 4:1–4:26. [Online]. Available: http://doi.acm.org/10.1145/1365815.1365816

[28] Z. Chen, H. T. Shen, X. Zhou, Y. Zheng, and X. Xie, "Searching trajectories by locations: An efficiency study," in Proceedings of the 2010 ACM SIGMOD International Conference on Management of Data, ser. SIGMOD '10. ACM, 2010, pp. 255–266. [Online]. Available: http://doi.acm.org/10.1145/1807167.1807197

[29] B.-K. Yi, H. V. Jagadish, and C. Faloutsos, "Efficient retrieval of similar time sequences under time warping," in Proceedings 14th International Conference on Data Engineering, Feb. 1998, pp. 201–208.

[30] R. Agrawal, C. Faloutsos, and A. Swami, "Efficient similarity search in sequence databases," in International conference on foundations of data organization and algorithms. Springer, 1993, pp. 69–84.

[31] T. Brinkhoff, "A framework for generating network-based moving objects," GeoInformatica, vol. 6, no. 2, June 2002, pp. 153–180. [Online]. Available: https://doi.org/10.1023/A:1015231126594

Superordinate Knowledge Based Comprehensive Subset of Conceptual Knowledge for Practical Geo-spatial Application Scenarios

Claus-Peter Rückemann
Westfälische Wilhelms-Universität Münster (WWU), Germany;
Knowledge in Motion, DIMF, Germany;
Leibniz Universität Hannover, Germany
Email: ruckema@uni-muenster.de

Abstract—**The results presented in this paper are based on the research conducted during the last years. Many multi-disciplinary and practical geo-spatial data and application solutions require to exploit holistically complex scenarios. In many cases, data and algorithms as well as workflows have to be created and tackled individually. The goal of this research is to create an innovative, comprehensive tool base of conceptual knowledge in geo-spatial application scenarios for arbitrary knowledge context in any media. The solution should be complementary to the commonly available geo-spatial features and should fulfill a range of further criteria, especially for a coherent system of knowledge, multi-disciplinary, and data-centric. The result should allow to create and refer to facetted knowledge focussed on geo-spatial scenarios. The paper presents the results of an implementation based on the fundamental methodology of superordinate knowledge. The solution is targeting geo-spatial application scenarios and has been used for many practical implementations over more than three decades. The resulting comprehensive subset of conceptual knowledge reference divisions, which was created from this long-term research, is available and first published with this paper.**

Keywords*–*Comprehensive Conceptual Knowledge; Geo-spatial Application Scenarios; Superordinate Knowledge Methodology; UDC; Advanced Data-centric Computing.

I. INTRODUCTION

It is a truth universally acknowledged, that geo-spatial disciplines are specialised and very much concentrating on providing solutions and tools for spatial data.

When it gets to more complex situations, then, spatial data based on numerical coordinate reference systems and domain only approaches may not be sufficient. This is, for example, the case when describing the target knowledge with mathematical spacial facets and dimensions is not sufficient. Many information and context maybe lost when knowledge is handled as plain data and mapped to preexisting attributes and categories. This is the case when a more holistic and more fundamental approach should be considered. In practice, associating different objectives and intentions, systematic knowledge, and physical features with knowledge, from methodology to implementation and realisation, can provide valuable solutions. The principles of superordinate knowledge provide such fundaments, from methodology to realisation.

The resulting solution should be complementary to the commonly available geo-spatial topologies, taxonomies, and features. In consequence, the means of describing spatial data, objects, entities, and context should be substantially extended.

The resulting solution should fulfill a range of criteria in order to provide a most sustainable, flexible fundament, e.g.:

- Covering a coherent system of knowledge.
- Consistent implementation, quasi-standardised.
- Providing facetted conceptual knowledge features.
- Multi-disciplinary knowledge spectrum.
- Features for multi-lingual implementation.
- Data-centric implementation / method.
- Extensible concept.

Therefore, these criteria should allow advanced features, e.g., documentation of data, objects, scenarios, concepts, algorithms, as well as universal context of knowledge criteria for all kind of knowledge in any media, knowledge documentation, knowledge consistent integration of publications and research data, knowledge mining, wide range of flexible implementation potential, supporting workflow features and documentation.

With this research, a comprehensive subset of conceptual knowledge reference divisions was created, further developed, and finally compiled from the practical application case studies, which have been conducted over the last decades.

The rest of this paper is organised as follows. Section II introduces the state of the art and motivation. Section III discusses previous work, components, and used resources. Section IV presents the required implementation features and sample scenarios. Section V presents the resulting conceptual knowledge solution. Section VI presents evaluation references to directly related implementations, research, development, and cases studies. Section VII summarises the lessons learned, conclusions, and future work.

II. STATE OF THE ART AND MOTIVATION

Geo-spatial practice is focussed on providing cartographic means for certain space and environment. Widely employed tools are Geoscientific Information Systems and Geographic Information Systems. Most of these tools use geo-referenced data in order to organise and reference information. Available topologies can also provide for the categorisation of geo-spatial entities. All together these means are very limited when seen in a larger context as required for many complex application scenarios. Regarding that, one of the major deficits is the lack of a consistent and holistic knowledge concept. The fundaments of terminology and understanding knowledge are layed out by Aristotle [1], being an essential part of 'Ethics' [2]. Information sciences can very much benefit from

Aristotle's fundaments and a knowledge-centric approach [3] but for building holistic and sustainable solutions, supporting a modern definition of knowledge [4], they need to go beyond the available technology-based approaches and hypothesis [5] as analysed in Platon's Phaidon.

In sciences, observation is one of the most important fundamental tasks [6]. But, as John Burroughs expressed "There is nothing in which people differ in more than in their powers of observation. Some are only half alive to what is going on around them." [7]. Triggered by the results of a systems cases study, it is obvious that superordinate systematic principles [8] are still widely missing in practice and education. Making a distinction and creating interfaces between methods and the implementation applications [9], the results of this research are illustrated here along with the practical example of the Knowledge Mapping methodology [10] enabling the creation of new object and entity context environments, e.g., implementing methods for knowledge mining context. This motivating background allows to build methods for knowledge mapping on a general methodological fundament.

The Organisation for Economic Co-operation and Development (OECD) has published principles and guidelines for access to research data from public funding [11]. The principles and guidelines are meant to apply to research data that are gathered using public funds for the purposes of producing publicly accessible knowledge. In this context, the OECD especially addresses knowledge, re-use, and knowledge generated from re-use. The means to achieve such recommendations even for complex scenarios is to use the principles of Superordinate Knowledge, which integrate arbitrary knowledge over theory and practice. Core assembly elements of Superordinate Knowledge [8] are methodology, implementation, and realisation. Separation and integration of assemblies have proven beneficial for building solutions with different disciplines, different levels of expertise. Comprehensive focussed subsets of conceptual knowledge can also provide excellent modular and standardised complements for information systems component implementations, e.g., for environmental information management and computation [12]. The conceptual knowledge reference divisions presented here are the result from more than three decades of scientific research in information science and multidisciplinary knowledge.

III. Previous Work, Components, and Resources

For the implementation of case studies, the modules are built by support of a number of major components and resources, which can be used for a wide range of applications, e.g., creation of resources and extraction of entities. The facility for consistently describing knowledge is a valuable quality, especially conceptual knowledge, e.g., using the Universal Decimal Classification (UDC) [13].

The UDC is the world's foremost document indexing language in the form of a multi-lingual classification scheme covering all fields of knowledge and constitutes a sophisticated indexing and retrieval tool. The UDC is designed for subject description and indexing of content of information resources irrespective of the carrier, form, format, and language. UDC is an analytico-synthetic and facetted classification. It uses a knowledge presentation based on disciplines, with synthetic features. UDC schedules are organised as a coherent system of knowledge with associative relationships and references between concepts and related fields. Therefore, the UDC represents a most flexible facetted classification system for all kinds of knowledge in any media. The UDC provides 70,000 subdivisions, in 50 languages, which provides more than 3 million entries and verbal descriptions. The UDC is up to now internationally used in 130 countries, for 150,000–200,000 document collections worldwide. The classification has shown up being especially important for complex, facetted, multidisciplinary, and long-term classification, e.g., with Knowledge Resources. The UDC is the best publicly available implementation of conceptual knowledge to illustrate the width and depth of knowledge dimensions. The UDC allows an efficient and effective processing of knowledge data and provides facilities to obtain a universal and systematical view on classified objects. Operational areas include author-side content classifications and museum collections, e.g., with documentation of resources, library content, bibliographic purposes on publications and references, for digital and realia objects. The Knowledge Resources objects and entities can refer to any conceptual knowledge, e.g., main UDC-based classes, which for this publication are taken from the multi-lingual UDC summary [13] released by the UDC Consortium under a Creative Commons license [14]. Facets can be created with any auxiliary tables, e.g., auxiliaries of place and space, time, language, and form as well as general characteristics, e.g., properties, materials, relations, processes, and operations, persons and personal characteristics.

IV. Implementation and Basic Examples

A. *Required conceptual knowledge features*

Data and objects result from public, commonly available, and specialised Knowledge Resources. The Knowledge Resources are containing factual and conceptual knowledge as well as documentation and instances of procedural and metacognitive knowledge. These resources contain multidisciplinary and multi-lingual data and context. UDC provides auxiliary signs [15], which represent kinds of standardised "operations". UDC allows the creation of facetted knowledge using these features. The conceptual knowledge in focus requires to provide references to any universal knowledge context. References to UDC codes are capable to provide all the required context. The main tables provide an entry point to universal knowledge context [16]. For practical use, classification references can refer to UDC reference codes based on science and knowledge organisation [17]. For conceptual knowledge of place and spatial context the implementation requires to provide references to classification codes. The UDC provides references based on the common auxiliaries of place of the UDC [18]. In that context, besides universal knowledge, additional closely related references are required. UDC can provide appropriate references, e.g., geodesy, surveying, photogrammetry, remote sensing, cartography (UDC:528) [19] and geography, exploration, travel (UDC:910) [20], and nonliterary, nontextual representations of a region (UDC:912) [21].

B. Examples of conceptual knowledge application

Examples of conceptual knowledge reference divisions according with UDC (UDC:913, Regional geography, [22]; UDC:94, General history, [23]; UDC:(1/9), Common auxiliaries of place, [18]) and UDC conventions are shown in the following four small sample groups:

UDC:913(3) ⇒ Geography of the ancient world
UDC:913(3/9) ⇒ Geography of the individual regions and countries of the ancient and modern world

UDC:94(3) ⇒ History of the ancient world
UDC:94(3/9) ⇒ History of individual places of the ancient and modern world

UDC:94(37) ⇒ History of ancient Rome and Italy (to 5th century)
UDC:94(38) ⇒ History of ancient Greece

UDC:(37)(24) ⇒ Ancient Rome and Italy, below sea level
UDC:(38)(24) ⇒ Ancient Greece, below sea level

A little more complex facetted example, a single data object entity of a ship wreck realia as referred in a container of extended Knowledge Resources, is shown in Figure 1.

```
Lindos [Archaeology, Geophysics, Remote Sensing, Seafaring]:
        Greek city, Rhodos Island, Dodekanese, Greece, ...
        Object: Ship wreck.
        Object-Type: Realia object.
        Object-Location: 500\UD{m} SE of Hagios Pavlos Harbor.
        %%IML: UDC:[902+903+...+904]+629.5+(38)+(4)+(24)...
        %%IML: cite: YES 19810000 {LXK:Lindos; Rhodes; Ancient Greece;
         Archaeology; Artefacts; Ship wreck;} {UDC:...} {PAGE:--45..--58} LXCITE:
         //Nikolitsis:1981:Rhodos
        %%IML: ...
        %%IML: OSMLocation: https://www.openstreetmap.org/...=36.08...%2C28.08...
        %%IML: GoogleMapsLocation: http://maps.google.com/maps...=...,...
```

Figure 1. Knowledge Resources, conceptual spatial and geo-references: Lindos object with ship wreck entity, Rhodes, Greece (excerpt).

Passages not relevant for demonstration and not adequate for privacy and safety reasons were shortened to ellipses. The object entity contains documentation, object categories and factual data, conceptual data references, a source reference [24], and data for geo-references. The conceptual knowledge comprises details of non geo-spatial domains, e.g., from main tables UDC:6 and UDC:9, and from geo-spatial context, e.g., auxiliary tables for place and space UDC:(24) UDC:(3/9). For this case, the object entity references can be resolved as:

UDC:902 ⇒ Archaeology
UDC:903 ⇒ Prehistory. Prehistoric remains, artefacts, antiquities
UDC:904 ⇒ Cultural remains of historical times
UDC:629.5 ⇒ Watercraft engineering. Marine engineering. Boats. Ships. Boatbuilding and shipbuilding
UDC:(38) ⇒ Ancient Greece
UDC:(4) ⇒ Europe
UDC:(24) ⇒ Below sea level. Underground. Subterranean

The references can hold further details and sub-contain additional information, e.g., UDC:903 further refers to artefacts in more detail. For a wider and deeper view, we have to refer to a number of successful projects, which were conducted by the author's group and various collaborators over the last decades. All these implementations are significantly based on the solution presented here.

V. RESULTING CONCEPTUAL KNOWLEDGE SOLUTION

Table I contains the compilation of a general comprehensive subset of resulting major conceptual knowledge reference divisions for geo-spatial application scenarios. All the conceptual knowledge reference divisions presented are referring to UDC codes, which have been made publicly available. Here, "UDC:" is the designated notation of references used with Knowledge Resources and objects in ongoing projects. The UDC illustrates the width and depth of knowledge dimensions. The full details of organisation and knowledge are available from the UDC. As far a possible, the original verbal descriptions (English for demonstration) were taken, even if the writing of terms and words may differ from the practice used for the rest of this paper. The resulting conceptual knowledge solution comprises a most comprehensive knowledge compendium of geo-spatially dominated facetted knowledge, which can be effectively and efficiently used in geo-spatial application scenarios. Besides the level of detail and arbitrary facetted knowledge, the respective conceptual knowledge reference divisions provide a focussed discipline coverage while spanning a large width and depth of knowledge reference divisions. For example, let us take an additional view on depth for UDC:004 (Computer science and technology. Computing. Data processing), UDC:51 (Mathematics), and UDC:528 (Geodesy. Surveying. Photogrammetry. Remote sensing. Cartography).

Besides the shown references, UDC:004 also comprises important subdivision context of data and structure, e.g., data handling (UDC:004.62), files (UDC:004.63), databases and their structures (UDC:004.65), and systems for numeric data (UDC:004.67). For practical references, UDC:004 can be used to also hold references to many application scenarios, e.g., algorithms for program construction, low level as well as high level and problem oriented languages, knowledge representation, artificial intelligence application systems, intelligent knowledge-based systems. For practical references with mathematical, geometrical, and topological context, UDC:51 can be used to also hold references to fundamental and general considerations of mathematics, number theory, algebra, geometry, topology, analysis, combinatorial analysis, graph theory, probability, mathematical statistics, computational mathematics, numerical analysis, mathematical cybernetics, operational research as well as mathematical theories and methods. For practical references with geoscience and spatial disciplines, UDC:528 can be used to also hold references to a much deeper discipline based knowledge, e.g., fundamentals derived from potential theory, level surfaces, geoids, geometric/static methods, use of longitudinal and latitudinal measurements, gravity measurement, astro-geodetic determination of position, geographical coordinates, topographic surveying, engineering surveys, special fields of surveying, applications of photogrammetry, fundamental and physical principles, data processing, and interpretation.

The result of conceptual knowledge reference divisions based on the methodology of superordinate knowledge is complementary to geo-spatial topologies and geo-referencing. It can be used complementary with any geoscientific and geo-spatial knowledge in any context.

TABLE I. COMPREHENSIVE SUBSET OF RESULTING CONCEPTUAL KNOWLEDGE REFERENCE DIVISIONS FOR GEO-SPATIAL APPLICATION SCENARIOS, PRACTICALLY USED MAIN CLASSIFICATION REFERENCES, UNIVERSAL DECIMAL CLASSIFICATION SAMPLES (UDC, ENGLISH; UDCC [13]; CC [14]).

CONCEPTUAL KNOWLEDGE REFERENCES FOR GEO-SPATIAL SCENARIOS			
Code / Sign Ref.	*Verbal Description (EN)*	*Code / Sign Ref.*	*Verbal Description (EN)*
	Common Auxiliary Signs		
+	Coordination. Addition (plus sign).	[]	Subgrouping (square brackets).
/	Consecutive extension (oblique stroke sign).	*	Introduces non-UDC notation (asterisk).
:	Simple relation (colon sign).	A/Z	Direct alphabetical specification.
::	Order-fixing (double colon sign).	.	[Reference listing, itemisation]
	Auxiliary Tables		
UDC:=...	Common auxiliaries of language.	UDC:(=...)	Common auxiliaries of human ancestry, ethnic grouping and nationality.
UDC:(0...)	Common auxiliaries of form.		
UDC:(1/9)	Common auxiliaries of place.	UDC:-0...	Common auxiliaries of general characteristics: Properties, Materials, Relations/Processes and Persons.
UDC:"..."	Common auxiliaries of time.		
	Place and Space		
UDC:(1/9)	Common auxiliaries of place.	UDC:(20)	Ecosphere
UDC:(1)	Place and space in general. Localization. Orientation	UDC:(21)	Surface of the Earth in general. Land areas in particular. Natural zones and regions
UDC:(100)	Universal as to place. International. All countries in general		
UDC:(1-0/-9)	Special auxiliary subdivision for boundaries and spatial forms of various kinds	UDC:(23)	Above sea level. Surface relief. Above ground generally. Mountains
UDC:(1-0)	Zones		
UDC:(1-1)	Orientation. Points of the compass. Relative position	UDC:(24)	Below sea level. Underground. Subterranean
UDC:(1-2)	Lowest administrative units. Localities	UDC:(25)	Natural flat ground (at, above or below sea level). The ground in its natural condition, cultivated or inhabited
UDC:(1-5)	Dependent or semi-dependent territories		
UDC:(1-6)	States or groupings of states from various points of view	UDC:(26)	Oceans, seas and interconnections
UDC:(1-7)	Places and areas according to privacy, publicness and other special features	UDC:(28)	Inland waters
		UDC:(29)	The world according to physiographic features
UDC:(1-8)	Location. Source. Transit. Destination	UDC:(3/9)	Individual places of the ancient and modern world
UDC:(1-9)	Regionalization according to specialized points of view	UDC:(3)	Places of the ancient and mediaeval world
UDC:(2)	Physiographic designation	UDC:(4/9)	Countries and places of the modern world
	Main Tables		
UDC:0	Science and Knowledge. Organization. Computer Science. Information. Documentation. Librarianship. Institutions. Publications	UDC:5	Mathematics. Natural Sciences
		UDC:6	Applied Sciences. Medicine, Technology
UDC:1	Philosophy. Psychology	UDC:7	The Arts. Entertainment. Sport
UDC:2	Religion. Theology	UDC:8	Linguistics. Literature
UDC:3	Social Sciences	UDC:9	Geography. Biography. History
	Science, Knowledge, Organisation		
UDC:001	Science and knowledge in general. Organization of intellectual work	UDC:007	Activity and organizing. Communication and control theory generally (cybernetics). 'Human engineering'
UDC:002	Documentation. Books. Writings. Authorship		
UDC:003	Writing systems and scripts	UDC:01	Bibliography and bibliographies. Catalogues
UDC:004	Computer science and technology. Computing. Data processing	UDC:02	Librarianship
UDC:004.4	Software	UDC:030	General reference works (as subject)
UDC:004.6	Computer data	UDC:050	Serial publications, periodicals (as subject)
UDC:004.7	Computer communication. Computer networks	UDC:06	Organizations of a general nature
UDC:004.8	Artificial intelligence	UDC:061	Organizations and other types of cooperation
UDC:005	Management	UDC:069	Museums. Permanent exhibitions
UDC:005.94	Knowledge management	UDC:070	Newspapers (as subject). The Press. Journalism
UDC:006	Standardization of products, operations, weights, measures and time	UDC:08	Polygraphies. Collective works
UDC:008	Civilization. Culture. Progress	UDC:09	Manuscripts. Rare and remarkable works
	Geo-spatial Focus Divisions From Main Tables		
UDC:51	Mathematics	UDC:550.3	Geophysics
UDC:528	Geodesy. Surveying. Photogrammetry. Remote sensing. Cartography	UDC:550.7	Geobiology. Geological actions of organisms
UDC:528.2	Figure of the Earth. Earth measurement. Mathematical geodesy. Physical geodesy. Astronomical geodesy	UDC:550.8	Applied geology and geophysics. Geological prospecting and exploration. Interpretation of results
UDC:528.3	Geodetic surveying	UDC:551	General geology. Meteorology. Climatology. Historical geology. Stratigraphy. Palaeogeography
UDC:528.4	Field surveying. Land surveying. Cadastral survey. Topography. Engineering survey. Special fields of surveying	UDC:551.8	Palaeogeography
UDC:528.7	Photogrammetry: aerial, terrestrial	UDC:778	Special applications and techniques of photography
UDC:528.8	Remote sensing	UDC:91	Geography. Exploration of the Earth and of individual countries. Travel. Regional geography (systematic geography). Theoretical geography
UDC:528.9	Cartography. Mapping (textual documents)		
UDC:528.94	Thematic cartography. Topical cartography		
UDC:53	Physics	UDC:912	Nonliterary, nontextual representations of a region
UDC:55	Earth Sciences. Geological sciences	UDC:913	Regional geography

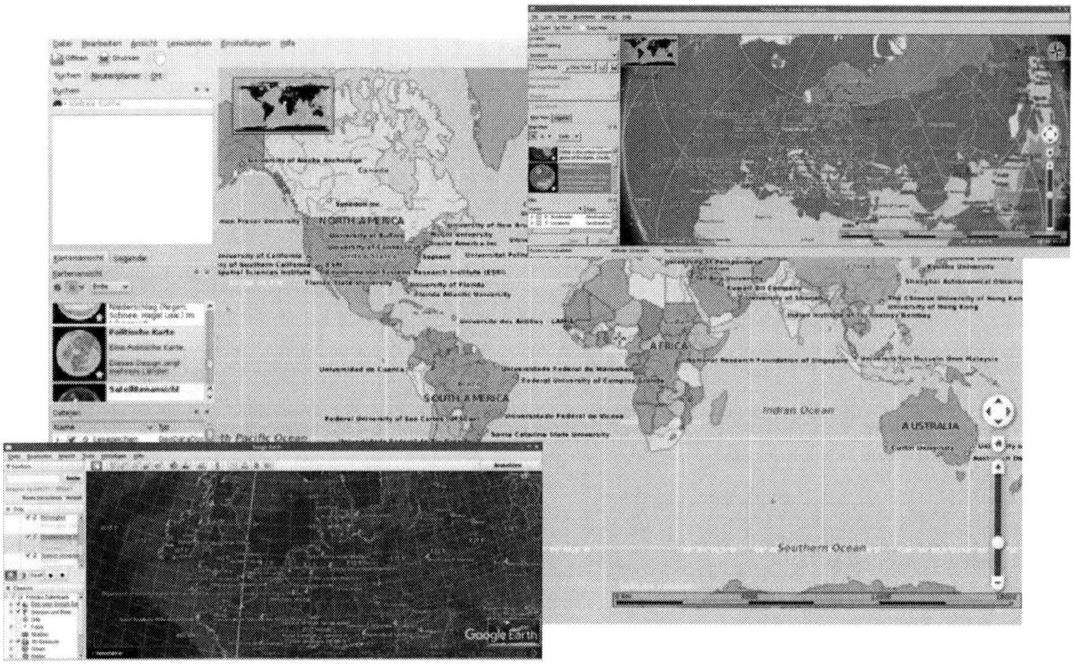

Figure 2. Collage of different implementation cases based on the resulting conceptual knowledge (Table I) from this research: Knowledge mapping, integration, mining; the samples illustrate context creation and dynamical visualisation. For technical details please see the references for the case studies given in the text.

The result can provide solutions wherever conceptual knowledge references are involved. The methodologies and implementations make sure that powerful sets of unique attributes and features are available. The number of possible use cases is practically unlimited. The case studies showed that a wide range of application scenarios can benefit from the principles of superordinate knowledge and considering conceptual knowledge as complementary means for consistently documenting and handling knowledge. The passages in the following section refer to discussions and details for an excerpt of successful implementations.

VI. EVALUATION FROM IMPLEMENTATION CASES

Many years of research and practical solution developments contributed to creating a comprehensive subset of conceptual knowledge, which is the fundament deployed for general practical solutions, e.g., with geo-spatial applications and with geo-data knowledge mining and processing. The conceptual knowledge framework employed here, especially UDC, has passed the test of time and is so mature and used in so many scenarios that the ongoing knowledge development itself is iterating with its application.

The previously unpublished results of practical conceptual knowledge are first presented here (Table I). The following case studies are based on these results and present small but illustrative excerpts (Figure 2) in form of a cross-section of conducted research and development, of Knowledge Resources, algorithms, intelligent workflows, and implementations. Here, for example, a knowledge mining process employing knowledge objects based on the referred conceptual knowledge can use all the width and depth of knowledge behind the comprehensive subset to automatically or semi-automatically create new context and visualisation for a data set containing non-georeferenced text entities (affiliations in floating text), e.g., geographical, political, and climate zone context.

Besides the knowledge fundament and framework being focus of this research paper, the references in the next passages contain further details for the practical case studies, the implemented methods and the technologies, which were used for the different case studies.

- *Knowledge integration* allows to create new views and insights by computing Spatial Cogwheel modules [25].
- *Knowledge mining:* Creating Knowledge Resources and employing classification and concordances can provide a base for advanced knowledge discovery and computational solutions [26]. The integration of Knowledge Resources and advanced association processing can be beneficial in many disciplines as it provides multi-disciplinary and multi-lingual support [27]. Methods like the Content Factor can be used for advanced knowledge processing [28]. The integration of appropriate methods can be used for further advancing the Knowledge Resources, as well as the mining processes [29].
- *The methodology of knowledge mapping* allows to create flexible methods in order to handle spatial representations and knowledge mining by creating a multi-dimensional context for arbitrary objects and entities [10].

- *Dynamical visualisation:* The methodology can be used for enabling knowledge based methods for computation and computational and dynamical visualisation [30].
- *Association and phonetic features:* The methodology supports phonetic association and mining methods [31].
- *Verbal description:* The employment of implemented methods can be supported and make use of multilingual verbal descriptions and concordances [32] as the conceptual knowledge is consistently available in 50 languages, providing millions of basic conceptual knowledge references.

VII. Conclusion

This research achieved to create a comprehensive tool base of conceptual knowledge in geo-spatial application scenarios for all kinds of knowledge context in any media. The implemented superordinate knowledge based solution fulfills all the required criteria as was presented and discussed in this paper. The result was employed to successfully implement a wide range of different geo-spatial cases.

With this research, a comprehensive subset of references to conceptual knowledge, allowing geo-spatially dominated facetted knowledge, was created, further developed, and finally compiled from the application case studies, which have been conducted over the last three decades. Knowledge based fundaments, e.g., those built on UDC, showed to have a very high impact on knowledge creation and mining in theory and practice, not only for spatial knowledge.

The knowledge approach proved to be a fundamental "enabler" and contributed significantly to many solutions. Covering a coherent system of knowledge provides a holistic and consistent environment for any scenario, which is supported by excellent features for facetted knowledge. The referenced conceptual knowledge itself is consistent due to its development and publication via editions. Implementations support fully multi-disciplinary context and multi-lingual instances for many languages. Solutions are extensible to integrate and fit special purposes. The methodology is data-centric and scalable for width and depth of knowledge as well as for infrastructure requirements. All the cases so far implementing the presented solution provided seamless integration with common geo-spatial practices and showed excellent sustainability, knowledge coverage, long-term characteristics, and scalability. In review of these results, all major institutions, e.g., libraries focussing on information science and research data management, are using and developing conceptual knowledge with their core tasks, which opens up a wide range of excellent knowledge sources, which can be considered high value resources. Moreover, such Knowledge Resources are complementary, independent of the fact that they can incorporate different methods and approaches, e.g., thesauri, semantic frameworks, ontologies, and phonetic interfaces for the content they handle.

Future research on theory and practice will concentrate on further developing the spectrum of references and creating knowledge reference based solutions for scenarios and disciplines.

Acknowledgements

We are grateful to the "Knowledge in Motion" (KiM) long-term project, Unabhängiges Deutsches Institut für Multidisziplinäre Forschung (DIMF), for partially funding this research, implementation, case studies, and publication under grants D2016F5P04648 and D2018F6P04938 and to its senior scientific members and members of the permanent commission of the science council, especially to Dr. Friedrich Hülsmann, Gottfried Wilhelm Leibniz Bibliothek (GWLB) Hannover, to Dipl.-Biol. Birgit Gersbeck-Schierholz, Leibniz Universität Hannover, to Dipl.-Ing. Martin Hofmeister, Hannover, and to Olaf Lau, Hannover, Germany, for fruitful discussion, inspiration, practical multi-disciplinary case studies, and the analysis of advanced concepts. We are grateful to Dipl.-Ing. Hans-Günther Müller, Cray, Germany, for his excellent contributions and assistance providing practical private cloud and storage solutions. We are grateful to all national and international partners in the Geo Exploration and Information cooperations for their constructive and trans-disciplinary support. We are grateful to the Science and High Performance Supercomputing Centre (SHPSC) for long-term support. / DIMF-PIID-DF98_007.

References

[1] Aristotle, Nicomachean Ethics, Volume 1, 2009, Project Gutenberg, eBook, EBook-No.: 28626, Rel. Date: Apr. 27, 2009, Digit. Vers. of the Orig. Publ., Produced by Sophia Canoni, Book provided by Iason Konstantinidis, Translator: Kyriakos Zambas, URL: http://www.gutenberg.org/ebooks/12699 [accessed: 2018-07-08].

[2] Aristotle, The Ethics of Aristotle, 2005, Project Gutenberg, eBook, EBook-No.: 8438, Rel. Date: Jul., 2005, Digit. Vers. of the Orig. Publ., Produced by Ted Garvin, David Widger, and the DP Team, Edition 10, URL: http://www.gutenberg.org/ebooks/8438 [accessed: 2018-01-01].

[3] L. W. Anderson and D. R. Krathwohl, Eds., A Taxonomy for Learning, Teaching, and Assessing: A Revision of Bloom's Taxonomy of Educational Objectives. Allyn & Bacon, Boston, MA (Pearson Education Group), USA, 2001, ISBN: 978-0801319037.

[4] C.-P. Rückemann, F. Hülsmann, B. Gersbeck-Schierholz, P. Skurowski, and M. Staniszewski, Knowledge and Computing. Post-Summit Results, Delegates' Summit: Best Practice and Definitions of Knowledge and Computing, Sept. 23, 2015, The Fifth Symp. on Adv. Comp. and Inf. in Natural and Applied Sciences (SACINAS), The 13th Int. Conf. of Num. Analysis and Appl. Math. (ICNAAM), Sept. 23–29, 2015, Rhodes, Greece, 2015, DOI: 10.15488/3409, URL: https://doi.org/10.15488/3409 [accessed: 2018-07-08].

[5] Plato, Phaedo, 2008, (Written 360 B.C.E.), Translated by Benjamin Jowett, Provided by The Internet Classics Archive, URL: http://classics.mit.edu/Plato/phaedo.html [accessed: 2018-07-08].

[6] T. Gooley, How to Read Nature: Awaken Your Senses to the Outdoors You've Never Noticed. New York, N.Y.: Experiment, 2017, ISBN: 978-1-61519-429-2.

[7] J. Burroughs, Leaf and Tendril, 1908, Ch. 1, The Art of Seeing Things.

[8] C.-P. Rückemann, "Principles of Superordinate Knowledge: Separation of Methodology, Implementation, and Realisation," in The Eighth Symp. on Adv. Comp. and Inf. in Natural and Applied Sciences (SACINAS), Proceedings of The 16th Int. Conf. of Num. Analysis and Appl. Math. (ICNAAM), Sept. 13–18, 2018, Rhodes, Greece. AIP Press, American Institute of Physics, Melville, New York, USA, 2019, ISSN: 0094-243X, (to appear).

[9] C.-P. Rückemann and F. Hülsmann, "Significant Differences: Methodologies and Applications," "Significant Differences: Methodologies and Applications", KiMrise, Knowledge in Motion Meeting, November 27, 2017, Knowledge in Motion, Hannover, Germany, 2017.

[10] C.-P. Rückemann, "Methodology of Knowledge Mapping for Arbitrary Objects and Entities: Knowledge Mining and Spatial Representations – Objects in Multi-dimensional Context," in Proceedings of The Tenth International Conference on Advanced Geographic Information Systems, Applications, and Services (GEOProcessing 2018), March 25–29, 2018, Rome, Italy. XPS Press, Wilmington, Delaware, USA, 2018, pp. 40–45, ISSN: 2308-393X, ISBN: 978-1-61208-617-0, URL: http://www.thinkmind.org/index.php?view=article&articleid=geoprocessing_2018_3_20_30078 [accessed: 2018-07-08].

[11] Organisation for Economic Co-operation and Development (OECD), "OECD Principles and Guidelines for Access to Research Data from Public Funding," 2007, URL: https://www.oecd.org/sti/sci-tech/38500813.pdf [accessed: 2018-07-08].

[12] C.-P. Rückemann, Sustainable Knowledge and Resources Management for Environmental Information and Computation. Business Expert Press, Manhattan, New York, USA, Mar. 2018, Ch. 3, pp. 45–88, in: Huong Ha (ed.), Climate Change Management: Special Topics in the Context of Asia, ISBN: 978-1-94784-327-1, in: Robert Sroufe (ed.), Business Expert Press Environmental and Social Sustainability for Business Advantage Collection, ISSN: 2327-333X (collection, print).

[13] "Multilingual Universal Decimal Classification Summary," 2012, UDC Consortium, 2012, Web resource, v. 1.1. The Hague: UDC Consortium (UDCC Publication No. 088), URL: http://www.udcc.org/udcsummary/php/index.php [accessed: 2018-07-08].

[14] "Creative Commons Attribution Share Alike 3.0 license," 2012, URL: http://creativecommons.org/licenses/by-sa/3.0/ [accessed: 2018-07-08], (first release 2009, subsequent update 2012).

[15] "UDC, Common Auxiliary Signs," 2018, Universal Decimal Classification (UDC), URL: https://udcdata.info/078885 [accessed: 2018-10-14].

[16] "UDC Summary Linked Data, Main Tables," 2018, URL: https://udcdata.info/078887 [accessed: 2018-10-14].

[17] "UDC 0: Science and knowledge. Organization. Computer science. Information. Documentation. Librarianship. Institution. Publications," 2018, URL: http://udcdata.info/13358 [accessed: 2018-10-14].

[18] "UDC (1/9): Common auxiliaries of place," 2018, URL: http://udcdata.info/001951 [accessed: 2018-10-14].

[19] "UDC 528: Geodesy. Surveying. Photogrammetry. Remote sensing. Cartography," 2018, Universal Decimal Classification (UDC), URL: http://udcdata.info/027504 [accessed: 2018-08-06].

[20] "UDC 910: General questions. Geography as a science. Exploration. Travel," 2018, URL: http://udcdata.info/068129 [accessed: 2018-08-06].

[21] "UDC 912: Nonliterary, nontextual representations of a region," 2018, URL: http://udcdata.info/068183 [accessed: 2018-08-06].

[22] "UDC 913: Regional geography," 2018, Universal Decimal Classification (UDC), URL: http://udcdata.info/068186 [accessed: 2018-10-14].

[23] "UDC 94: General history," 2018, Universal Decimal Classification (UDC), URL: http://udcdata.info/068284 [accessed: 2018-10-14].

[24] N. T. Nikolitsis, "Archäologische Unterwasser-Expedition bei Rhodos, (English: Archaeological Underwater-Expedition at Rhodes)," Antike Welt, Zeitschrift für Archäologie und Kulturgeschichte, (English: Antique World, Magazine for Archaeology and Cultural History), 1981, 12. Jg., Heft 1, (English: 12th Year, Issue 1), pp. 45–58.

[25] C.-P. Rückemann, "Creating New Views and Insights by Computing Spatial Cogwheel Modules for Knowledge Integration," Int. Journ. on Adv. in Intell. Syst., vol. 10, no. 3&4, 2017, pp. 314–326, ISSN: 1942-2679, URL: http://www.thinkmind.org/index.php?view=article&articleid=intsys_v10_n34_2017_13/ [accessed: 2018-07-08].

[26] C.-P. Rückemann, "Advanced Knowledge Discovery and Computing based on Knowledge Resources, Concordances, and Classification," Int. Journ. on Adv. in Intell. Syst., vol. 9, no. 1&2, 2016, pp. 27–40, ISSN: 1942-2679, URL: http://www.thinkmind.org/index.php?view=article&articleid=intsys_v9_n12_2016_3/ [accessed: 2018-07-08].

[27] C.-P. Rückemann, "Integration of Knowledge Resources and Advanced Association Processing for Geosciences and Archaeology," Int. Jour. on Adv. in Systems and Measurements, vol. 9, no. 3&4, 2016, pp. 485–495, ISSN: 1942-261x, URL: http://www.thinkmind.org/index.php?view=article&articleid=sysmea_v9_n34_2016_22/ [accessed: 2018-07-08].

[28] C.-P. Rückemann, "Knowledge Processing and Advanced Application Scenarios With the Content Factor Method," International Journal on Advances in Intelligent Systems, vol. 9, no. 3&4, 2016, pp. 485–495, ISSN: 1942-2679, URL: http://www.thinkmind.org/index.php?view=article&articleid=intsys_v9_n34_2016_22/ [accessed: 2018-07-08].

[29] C.-P. Rückemann, "Progressive Advancement of Knowledge Resources and Mining: Integrating Content Factor and Comparative Analysis Methods for Dynamical Classification and Concordances," Int. Journal on Adv. in Systems and Measurements, vol. 11, no. 1&2, 2018, ISSN: 1942-261x, URL: http://www.thinkmind.org/index.php?view=article&articleid=sysmea_v11_n12_2018_5/ [accessed: 2018-07-08].

[30] C.-P. Rückemann, "Creating Knowledge-based Dynamical Visualisation and Computation," in Proc. of The Seventh International Conference on Advanced Geographic Information Systems, Applications, and Services (GEOProcessing 2015), February 22–27, 2015, Lisbon, Portugal. XPS Press, 2015, pp. 56–62, ISSN: 2308-393X, ISBN: 978-1-61208-383-4, URL: http://www.thinkmind.org/index.php?view=article&articleid=geoprocessing_2015_3_40_30063 [accessed: 2018-07-08].

[31] C.-P. Rückemann, "Archaeological and Geoscientific Objects used with Integrated Systems and Scientific Supercomputing Resources," Int. Jour. on Adv. in Systems and Measurements, vol. 6, no. 1&2, 2013, pp. 200–213, ISSN: 1942-261x, URL: http://www.thinkmind.org/download.php?articleid=sysmea_v6_n12_2013_15 [accessed: 2018-07-08].

[32] C.-P. Rückemann, "Methodology Enabling Knowledge Mining Computation Based on Conceptual Knowledge and Verbal Description," in The Seventh Symposium on Advanced Computation and Information in Natural and Applied Sciences (SACINAS), Proc. of The 15th Int. Conf. of Num. Analysis and Appl. Math. (ICNAAM), Sept. 25–30, 2017, Thessaloniki, Greece, AIP Conference Proceedings, Vol. 1728, no. 1. AIP Press, Melville, New York, USA, Jul. 2018, ISBN: 978-0-7354-1690-1 (Book), ISSN: 0094-243X, DOI: 10.1063/1.5043723.

A Proposal for Discovering Hotspots Using 3D Coordinates from Geo-tagged Photographs

Masaharu Hirota
Faculty of Informatics
Okayama University of Science
Okayama-shi, Okayama
Email: hirota@mis.ous.ac.jp

Masaki Endo
Division of Core Manufacturing
Polytechnic University
Kodaira-shi, Tokyo
Email: endou@uitec.ac.jp

Hiroshi Ishikawa
Faculy of System Design
Tokyo Metropolitan University
Hino-shi, Tokyo
Email: ishikawa-hiroshi@tmu.ac.jp

***Abstract*—A hotspot is an interesting place where many people go for sightseeing. To extract hotspots, most of the existing research applies a density-based clustering algorithm, such as Density-based spatial clustering of applications with noise (DBSCAN) with latitude and longitude as its features. Therefore, the extracted hotspots are visualized as a two-dimensional space. However, large areas, landmarks, and buildings may include high hotspots or multiple hotspots with different altitudes. Therefore, in this research, we propose extracting hotspots based on altitude in addition to latitude and longitude and visualize these extracted hotspots in a three-dimensional space. To use those features, we apply ST-DBSCAN to extract hotspots and discuss the usefulness of extracting hotspots using altitude. In addition, as an application example, we classified hotspots as shooting spots, observation spots, areas of interest, among others and visualized the results.**

***Keywords*–area of interest;photograph location;photograph orientation**

I. Introduction

Owing to the increasing popularity of mobile devices such as digital cameras and smartphones, numerous photographs taken by photographers have been uploaded to photo-sharing web services, such as Flickr [1]. In addition, these digital devices have been equipped recently with Global Positioning System (GPS) sensors; thus, many photographs are annotated with latitude and longitude information. A photographic location represented by the latitude and longitude shows the place where the photographer took a photograph. If many people take photographs at the same location, this represents an area of interest to users. Analyzing such areas using photographs given a photographic location on social media sites is useful for analyzing geographical characteristics, such as obtaining information on sightseeing spots that the photographer finds interesting.

Many people take photographs of subjects or landscapes that satisfy their own interests. Subsequently, some of them upload their photographs to websites. As places from which many photographs have been taken, these locations might also be interesting places for other people to visit. As described in this paper, we define such places as hotspots. Most of the existing research for extracting hotspots are based on a density-based clustering method, such as density-based spatial clustering of applications with noise (DBSCAN) [2] and mean shift [3]. In addition, those researches that use such density-based clustering methods use latitude and longitude as features to extract hotspots and the extracted clusters are then defined as hotspots. However, clusters obtained by such a method only using latitude and longitude do not consider altitude. Therefore, there are some cases wherein multiple hotspots at different altitudes are extracted as one hotspot. For example, in a sightseeing spot such as the Eiffel Tower, the latitude and longitude for the observatory and area around the building are almost the same, but there are some hotspots with different altitudes. Even if the altitude is different, because these latitudes and longitudes are almost equally located, it is difficult to distinguish between these hotspots.

In this research, when extracting a hotspot, we propose not only the width of a hotspot represented by the latitude and the longitude to extract hotspots but also the height of the hotspot by adding the altitude. In recent years, the metadata annotated to a photograph captured by smartphones includes altitude in addition to latitude and longitude. For this reason, in this research, we extract hotspots taking into consideration such metadata using the photographs given the information obtained from Flickr. As DBSCAN and mean shift, which is commonly used for extracting hotspots, treat the distance for evaluating the density around the data as one dimension, we consider those methods inappropriate for clustering with feature quantities with the metadata. Therefore, in this paper, we use ST-DBSCAN [4], which was proposed to deal with time in addition to latitude and longitude. When we apply ST-DBSCAN, we adopt altitude instead of time to extract hotspots, thereby considering the height of the hotspot.

In addition, hotspots can be classified into three types: an area of interest, a shooting spot, and an observation spot [5][6]. The areas of interest for people are tourist spots (e.g., the Colosseum or the Statue of Liberty). In such areas, many photographs have been taken inside the monument or at a nearby location. Also, when people take a photograph of such an area of interest, they will take it at a place that is at a distance from the area of interest. Such places are also extracted as hotspots and are defined as shooting spots. Observation spots are hotspots for photographing the surroundings of the hotspot. In this research, we classify hotspots extracted considering the altitude in addition to latitude and longitude into three classes by considering multiple information sources, such as the direction of photography and we then visualize the results.

The remainder of this paper is organized as follows. Section II presents works related to this topic. Section III describes our proposed method for extracting hotspots based on altitude in addition to latitude and longitude. Section IV explains several examples of visualization result. Section V conclude the paper with a discussion of results and future works.

II. RELATED WORKS

Some methods have been proposed to extract hotspots from the many photographs with the photographic location available on social media sites.

Density-based clustering algorithms, such as DBSCAN [2] or mean shift [3] can be used to extract hotspots from a dataset that includes huge numbers of photographs annotated with photographic location. Crandall et al. presented a method to extract hotspots using mean shift based on many photographs annotated with photographic location [7]. Kisilevich et al. proposed P-DBSCAN, an improved version of DBSCAN, for the definition of a reachable point, to extract hotspots using the density of photographic locations [8]. Ankerst et al. proposed a clustering method of OPTICS, which is a variation of DBSCAN used to create a cluster using different subspaces extracted from various parameters [9]. Sander et al. proposed GDBSCAN, which extends DBSCAN to enable the correspondence to both spatial and non-spatial features [10]. Shi et al. proposed a density-based clustering method to extract places of interest using spatial information and the social relationships between users [11].

The previously described research extracts hotspots using a density-based clustering method, such as DBSCAN based on latitude and longitude. However, in some cases, actual hotspots have a concept of height and are distributed in a three-dimensional space rather than a two-dimensional space. In this paper, we propose a new approach to extract and visualize hotspots using ST-DBSCAN by adding altitude.

III. PROPOSED METHOD

In this section, we describe our proposed method for extracting hotspots considering the altitude in addition to latitude and longitude from photographs and classifying the hotspots into one of three types: area of interest, shooting spot, and observation spot.

A. Extracting hotspots with altitude

Here, we describe why we adopt ST-DBSCAN to extract hotspots with altitude in addition to latitude and longitude. In most of the previous research, DBSCAN has been used for extracting hotspots. At this time, latitude and longitude are used as the features for representing the distance between two points. As we need to consider altitude in this research to extract hotspots, we infer that DBSCAN is not an appropriate method in this case. This is because the Eps, which is the parameter of DBSCAN for evaluating the distance between two points, is a one-dimensional threshold. As previously described, there are hotspots with different altitudes but almost equal latitude and longitude. Therefore, although DBSCAN is an appropriate method to use latitude and longitude as one feature for evaluating the distance between two points, it is not appropriate to add altitude to the feature. As a result, the altitude should be regarded as a different feature to latitude and longitude, and we adopt ST-DBSCAN to achieve this.

ST-DBSCAN is one of the improved methods of DBSCAN that considers time in addition to the spatial feature of latitude and longitude. ST-DBSCAN has three parameters $Eps1$, $Eps2$, and $MinP$, where $Eps1$ is a threshold of distances of spatial features of two data, $Eps2$ is a threshold of distances of other features, and $MinP$ is a threshold of the number of data included in the cluster. In this research, we apply ST-DBSCAN with $Eps1$ as latitude and longitude and $Eps2$ as altitude.

B. Classification of hotspot

In this paper, a hotspot is classified as an area of interest, a shooting spot, or an observation spot as shown in Figure 1 using the photograph orientation annotated to the photographs included in the extracted hotspots. However, in addition to the latitude and longitude, the number of photographs with the photograph orientation is miniscule compared with the photographs with only the latitude and longitude. As a result, the classification of hotspots that have fewer photographs may be difficult. Therefore, we classify hotspots into four groups: areas of interest, shooting spots, observation spots, and others. In this research, we assume that hotspots with less than 10 photographs with photograph orientation as other, and we do not perform the following processes.

First, we classify a hotspot as a shooting spot or others. In this case, many photographs are taken with a specific orientation. Therefore, we calculate the bias of the photograph orientation based on a frequency distribution related to photograph orientation. We divided the value of photograph orientation by 10 degrees and counted the number of photographs for each class. We consider that these hotspots are focused on a specific orientation if the top class includes 15% of the photographs belonging to hotspots.

Next, we classify the remaining hotspots into either an area of interest or observation spot. This classification is based on the ratio of inward and outward photographs in the hotspot. Figure 2 shows examples of inward and outward photographs. In this research, if the photograph orientation and orientation to the center of gravity of the hotspot are close, we regard the photograph as an inward photograph; otherwise, we classify it as an outward photograph.

We set the orientation with the true north given to photograph as 0° to θ_i and the coordinates of the center of gravity of the hotspot h for the coordinates (x_i, y_i) of the latitude and longitude at the shooting position. We calculate the orientation θ_d in which (x_h, y_h) exists using the following equation:

$$\theta_d = \tan^{-1} \frac{\cos y_i \times \sin(x_h - x_i)}{\cos y_1 \times \sin y_h - \sin y_i \times \cos y_h \times \cos(x_h - x_i)} \quad (1)$$

Next, we classify each photograph in a hotspot as an inward or outward photograph based on the difference between θ_d and θ_i, as follows:

$$\begin{cases} inward & |\theta_i - \theta_d| < \theta \\ outward & \text{otherwise} \end{cases} \quad (2)$$

In this study, we set the threshold for classifying inward photographs and outward photographs as $\theta = 50$. If the number of photographs classified as inward photographs in a hotspot is larger than the number of outward photographs, the hotspot is classified as an area of interest; otherwise, it is classified as an observation spot.

IV. EXPERIMENT

A. Dataset

Here, we describe the dataset for the experiment of extracting hotspots using latitude, longitude, and altitude. Photographs for experiments were obtained from Flickr. Those photographs include metadata for latitude, longitude, altitude, and orientation. We obtained photographs taken during January 1, 2011–May 10, 2016. We use the photographs taken in

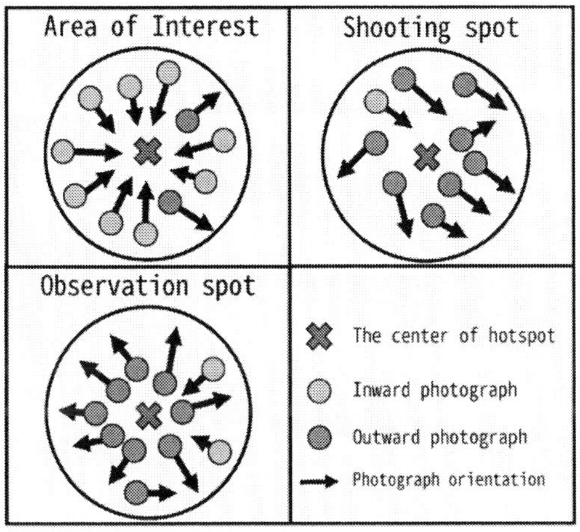

Figure 1. Classification of hotspots.

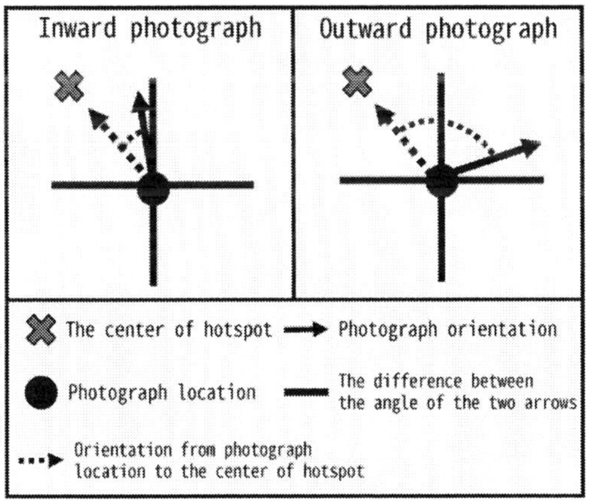

Figure 2. Inward photograph and outward photograph.

the area of Westminster in London. There are some famous landmarks in this area, such as the Big Ben (latitude: 51.500729; longitude: −0.124625) and the London Eye (latitude: 51.503324; longitude: −0.119543).

To deal with altitude errors, we set the threshold of altitude and remove photographs having an altitude higher or lower than the threshold. In this experiment, we set the parameter based on the height of buildings around the area to be analyzed. In addition, we removed photographs with an altitude of 0 m or less.

Furthermore, we excluded photographs in which the latitude, longitude, and altitude all overlap. This might occur as a result of an incorrect GPS positioning or device configuration. The point where there is much inappropriate metadata is excessively evaluated when extracting a hotspot. As a result, the number of photographs used in this experiment is 13,911.

B. Visualization of hotspots

Figure 3 shows the clustering results by ST-DBSCAN based on the latitude, longitude, and altitude of photographs. The parameters used in ST-DBSCAN were $Eps1 = 0.0001$, $Eps1 = 5$, and $MinP = 30$, respectively. The number of extracted clusters in Figure 3 is 35. Each color in this Figure represents a cluster (the colors are only an easy-to-view representation to distinguish between clusters).

In Figure 3, some clusters with different altitudes are extracted from areas with almost the same latitude and longitude. In particular, several clusters were extracted near an altitude of 130 m, latitude of 51.504, and longitude of −0.120. This is because the highest point of the London Eye is 135 m. Therefore, many people take photographs around there, and the area was extracted as a hotspot.

Figure 4 is a two-dimensional representation of the clustering result (i.e., the Figure shows that the clusters in Figure 3 map two dimensions without altitude). Some clusters are displayed overlapping in multiple areas in this Figure. Therefore, in such areas, points with different altitudes should be extracted as distinguished hotspots. Naturally, the latitude and longitude of the photographs taken in such areas are almost equal. As a result, unless we extract hotspots by considering the altitude in addition to latitude and longitude, it is difficult to distinguish between and extract these clusters.

Although it may be possible to distinguish these hotspots by clustering with only latitude and longitude in some cases, much time and effort are required to tune parameters of Eps and $MinP$ in DBSCAN. In addition, when latitude- and longitude-annotated photographs are used, those metadata include errors. Therefore, the photographs that should originally belong to different hotspots may belong to the same hotspots erroneously. Therefore, in Figures 3 and 4 we show that it is possible to distinguish between the hotspots in areas of similar latitude and longitude by considering the altitude even in such a state.

Next, Figure 5 shows the result of the classification of hotspots. In this Figure, the green point shows a photograph in a hotspot classified as an observation spot. In addition, the red point is a shooting spot and the orange point is an area of interest. In Figure 5, many observation spots were extracted. For example, the highest location of the London Eye is an observation spot. It seems that people are shooting the periphery from the top of the Ferris wheel. In addition, there are two chunks of orange points: under the London Eye and around the Big Ben. These hotspots should probably be classified as shooting spots because the hotspots include photographs of these landmarks. The area around latitude 51.502 and longitude −0.121 is extracted as a shooting spot as it includes many photographs of the Big Ben. It seems that other areas are also classified as shooting spots because they contain many photographs of landmarks, such as the London Eye and the Big Ben.

In the above description, we explained the classification results regarding hotspots. At this stage, quantitative analysis of the classification is not done. In these results, there are some hotspots misclassified. Therefore, we think the need for improvement of the method and evaluation for classifying hotspots in a future study.

V. Conclusion

In this paper, we have discussed the extraction of hotspots that can be extracted as one cluster when considering only latitude and longitude by using latitude and longitude in addition to the altitude information of a photograph. We used ST-DBSCAN for extracting hotspots while also considering the altitude. In addition, we visualized clustering results using ST-DBSCAN using the metadata of photographs taken in London.

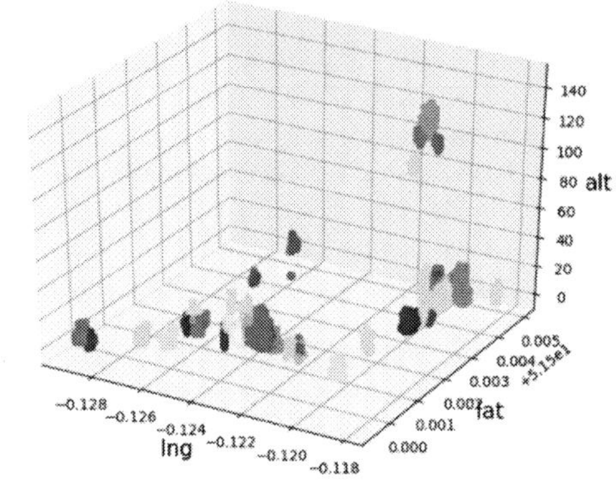

Figure 3. The clustering result in three-dimensional.

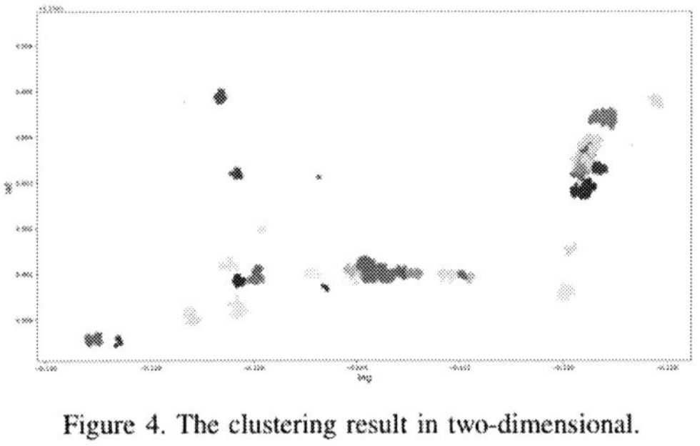

Figure 4. The clustering result in two-dimensional.

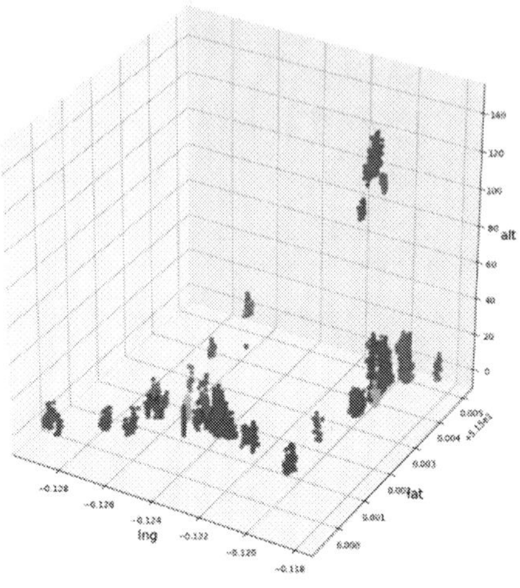

Figure 5. Classification result of hotspot.

In addition, we classified the hotspots as areas of interest, shooting spots, observation spots, and others and visualized the results.

As future work, we aim to compare our approach with density-based clustering methods other than ST-DBSCAN. In this paper, ST-DBSCAN has been applied only using latitude, longitude, and altitude as a feature quantity, and it has not yet been revealed to be superior to other clustering methods, such as DBSCAN. In addition, we performed classification of hotspots in one of the application examples of hotspots and have not been evaluated the result yet. Thus, further improvements in our proposed method is necessary.

ACKNOWLEDGMENT

This work was supported by JSPS KAKENHI Grant Numbers 16K00157 and 16K16158, and Tokyo Metropolitan University Grant-in-Aid for Research on Priority Areas "Research on social big data."

REFERENCES

[1] "Flickr," 2014, URL: https://www.flickr.com [accessed: 2019-01-11].

[2] M. Ester, H.-P. Kriegel, J. Sander, and X. Xu, "A density-based algorithm for discovering clusters in large spatial databases with noise," in Proceedings of the Second International Conference on Knowledge Discovery and Data Mining, ser. KDD '06, 1996, pp. 226–231.

[3] D. Comaniciu and P. Meer, "Mean shift: a robust approach toward feature space analysis," IEEE Transactions on Pattern Analysis and Machine Intelligence, vol. 24, no. 5, May 2002, pp. 603–619.

[4] D. Birant and A. Kut, "St-dbscan: An algorithm for clustering spatial-temporal data," Data & Knowledge Engineering, vol. 60, no. 1, 2007, pp. 208 – 221, intelligent Data Mining.

[5] M. Shirai, M. Hirota, H. Ishikawa, and S. Yokoyama, "A method of area of interest and shooting spot detection using geo-tagged photographs," in Proceedings of The First ACM SIGSPATIAL International Workshop on Computational Models of Place, ser. COMP '13. ACM, 2013, pp. 34:34–34:41.

[6] M. Hirota, M. Shirai, H. Ishikawa, and S. Yokoyama, "Detecting relations of hotspots using geo-tagged photographs in social media sites," in Proceedings of Workshop on Managing and Mining Enriched Geo-Spatial Data, ser. GeoRich '14. ACM, 2014, pp. 7:1–7:6.

[7] D. J. Crandall, L. Backstrom, D. Huttenlocher, and J. Kleinberg, "Mapping the world's photos," in Proceedings of the 18th International Conference on World Wide Web, ser. WWW '09. ACM, 2009, pp. 761–770.

[8] S. Kisilevich, F. Mansmann, and D. Keim, "P-dbscan: A density based clustering algorithm for exploration and analysis of attractive areas using collections of geo-tagged photos," in Proceedings of the 1st International Conference and Exhibition on Computing for Geospatial Research & Application, ser. COM.Geo '10. ACM, 2010, pp. 38:1–38:4.

[9] M. Ankerst, M. M. Breunig, H.-P. Kriegel, and J. Sander, "Optics: Ordering points to identify the clustering structure," in Proceedings of the 1999 ACM SIGMOD International Conference on Management of Data, ser. SIGMOD '99. ACM, 1999, pp. 49–60.

[10] J. Sander, M. Ester, H.-P. Kriegel, and X. Xu, "Density-based clustering in spatial databases: The algorithm gdbscan and its applications," Data Mining and Knowledge Discovery, vol. 2, no. 2, 1998, pp. 169–194.

[11] J. Shi, N. Mamoulis, D. Wu, and D. W. Cheung, "Density-based place clustering in geo-social networks," in Proceedings of the 2014 ACM SIGMOD International Conference on Management of Data, ser. SIGMOD '14. ACM, 2014, pp. 99–110.

Analysis of the Difference of Movement Trajectory by Residents and Tourists using Geotagged Tweet

Shintaro Fujii
Faculty of System Design
Tokyo Metropolitan University
Hino-shi, Tokyo
Email: fujii-shintarou@ed.tmu.ac.jp

Masaharu Hirota
Faculty of Informatics
Okayama University of Science
Okayama-shi, Okayama
Email: hirota@mis.ous.ac.jp

Daiju Kato
WingArc1st Inc.
Shibuya-ku, Tokyo
Email: kato.d@wingarc.com

Tetsuya Araki
Faculty of System Design
Tokyo Metropolitan University
Hino-shi, Tokyo
Email: araki@tmu.ac.jp

Masaki Endo
Division of Core Manufacturing
Polytechnic University
Kodaira-shi, Tokyo
Email: endou@uitec.ac.jp

Hiroshi Ishikawa
Faculty of System Design
Tokyo Metropolitan University
Hino-shi, Tokyo
Email: ishikawa-hiroshi@tmu.ac.jp

***Abstract*—In recent years, tourism industry has been drawing attention in various countries. Tourists are on an increasing trend all over the world, and it is estimated that the value exceed 1.8 billion in 2030. Consumer behavior by tourists brings high economic effects to many industries such as transportation, lodging, manufacturing. Therefore the increase in tourists is an important issue for governments and tourism agency. According to a survey by tourism agency, 60% of foreign tourists visiting Japan are repeaters. In other words, it is considered important to increase repeaters to increase tourists. Compared with the first tourist, there is a need for repeaters to visit sightseeing spot that many residents visit and tourists do not know. One must analyze data of resident to discover these sightseeing spots. Nevertheless, most studies conducted to extract hotspots (areas where many photographs are taken) and recommend sightseeing routes using movement trajectories do not consider user attributes. Therefore, by considering user attributes, this study was conducted to extract hotspots that many residents visit but are not know to tourists. Additionally, we extract movement trajectories from residents and tourists to ascertain differences in sightseeing areas and to analyze them by visualizing those results on a map.**

***Keywords*—Tourism; Geospatial analysis; Cities and towns.**

I. INTRODUCTION

The number of tourists worldwide is increasing every year. It is predicted that they will be 1.8 billion in 2030 [1]. Tourism occupies an important position as a key industry in many countries. Consumption activities related to tourism positively affect industries such as transportation, lodging, and manufacturing. Therefore, increasing the number of tourists represents an important issue for governments and companies. In Japan, where the Tokyo Olympics Games are to be held in 2020, the Japanese Government and companies are actively conducting activities to increase foreign visitors to Japan, such as the Visit Japan Campaign [2] and promotion [3]. As a result, foreign visitors Japan have increased year by year, reaching a record high of 28.69 million in 2017 [4]. It is necessary to analyze tourists data to increase tourism. According to a survey by the Tourism Agency, 60% of foreign visitors to Japan are repeaters [5]. We consider that increasing repeaters is important to increase tourists. The repeater described here refers to a person who visits a specific sightseeing area more than once. The need exists for repeaters to experience more local culture and visit local spots more than first-time tourists do [6]. The local spot described here refers to a place that many residents know: not famous sightseeing spots that many tourists visit. For this study, we define a local spot as a hotspot that many residents visit but few tourists visit. Discovering local spots is important to increase tourists. Therefore, we extract hotspots that many residents visit but few tourists visit.

Additionally, several needs exist for tourism agencies as tourists increase. It is necessary to ascertain the movements and interests of tourists in sightseeing areas. Tourism agencies perform more effective PR methods for sightseeing areas and recommend sightseeing plans to satisfy tourist needs and attract more tourists in sightseeing areas by knowing the movements and interests of tourists in sightseeing areas. We extract hotspots and movement trajectories of tourists to analyze the movements and interesting spots of tourists in sightseeing areas. Therefore, one must extract the respective hotspots and movement trajectories of residents and tourists to satisfy the needs of tourism agencies and tourists.

Several studies have been conducted to extract hotspots and recommend sightseeing routes using movement trajectories [7]–[9]. Nevertheless, these studies do not consider user attributes. Many tourists visit famous sightseeing spots in sightseeing areas and post many contents from those locations. Tourist contents continue to increase in sightseeing areas year by year. By contrast, contents of residents for sightseeing areas have not changed much numerically. These indicate that more contents uploaded in sightseeing areas to social media site are posted by tourists than by residents. Therefore, when we do not consider user attributes and extract hotspots from their contents, it is difficult to extract local spots in sightseeing areas because tourists post the most contents in sightseeing areas. Therefore, for this study, we extract hotspots of residents and tourists respectively using geotagged tweets to discover local spots. Furthermore, when classifying users, we adapt the method proposed in [10] because our research goal is discovering local spots and not user classification.

Actually, [11] and [12] are studies applying [7] and [8]. Also, [11] and [12] extract sightseeing spot by considering user attributes. For this study, in addition to discovering hotspots considering user attributes, we extract movement trajectories of residents and tourists. Considering user attributes, we combine hotspot and movement trajectories and thereby discover sightseeing routes that many residents use, but which tourists do not use. Discovering these routes contributed to recommendation of new sightseeing routes that many residents know, thereby relieving congestion in sightseeing areas. Therefore, for this study, we extract sightseeing routes that many residents use and tourists do not use by clustering and visualizing resident and tourist movement trajectories.

The structure of this paper is the following. In Section II, this report presents some related research efforts. In Section III, we describe our proposed method to discover local spots and to assess differences of residents' and tourists' movement trajectories. Section IV presents experiments and results obtained using the proposed method. Section V, presents discussion of the results of visualizing hotspots and movement trajectories of residents and tourists obtained using our proposed method. Section VI, we conclude this paper and describe avenues for future work.

II. RELATED WORK

In this section, we describe research related to this research.

A. Hotspot

Research on hotspot extraction is actively conducted using geotagged tweets and photographs posted on social media. Crandall et al. [7] proposed a method to discover popular spots using spatial clustering with large amounts of geotagged photographs and image features. Kisilevich et al. [8] proposed a method to discover hotspots using PDBSCAN: an improved DBSCAN algorithm. Yang et al. [13] proposed an algorithm to extract hotspots of various sizes: Self-Tuning Spectral Clustering. Lacerda et al. [14] extracted hotspots using geotag information and intersections of photograph orientations. Zhijun et al. [15] divided areas into grids and extracted and visualized geographical features in the grid using geotag information and text tags attached to photographs. Li et al. [16] proposed a method to classify Flickr [17] users as residents or tourists, calculate their relative proportions in each of the five cities, and compare them to ascertain and analyze differences in cities. Zhuang et al. [11] proposed a method to discover Anaba (sightseeing spots that are less well-known, but still worth visiting) using geotagged photos. They evaluate the scenery quality by considering both social appreciation and the contents of images shot around there. Van et al. [18] first extracted hotspots by clustering Flickr photographs. Then they analyzed Twitter [19] text and extracted areas of interest. Furthermore, they confirmed and investigated the places using data from Foursquare [20]. Zhuang et al. [12] proposed a method to discover obscure sightseeing spots that are less well-known, but which are still worth visiting. They aimed to overcome challenges that classical authority analysis based methods do not encounter: how to discover and rank spots based on popularity (obscurity level) and on scenery quality. For the present research, we extract hotspots of residents and tourists and discover local spots in sightseeing areas.

B. Movement trajectory

Actively conducted research efforts contribute to each industry by analyzing movement trajectories from geotagged data. Yuan et al. [21] proposed a method to discover areas of different functions in the city by combining taxi trajectory data and data of a person's area of interest obtained from social media. Nanni et al. [22] proposed a method to adapt density-based clustering algorithms to trajectory data based on the simple concept of distance between trajectories. Additionally, to improve trajectory clustering, they proposed an algorithm incorporating time information. Kori et al. [23] proposed a method to recommend sightseeing routes using user blogs to extract movement trajectories that are produced during sightseeing. Sun et al. [24] proposed a system that recommends the best sightseeing route for users using geotagged photographs that had been posted on Flickr. They defined the best sightseeing route recommendations as one for which many users visit and for which each landmark distance is close. Memon et al. [25] proposed a method to recommend sightseeing routes particularly addressing the posting times of geotagged photographs posted on Flickr. Garcia et al. [26] proposed a method to examine route generation and route customization and to analyze them to solve the tourist planning problem. They present an heuristic that is able to solve a tourist planning problem in real-time using public transportation information and the Time Dependent Team Orienteering Problem with Time Windows (TDTOPTW). Zhang et al. [27] proposed an efficient tourist route search system that not only recommends a route simply connecting several tourist spots, but which also recommends a route with beautiful scenic sights. Xin et al. [28] propose to leverage existing travel clues recovered from 20 million geo-tagged photographs to suggest customized travel route plans according to user preferences. For the present study, we extract movement trajectories of residents and tourists and discover sightseeing routes that many residents use and which many tourists do not use.

III. PROPOSED METHOD

In this section, we describe our proposed method to extract hotspots of residents and tourists and their respective movement trajectories in the sightseeing area. The procedure that is followed to accomplish the proposed method is the following.

1) We apply preprocessing.
2) We classify users as residents and tourists.

3) We cluster movement trajectories.
4) We visualize the hotspots and movement trajectories of residents and tourists.

For this study, we define users who post many tweets in specific sightseeing areas as residents, and users who post many tweets outside specific sightseeing areas as tourists.

TABLE I. DESCRIPTION OF GRID COLOR-CODED INTO 7 COLORS.

Grid color	Difference in proportion of users between residents and tourists
Green	low order 2%
Blue	low order 2 ~4%
Purple	low order 4 ~6%
No color	other
Yellow	superior 6 ~4%
Orange	superior 4 ~2%
Red	superior 2%

A. Preprocessing

This section specifically explains how to obtain data and how to preprocess the data. From Twitter, we obtained tweets with annotated geo-tag information. At that time, we eliminated tweets posted from countries other than Japan. Next, we applied preprocessing to the tweets we obtained. We deleted tweets including auto-generated texts from other social media sites, replies, retweets and tweets by bots.

B. Classification of users

This section presents a description of methods used to characterize users as residents and tourists and methods of extracting a series of tweets within a specific sightseeing area. First, we sort the user tweets to arrange them in chronological order. Additionally, we calculate the proportion of tweets by latitude and longitude within a specific sightseeing area. Subsequently, we define specific sightseeing areas by latitude and longitude. Nozawa et al. [10] classified Twitter users as residents or tourists. Users who posted over 30% of tweets within a specific sightseeing area were inferred as residents, and were otherwise inferred as tourists. We apply this classification method to classify users as residents or tourists because our research is not aimed at user classification. Next, we extract tweets posted during a specified sightseeing period. We extract a series of tweets posted from the time tourists start tweeting within this area until they are out of range. For this research, a series of tweets within the area is called as a tourism tweet. Furthermore, for residents, we extract tourism tweets by classifying everyday tweets within a range. Through this process, we extract many movement trajectories suggested by tourism tweets posted by residents and tourists.

C. Clustering of movement trajectories

This section presents an explanation of a method to cluster tourism tweets extracted in Section III-B. The purpose of clustering is to clarify differences in movement trajectories between residents and tourists. First, we ascertain tourism tweets as those of residents or tourists. Subsequently, we classify them accordingly. Next, for each tourism tweet of residents and tourists, we extract the distance of each tourism tweet using Dynamic Time Warping (DTW) for every round. Then, we calculate the distance of all tweets included in tourism tweets. We adopted DTW in this study because the length of tourism tweets is different depending on the user. DTW allows duplication of correspondence between two time series and is applied to time series data of different lengths. We use this extracted distance to cluster tourism tweets using kmeans++. Kmeans that is non-hierarchical clustering depends on the initial value because the initial centroid is allocated as a random number. Therefore, we adopted kmeans++ in this study to avoid the problem of assigning the cluster to the one in which the kmeans method should not be frequently used as a cluster. The clustered movement trajectories show where the residents and tourists frequently move.

D. Visualize hotspots and moving trajectories on the map

This section describes a method to discover local spot and sightseeing routes that many residents use and which many tourists do not use. We visualize hotspots based on the posting position of tweets to analyze areas where a user is interested in the sightseeing area. To analyze details of the visited places, we map areas into sixth-order meshes (125-meter square grids), which is the smallest grid size provided by the Geographical Survey Institute in Japan. We count the users in each cell. We define a threshold in the cell and a hotspot cell according to the proportion of the number of users.

To assess movement trajectories, we visualize the resident and tourist tourism tweets as clustered in Section III-C on the map. First, for all the clusters classified in Section III-C, we calculate the movement proportion of the user between the grids. Next, as a result of clustering, in clusters classified in the same sightseeing area, we calculate the difference of the movement proportion between the resident and the tourist grids. The one that exceeds the threshold is visualized.

IV. EXPERIMENT

In this section, we describe experiment conducted based on the proposed method.

A. Data set

We compiled and used a data set that was especially intended for this experiment. We obtained geotagged tweets for Twitter using Twitter API [29]. The data collection period was January 1, 2017 to December 31, 2017. The total number of data was 2,793,207. We used these data to classify users as residents or tourists. Data used for the visualization of hotspots and movement trajectory were tweets posted in Tokyo during April 1, 2017 – May 31, 2017. For that time, we deleted replies, retweets, tweets posted by bots and tweets that included auto-generated texts from other social media sites such as FourSquare. We consider these tweets are noise because we analyze hotspots and consider users' text. In addition, we deleted tourism tweets that were only single tweets or tweets sent from the same place because we need to analyze the movement trajectory and extract consecutive tweets. Results show that resident tweets were 190,091, users as resident were 27,231, tourist tweets were 100,444, and users as tourist were 13,712. Tourism tweets classified using the proposed method were 14,582 for residents and 17,119 for tourists.

B. Clustering

This section presents a description of procedures used for clustering tourism tweets posted by residents and tourists after extraction using this proposed method. We used the elbow method to ascertain the optimal number of clusters because kmeans++ must be determined beforehand. The elbow method is widely used as a method for determining the optimum number of clusters. We adopted widely used methods because our goal is analysis of sightseeing areas. Results show that the number of clusters of resident movement trajectories was 34; that of tourist movement trajectories was 29. The movement proportion between the grids is calculated by dividing the number of movements between the grids by the total movement number for each cluster. We explain related details with Figure 1 as an example. We extract movements between grids when users tweet on different grids. In Figure 1, the respective grid movement numbers of residents and tourists are 100 and 200. This grid movement number is the result of clustering and is classified in the same area. The top two figures in Figure 1 show the number of residents and tourist movements in the grid. The numbers in parentheses represent the movement proportion. The difference between residents and tourists is calculated as shown in the figure below. We calculated the difference between residents and tourists and visualized the movement trajectory of the top 0.5%. Hotspots and movement trajectories of residents and tourists extracted using the proposed method are portrayed in Figure 2, Figure 3 and Figure 4. Figure 2 presents the difference between the proportion of residents and tourists in each grid around the Tokyo Skytree. In Figure 2, the relation between the grid color and the difference in proportion of users between residents and tourists is presented in Table I. As a result of the difference in proportion of users between residents and tourists, more than 90% of the grids existed at 25% or less. Therefore, we visualized result as shown in Table I. Additionally, if no user exists in the grid, then the grid itself is not displayed in Figures 2–4. The area around the Tokyo Skytree is a popular sightseeing area in Tokyo that many tourists visit.

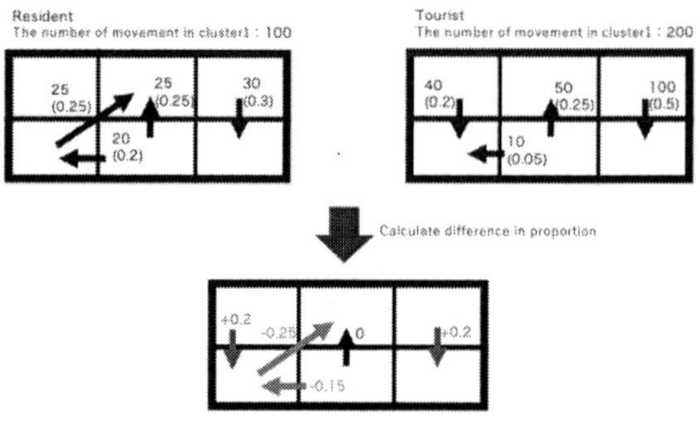

Figure 1. Movement trajectories of residents(Blue) and tourists(Red).

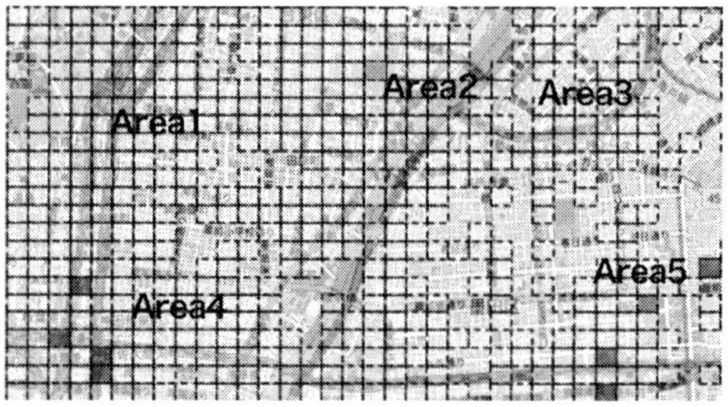

Figure 2. Difference between hotspots of resident and tourist around Tokyo Skytree.

V. DISCUSSION

In this section, we discuss the results presented in Section IV-B. First, we explain Figure 2. Figure 2 portray the area surrounding Tokyo Skytree. We show Figure 2, Figure 3 and Figure 4 in five areas to support several points of the discussion. We shall specifically discuss areas numbered as Area1, Area2, ..., Area5 and describe each area in Table II. From Figure 2, it is proven that many tourists visit Ueno in Area1, but fewer residents there. Many sightseeing spots exist around Ueno, such as Shinobazu-no-ike Pond and the Ueno Zoological Gardens. Especially at the Ueno Zoological Gardens, attendance has increased recently [30] because of the birth of a panda. Results demonstrate that it has become a popular sightseeing spot for tourists.

Therefore, we regard the area around Ueno as a sightseeing area of interest for tourists rather than residents. Conversely, many residents visit Kameido Temple and Kinshicho Park in Area5, but there appear to be few tourists among the users. Kameido Temple, located near the Tokyo Skytree in Area3, is a sightseeing spot where the main shrine and the Tokyo Skytree can be photographed together. In addition, because many wisteria flowers grow within its precincts, it is possible in the spring to take photographs of the Tokyo Skytree as well as wisteria flowers in the main shrine. A festival, called the Fuji Festival, is held there and is visited by many people. As Kinshicho Park is famous for cherry blossoms, many people visit in spring. Therefore, the possibility exists that these sightseeing spots are the local spot that is an object of this research.

Next, we discuss Figure 3. Many more tourists than residents move to Ueno in Area1, Asakusa in Area2, and Tokyo Skytree in Area3. The reason for this result is that many pamphlets and web sites have presented this area as a series of sightseeing areas. However Kameido Temple and Kinshicho

TABLE II. DESCRIPTION OF THE AREA AROUND SHIBUYA AND ASAKUSA.

Area	Area description
Area1	Near Ueno, with the Ueno Zoological Gardens and their well-known panda attraction
Area2	Near Asakusa, with its many temples such as Sensoji Temple
Area3	Near Tokyo Skytree
Area4	Near Akihabara, with its many famous electronics mass merchandisers and animation goods retailers
Area5	Near Kinshichou that has many taverns and restaurants
Area6	Near Shimokitazawa that is famous as a fashion like old clothes
Area7	Near Shibuya where many young people visit
Area8	Near Harajyuku where there are many stylish cafes and shops

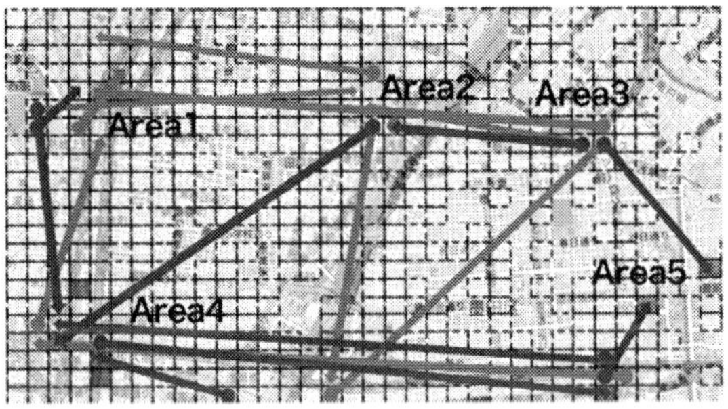

Figure 3. Movement trajectories of residents(Blue) and tourists(Red) around Tokyo Skytree.

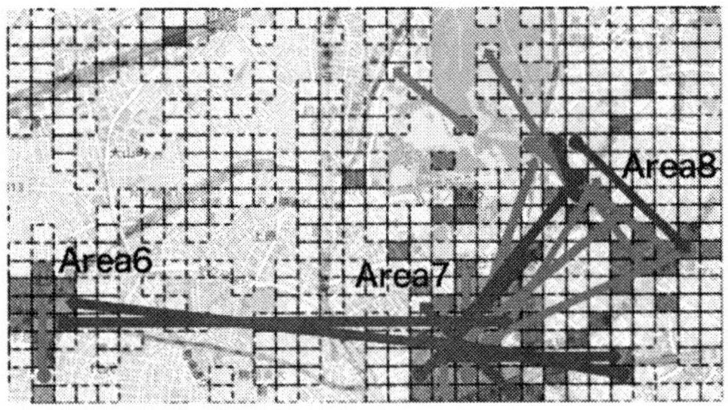

Figure 4. Movement trajectories of residents(Blue) and tourists(Red) around Shibuya.

Park in Area5 is near the Tokyo Skytree in Area3 by movement trajectory of residents and sightseeing spots that many tourist visit. We infer the possibility that the route of Kameido Temple and Kinshicho Park is a sightseeing route that many residents know, but tourists do not know. These results are regarded as useful information for tourism agencies when recommending sightseeing plans and sightseeing spots for tourists.

Next, we discuss Figure 4. Figure 4 portrays the area surrounding Shibuya and Harajyuku. We show Figure 4 in three areas to support several points of the discussion. We shall specifically discuss areas numbered as Area6, Area7, and Area8 and describe each area in Table II. Many more residents than tourists move to Shimokitazawa in Area6 and Shibuya in Area7. Conversely, many more tourists than residents move to Harajyuku in Area8 and Shibuya in Area7, although both Shimokitazawa in Area6 and Harajyuku in Area8 are famous for fashion. The reason for this result is that Harajyuku is known to many more people than Shimokitazawa because Harajyuku is reported frequently in media such as television and dramas. However, Shimokitazawa is a fashion town that anyone living in Tokyo knows. Many magazines publish the area and many residents are visit there. Possibly, the route of Shimokitazawa and Shibuya is a sightseeing route that many residents know, but which tourists do not know. In addition, many reviews [31] state dissatisfaction with sightseeing because Shibuya and Harajyuku are extremely crowded by many tourists on holidays. The result of our experiment points to resolution of this difficulty if tourism agencies have performed PR for Shimokitazawa, Shibuya, and Harajyuku as a series of sightseeing areas and if tourists who visit Harajyuku visit Shimokitazawa.

As for the implementation of discussion, we discover hotspots and sightseeing routes that many residents use but many tourists do not use. These result have the possibility of local spots and new sightseeing routes. As reported herein, we have discovered differences in the movement trajectories of residents and tourists in sightseeing areas.

VI. CONCLUSIONS

This study used latitude and longitude information given along with huge volumes of data obtained from social media sites. By classifying contents into those of residents and those of tourists, and by performing DTW and kmeans++ analyses, we clustered the movement trajectories, visualized hotspots and movement trajectories, and analyzed them further. Based on those results, we were able to discover sightseeing spots that many residents and tourists visit respectively around the Tokyo Skytree. Especially, sightseeing spots that many residents visit, other than tourists, can become new sightseeing spots for increased tourists. We also discovered sightseeing route that many residents use and few tourists use around Shibuya by movement trajectories.

As future work, we expect to conduct quantitative evaluation experiments and improve the proposed method. As described in this paper, we consider different hotspots and movement trajectories of residents and tourists based on visualization results. However, in future work, we plan to evaluate them more quantitatively. For improvement of the method, we focus on a certain cell, calculate the movement proportion of the next cell, and extract the ranking of the cell movement proportion. Then we must adapt this method to all resident and tourist cells. By adapting the Spearman's rank correlation coefficient to the calculated data, the difference between the movement trajectories of residents and tourists is quantified. As a different method, map matching are regarded as revealing details of differences between residents and tourists when assessing the roads that they used. Additionally, for this study, users were classified as residents or tourists, but user attributes of many types exist. Studies assessing them and their characteristics are being conducted actively. The main targets of estimation are gender [32], age [33] and residence [34]. As future work, we expect to consider these user classifications and to analyze their movement trajectories in sightseeing areas. Additionally, we do not consider the user's preference in this study, however we also experiment with them in future work.

ACKNOWLEDGMENT

This work was supported by JSPS KAKENHI Grant Number 16K00157, 16K16158, and Tokyo Metropolitan University Grant-in-Aid for Research on Priority AreasResearch on social big data.

REFERENCES

[1] "By 2030 overseas travelers expand to 1.8 billion people annually," 2019, URL: https://www.travelvoice.jp/20171005-97777 [accessed: 2019-01-09].

[2] "Tourism promotion business to Japan," 2019, URL: http://www.mlit.go.jp/kankocho/shisaku/kokusai/vjc.html [accessed: 2019-01-09].

[3] "Some tourism promortions," 2019, URL: http://www.sangyo-rodo.metro.tokyo.jp/plan/tourism/chapter6_3_2018.pdf [accessed: 2019-01-09].

[4] "The number of foreign visitors Japan records 28.69 million," 2019, URL: https://www.travelvoice.jp/20180116-104077 [accessed: 2019-01-09].

[5] "60% of foreign visitors to Japan are repeaters," 2019, URL: https://www.travelvoice.jp/20180403-108446 [accessed: 2019-01-09].

[6] "The need of repeaters," 2019, URL: http://www.mlit.go.jp/kankocho/news02_000346.html [accessed: 2019-01-09].

[7] D. J. Crandall, L. Backstrom, D. Huttenlocher, and J. Kleinberg, "Mapping the world's photos," in *Proceedings of the 18th international conference on World wide web*. ACM, 2009, pp. 761–770.

[8] S. Kisilevich, F. Mansmann, and D. Keim, "P-dbscan: a density based clustering algorithm for exploration and analysis of attractive areas using collections of geo-tagged photos," in *Proceedings of the 1st international conference*, 2010, pp. 38:1–38:4.

[9] H. Yin, X. Lu, C. Wang, N. Yu, and L. Zhang, "Photo2trip: an interactive trip planning system based on geo-tagged photos," in *Proceedings of the 18th ACM international conference on Multimedia*. ACM, 2010, pp. 1579–1582.

[10] N. Yuya, E. Masaki, E. Yo, H. Masaharu, Y. Syohei, and I. Hiroshi, "Inferring tourist behavior and purposes of a twitter user," *AIAI*, 2016.

[11] C. Zhuang, Q. Ma, X. Liang, and M. Yoshikawa, "Anaba: An obscure sightseeing spots discovering system," in *2014 IEEE International Conference on Multimedia and Expo (ICME)*. IEEE, 2014, pp. 1–6.

[12] ——, "Discovering obscure sightseeing spots by analysis of geo-tagged social images," in *Proceedings of the 2015 IEEE/ACM International Conference on Advances in Social Networks Analysis and Mining 2015*. IEEE, 2015, pp. 590–595.

[13] Y. Yang, Z. Gong, and H. U. Leong, "Identifying points of interest by self-tuning clustering," in *Proceedings of the 34th International ACM SIGIR Conference on Research and Development in Information Retrieval*. ACM, 2011, pp. 883–892.

[14] Y. A. Lacerda, R. G. F. Feitosa, G. Á. R. M. Esmeraldo, C. d. S. Baptista, and L. B. Marinho, "Compass clustering: A new clustering method for detection of points of interest using personal collections of georeferenced and oriented photographs," in *Proceedings of the 18th Brazilian symposium on Multimedia and the web*. ACM, 2012, pp. 281–288.

[15] Z. Yin, L. Cao, J. Han, C. Zhai, and T. Huang, "Geographical topic discovery and comparison," in *Proceedings of the 20th international conference on World wide web*. ACM, 2011, pp. 247–256.

[16] D. Li, X. Zhou, and M. Wang, "Analyzing and visualizing the spatial interactions between tourists and locals: A flickr study in ten us cities," *Cities*, vol. 74, pp. 249–258, 2018.

[17] "Flickr," 2019, URL: https://www.flickr.com [accessed: 2019-01-09].

[18] S. Van Canneyt, S. Schockaert, and B. Dhoedt, "Discovering and characterizing places of interest using flickr and twitter," *International Journal on Semantic Web and Information Systems (IJSWIS)*, vol. 9, no. 3, pp. 77–104, 2013.

[19] "Twitter," 2019, URL: https://www.twitter.com [accessed: 2019-01-09].

[20] "Foursquare," 2019, URL: https://ja.foursquare.com [accessed: 2019-01-09].

[21] J. Yuan, Y. Zheng, and X. Xie, "Discovering regions of different functions in a city using human mobility and pois," in *Proceedings of the 18th ACM SIGKDD international conference on Knowledge discovery and data mining*. ACM, 2012, pp. 186–194.

[22] M. Nanni and D. Pedreschi, "Time-focused clustering of trajectories of moving objects," *Journal of Intelligent Information Systems*, vol. 27, no. 3, pp. 267–289, 2006.

[23] H. Kori, S. Hattori, T. Tezuka, and K. Tanaka, "Automatic generation of multimedia tour guide from local blogs," in *International conference on multimedia modeling*. Springer, 2007, pp. 690–699.

[24] Y. Sun, H. Fan, M. Bakillah, and A. Zipf, "Road-based travel recommendation using geo-tagged images," *Computers, Environment and Urban Systems*, vol. 53, pp. 110–122, 2015.

[25] I. Memon, L. Chen, A. Majid, M. Lv, I. Hussain, and G. Chen, "Travel recommendation using geo-tagged photos in social media for tourist," *Wireless Personal Communications*, vol. 80, no. 4, pp. 1347–1362, 2015.

[26] A. Garcia, O. Arbelaitz, M. T. Linaza, P. Vansteenwegen, and W. Souffriau, "Personalized tourist route generation," in *International Conference on Web Engineering*. Springer, 2010, pp. 486–497.

[27] J. Zhang, H. Kawasaki, and Y. Kawai, "A tourist route search system based on web information and the visibility of scenic sights," in *Universal Communication, 2008. ISUC'08. Second International Symposium on*. IEEE, 2008, pp. 154–161.

[28] X. Lu, C. Wang, J.-M. Yang, Y. Pang, and L. Zhang, "Photo2trip: generating travel routes from geo-tagged photos for trip planning," in *Proceedings of the 18th ACM international conference on Multimedia*. ACM, 2010, pp. 143–152.

[29] "Twitter API," 2019, URL: https://help.twitter.com/ja/rules-and-policies/twitter-api [accessed: 2019-01-09].

[30] "Tourists visiting the Ueno Zoological Gardens has increased," 2019, URL: https://www.nikkei.com/article/DGXMZO28548380U8A320C1000000/ [accessed: 2019-01-09].

[31] "Reviews of Shibuya and Harajyuku," 2019, URL: http://xayataka.hatenablog.com/entry/2017/10/15/114420 [accessed: 2019-01-09].

[32] J. D. Burger, J. Henderson, G. Kim, and G. Zarrella, "Discriminating gender on twitter," in *Proceedings of the conference on empirical methods in natural language processing*. Association for Computational Linguistics, 2011, pp. 1301–1309.

[33] D. Rao, D. Yarowsky, A. Shreevats, and M. Gupta, "Classifying latent user attributes in twitter," in *Proceedings of the 2nd international workshop on Search and mining user-generated contents*. ACM, 2010, pp. 37–44.

[34] Z. Cheng, J. Caverlee, and K. Lee, "You are where you tweet: a content-based approach to geo-locating twitter users," in *Proceedings of the 19th ACM international conference on Information and knowledge management*. ACM, 2010, pp. 759–768.

Geospatial Web Portal for Regional Evacuation Planning

Chee-Hung Henry Chu
Informatics Research Institute
University of Louisiana at Lafayette
Lafayette, Louisiana, USA
Email: chu@louisiana.edu

Ramesh Kolluru
School of Computing and Informatics
University of Louisiana at Lafayette
Lafayette, Louisiana, USA
Email: kolluru@louisiana.edu

Abstract— **Evacuation of a regional population is often necessary when a disaster, such as wildfire or coastal flooding, is in the forecast. We build a map-based web portal for the planning of an evacuation of a region. A user marks a polygon on the map to indicate the extent of the region that will be evacuated. The population affected and the home value that will be impacted is calculated. The system then assigns local communities to different shelters. The evacuation plan for each local community in the region is then displayed. Underpinning the web portal is a data structure organized geographically by the U.S. postal service zip code that contains the population and a home value index. The implementation uses the Mapbox GL JS library.**

Keywords- Evacuation planning; geospatial web portal.

I. Introduction

When a major disaster due to a natural event or other causes or an emergency is imminent, it is useful to have an approximate estimate of the preliminary damage assessment and to have an evacuation plan [1-4]. In this paper, we present a web tool that assist in these two tasks.

There are different platforms to develop map-based web portals. Google Maps allow a user to display maps as images [5]. It supports JavaScript (JS) code to interact with users. Mapbox is similarly a geospatial platform. Mapbox GL is a set of libraries for different deployment platforms [6]. Mapbox GL JS is the library for Web applications. A JavaScript library for spatial analysis that works with Mapbox GL JS on the browser is turf.js [7]. These technology, when coupled with traditional map creation considerations, can bring cartography to a variety of devices [8]

A map is displayed using the Mapbox platform as an HTML file [3]. Figure 1 shows the HyperText Markup Language (HTML) code segment and the JavaScript code to display a map (Figure 2).

Our example tool operates at the level of local communities. We use the U.S. postal service zip code as the basic geographic unit. There are 508 zip codes in Louisiana that have inhabitants (vs. zip codes that are business or post office box addresses). We have the location (latitude, longitude) and population of each zip code. In Mapbox GL JS, data are organized using the GeoJSON format [9]. The set of all zip codes are collected in a FeatureCollection (Figure 3), which is an object using the JavaScript Object Notation (JSON). The features in the collection is collected as an array keyed by 'features'. Each zip code is represented as a point with the coordinates, and with "Name" and "Population" as properties. The FeatureCollection is displayed as an added layer of each zip code as a circle (Figure 4).

```
<div id='map'></div>

<script>
mapboxgl.accessToken = 'token from mapbox.com';
var map = new mapboxgl.Map({
    container: 'map',
    style: 'mapbox://styles/mapbox/streets-v9',
    center: [-92.02, 30.22], // starting position
    zoom: 7 // starting zoom level
});
</script>
```

Figure 1. HTML and JavaScript for displaying a map.

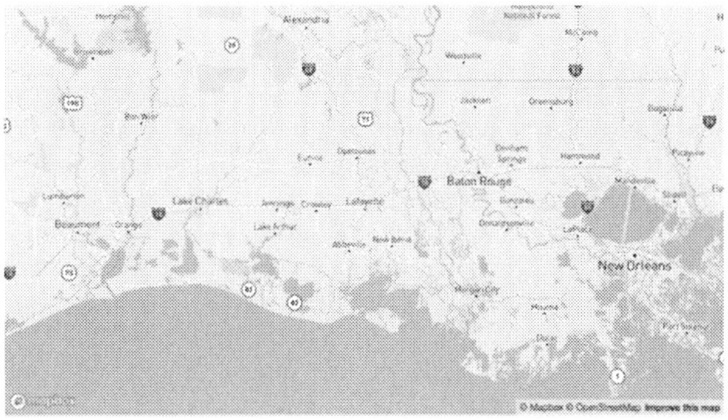

Figure 2. Map displayed based on code in Figure 1.

```
<script>
var zips={
  type: 'FeatureCollection',
  features: [
   {type:'Feature',
    properties:{Name:'70501',population:30867},
    geometry:{
      type:'Point',
      coordinates:[- 92.00959,30.2334]
    }},
    ...
  ]
};
</script>
```

Figure 3. GeoJSON object to hold zip code data.

The rest of the paper is organized as follows. In Section II, we describe the sources of the data sets that we use. In Section III, we describe the implementation as a client (browser)-side tool using the JavaScript programming language. In Section IV, we describe the implementation as a web application, using processing at the server and client sides for better performance. We draw our conclusions in Section V.

```
// plot zip points
map.on('load', function() {
  map.addLayer({
    id: 'zips',
    type: 'symbol',
    source: {
      type: 'geojson',
      data: zips
    },
    layout: {
      'icon-image': 'circle-11'
    },
    paint: {}
  });
});
```

Figure 4. JavaScript code to display the zip code nodes as a new layer.

II. DATA SOURCES

In this example tool, we would like to know for a given area, what is the population and what is the estimated home value. The population data for each zip code are available from the Census Bureau [10] and other web sites [11].

Getting the home value of a zip code is more challenging, unless one has access to, e.g., the tax assessor's data. We use the Zillow Home Value Index (ZHVI) [12], which as a home value index is an approximation to the median home value in a locality. To obtain the total of home values, we need to estimate the number of homes in a zip code. Since on average there are 2.8 persons in a U.S. household, we estimate the number of homes to be occupied by an average household of 2.8 persons, so that the total value V is given by

$$V = Z \times P / P_h \qquad (1)$$

where Z is the ZHVI for a zip code area, P is the total population in the zip code area, and P_h is the average household size, set to 2.8 in our examples.

In order to determine the evacuation plan, we need a number of shelters. We set the number of shelters to 3 and locate them in Houston, Little Rock, and Jackson, corresponding to the west, north, and east. Considering the capacity of shelters, Houston and Jackson would have larger ones than Little Rock. We note that in practice, planning requires more local analysis for more precise decisions. Thus, decisions about choice of shelters as well as assignment of shelters form the basis of network analyses.

III. IMPLEMENTATION OF CLIENT-SIDE ONLY TOOL

A. Impacted Population and Home Value Estimate

We use the Mapbox GL JS tool to enable the user to draw a polygon (Figure 5). A function updateArea() is called when the drawn object is created, deleted, or updated. When a polygon is created, the operations we want to do are:

1. determine the enclosed area;
2. determine which of the zip codes are included;
3. determine the population of the included zip codes;
4. determine the home values of the included zip codes.

The function updateArea() calculates these and reports them to the web page.

```
var draw = new MapboxDraw({
    displayControlsDefault: false,
    controls: {
        polygon: true,  // draw polygon
        trash: true
    }
});

map.addControl(draw);  // tool control panel
map.on('draw.create', updateArea);
```

Figure 5. JavaScript code to add the drawing tool to mark a polygon.

The @turf/turf library makes these spatial analysis steps simpler. Step (1) is accomplished by the turf.area(data) call, where data is the drawn FeatureCollection object. To perform Step (2), we use the turf.pointsWithinPolygon() function, which takes a FeatureCollection (the zip codes in our example) and a polygon. It returns a FeatureCollection containing all of the points that the polygon contains. The calculations for steps (3) and (4) are straightforward.

An example output is shown in Figure 6. Only the enclosed zip codes are displayed. The information for (1), (3), and (4) are shown inside a box on the lower left of the browser.

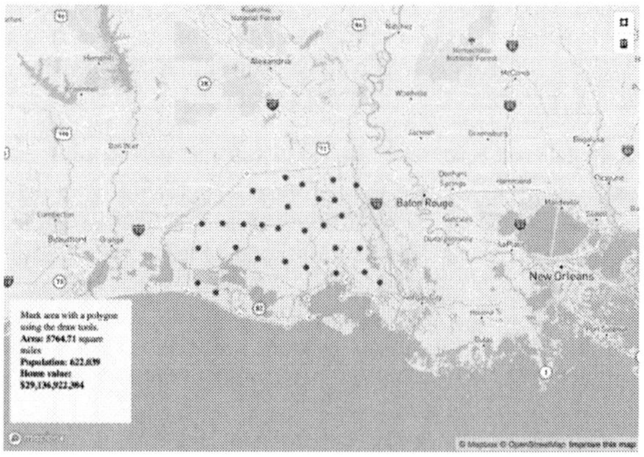

Figure 6. Map showing the zip codes within the drawn polygon (shaded).

B. *Evacuation Planning*

Given a set of zip code points, each with a population that should be evacuated. Given another set of shelter points, each with a capacity for handing evacuees. The distance between the zip code points and the shelter points and the roadway capacity between them together form the cost of transporting the evacuees to a shelter. As such, the problem can be set up as a classic transportation problem and an optimal solution using linear programming is possible. It, however, requires computational resources when the number of zip codes is large for a client-side implementation.

We might consider a heuristic solution because of the relatively similar costs due to the proximity of many of the zip codes to each other, to accommodate the limited computational resources in a client-side tool implementation. For instance, we could use a nearest neighbor approach to assign a shelter to a zip code. This is too simplistic, however, since the more capacious shelters in Houston are further away than Jackson for many zip codes.

We propose a compromise solution between ease of calculation and realistic performance. We map the bounding boxes of the shelters and the impacted zip codes. We would like to "embed" the shelters inside the polygon and then use the nearest assignment method. For each shelter, after using bilinear scaling to map it to the bounding box of the impacted zip codes, we use a scale factor to bring it to the interior of the bounding box. The more capacious the shelter is, the smaller the scale factor we assign, so that the shelter will be closer to the center of the zip code bounding box.

The turf library functions bbox() and nearest() respectively perform the bounding box and nearest point calculations.

An example is shown in Figure 7, where the enclosed zip code points are color coded, depending on which shelter it is assigned to. Two other examples (Figure 8 and Figure 9) with different shapes and at different locations are shown to illustrate that the shelter assignments are reasonably robust. In these examples, nodes marked in gold are assigned to the shelter in the west ("Houston"); those in dark blue are assigned to the shelter in the north ("Little Rock"); and the rest are assigned to the northeast ("Jackson").

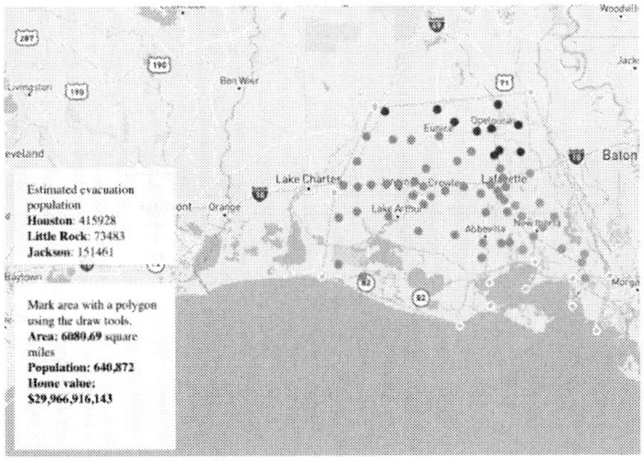

Figure 7. Map showing the zip codes color coded to indicate which shelter the population should head to.

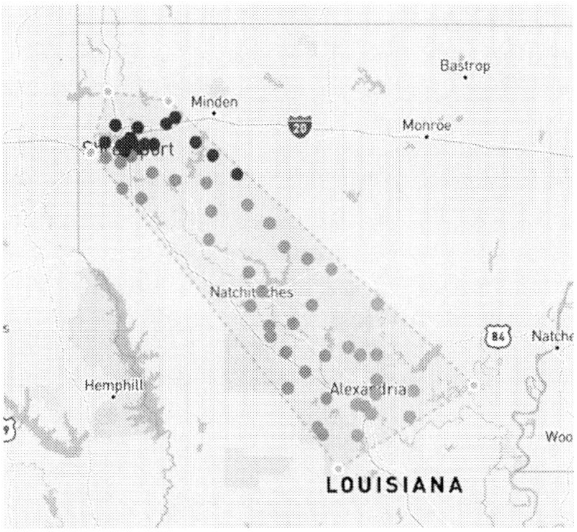

Figure 8. The zip codes in the northwestern corner of the state.

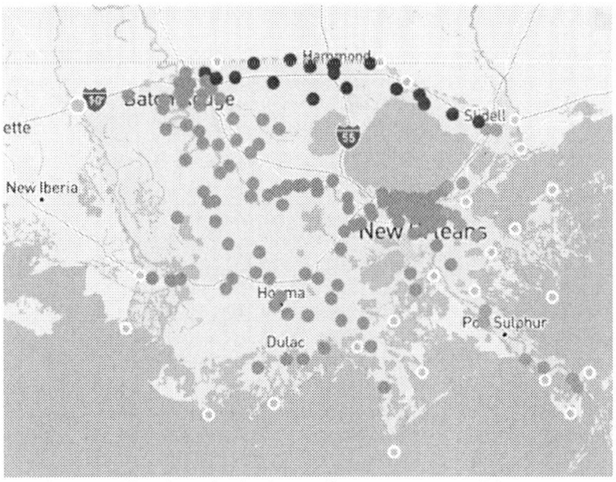

Figure 9. The zip codes in the southeastern corner of the state.

IV. WEB APPLICATION IMPLEMENTATION

The foregoing discussion assumes the portal does all of the processing on the client-side, using the rich functionalities enabled by the @turf.turf library. An advantage of having a client-side web page is that there is minimal communication between the browser and the server. The disadvantage is that all the data have to be loaded, whether they are needed or not. As an example, the data associated with all 508 zip codes in the State of Louisiana have to be pre-loaded, resulting in an HTML file that is 73K bytes. A more serious challenge to client-side processing is that some more sophisticated shelter assignment algorithms may not be able to be ported to the client-side. An example is an algorithm that requires linear programming optimization.

We refactored our application to a web application that uses the node.js framework. We divide the data, the presentation, and logic control in the model-view-controller pattern. The zip code (population, home value, location) data and the shelter data are stored on the server side. The map display and the polygon drawing interface are shown on the browser to interact with the user. Once the user has drawn the polygon on the map, the polygon data are sent to the server as a geoJSON "featureCollection" object. The server app contains the logic to find enclosed area, the zip codes enclosed, etc., i.e. the steps referenced in the updateArea() function as mentioned in III.A. The output is then generated as a map drawing HTML file and sent to the browser for the user.

The key challenge is to send the polygon data from the client to the server. Because MapBoxDraw() returns a geoJSON object containing the polygon coordinates, a straightforward way to send it to the server is to use an XMLHttpRequest(), as shown in Figure 10. Upon creation of a polygon, updateArea() is executed and the polygon geoJSON is sent to the server. The difference between the implementation here and the one in Section III is that updateArea() now does not do any further processing. On the server side, the app receives the JSON data as the request body (Figure 12); other processing steps are similar to the discussion in III.A by using the @turf.turf node.js module (Figure 11).

```
function updateArea() {
    var polygon = draw.getAll();
    // send to server
    var xhttp = new XMLHttpRequest();
  xhttp.open('POST', {{{url}}} , true);
    xhttp.setRequestHeader('Content-Type',
'application/json');
    xhttp.send(JSON.stringify(polygon));

    return;
}
```

Figure 10. JavaScript code to send the drawn polygon data to the server from the client-side.

```
// holds polygon data from browser
var polygon={};

app.post('/', jsonParser, function(req,res){
   polygon = req.body;
   res.send('received data');
});
```

Figure 11. JavaScript code in the server app that receives the polygon geoJSON data and holds the data as a geoJSON ("polygon") to be passed to other routes.

V. CONCLUSIONS

Web-based map tools open the geospatial information display and manipulation door to more data scientists. We demonstrate an example tool that determines the estimates of population affected, impacted home values, and assigned shelter locations based on a user marking the potential disaster area. We further refactor the HTML and client side JavaScript code to a JavaScript node.js server side app.

Ongoing work includes taking into account the impacted public facilities, the road capacity and fuel availability on the evacuation paths, size and locations of temporary populations such as tourists and temporary workers.

ACKNOWLEDGMENT

The authors gratefully acknowledge their colleague Dr. Michael Dunaway, Director of the National Incident Management Systems and Advanced Technologies Institute, for valuable discussions on disaster management. They further thank the anonymous reviewers whose comments help us to improve the manuscript.

REFERENCES

[1] S. M. Rahat Rahman, M. S. Mamun, M. A. Basit, and M. M. Rahman, "Evacuation plan for the solution to disaster management for the coastal region of Bangladesh: A review," International Conference on Engineering Research, Innovation and Education, 2017, Sylhet, Bangladesh, 6 pages.

[2] R. Alsnih and P. Stopher, "A review of the procedures associated with devising emergency evacuation plans," Transportation Research Record, vol. 1865, no. 1, pp. 89-97, 2004.

[3] G. Ayfadopoulou, I. Stamos, E. Mitsakis, and J.M.S. Grau, "Dynamic traffic assignment based evacuation planning for CBD areas," Procedia – Social Behavioral Sciences, vol. 48, pp. 1078-1087, 2012.

[4] G. Li, L. Zhang, and Z. Wang, "Optimization and planning of emergency evacuation routes considering traffic control," Scientific World Journal, 15 pages, 2014.

[5] Google Maps Platform, https://cloud.google.com/maps-platform/maps/ [Accessed: January 2019]

[6] Application programming interface specifications of the Mapbox GL JS library, https://www.mapbox.com/mapbox-gl-js/api/ [Accessed: January 2019]

[7] Turf.js: A JavaScript library for spatial and statistical analysis, https://www.mapbox.com/help/analysis-with-turf/ [Accessed: January 2019]

[8] I. Muelenhaus, Web Cartography: Map Design for Interactive and Mobile Devices, CRC Press, Boca Raton, Fla., 2014.

[9] The GeoJSON format for geospatial data interchange, https://tools.ietf.org/html/rfc7946 [Accessed: January 2019]

[10] ZIP code tabulation areas, https://www.census.gov/geo/reference/zctas.html [Accessed: January 2019]

[11] United States population by ZIP code, https://www.kaggle.com/census/us-population-by-zip-code [Accessed: January 2019]

[12] Zillow home value index: Methodology, https://www.zillow.com/research/zhvi-methodology-6032/ [Created: January 2014; Accessed: November 2018]

Geoprocessing of the Trends of the ENSO Phenomenon, from Peru to the Atlantic Ocean in Brazil.

Newton Silva de Lima*, Eriberto Façanha*, Robson Matos Calazães*, Ricardo Figueiredo*, William Dennis Quispe*, Aldemir Malveira†, Roseilson Souza do Vale‡

*Lutheran University Center of Manaus (Geosciences - Mathematics) / †Federal University of Amazonas (Mathematics)/ ‡Federal University of Western Pará (Geosciences)
* †Manaus/ ‡Santarém (Brazil)
(newtonulbra@gmail.com, eribertofacanha@seduc.net, matoscalazaes@gmail.com, rics.fig@gmail.com, William.exner@bol.com.br, amoliveira@gmail.com, roseilsondovale@gmail.com)

Abstract — **This research investigated 39 cities in the Amazônia, with the purpose of showing the high temperatures of the waters of the Amazon River, using remote sensors (Global Positioning System - GPS and Globalnaya Navigatsionnaya Sputnikovaya System - GLONASS), besides digital weather station and ship navigation, as a contribution to the trends of the El Niño phenomenon in the Amazon. It collected information on water quality, weather and climate, georeferencing of the route and localities during a drought period on the Amazon River, from Iquitos in Peru, to the city of Macapá in Brazil (Atlantic Ocean) in 2016, all data are presented in tables and thematic maps. The results obtained with temporal temperature series, compared to satellite images of temperature gradients, georeferenced map and water quality analysis showed high water temperatures along the river during the entire observation period, probably due to the prolonged El Niño event in 2014, 15 and 16.**

Keywords - GPS; satellite images; Amazon River; warming.

I. INTRODUCTION

Changes in atmospheric circulation in the tropical zone (Walker cell) induce changes in rainfall patterns, devastating floods, and severe droughts that can drastically affect the lives of millions of people [1]. In the mosaic of landscapes that is tropical South America, the tendencies for rainfall in the Amazon in eastern Brazil, to the northwest of Peru are well-defined by long-term hydrological data for the Amazon basin that were recorded during the 20th century. During this period the tendency for rainfall during the three most humid months and for the subsequent superficial runoff rate during the three months with the greatest runoff for the northeastern region of Brazil demonstrated a slow increase over long periods [2]. In 2016 the Amazon River Expedition from Peru to Brazil observed tendencies in which a prolonged El Niño Southern Oscillation (ENSO), event combined with a trend of regional warming increased the demand for water from the reservoirs of Brazilian hydroelectric plants in the Northeast, Central-West, and Southeastern regions of Brazil [3], and caused strong rains in the Southern region of Brazil [4]. According to the authors of [5] [6] [7], this event was associated with warming that was without precedent and an extreme drought in the Amazon, compared to other strong ENSO events in 1982/83 and 1997/98. The typical conditions of drought caused by the ENSO were observed and described by [5], as occurring only in the eastern Amazon, while in the western region of the Amazon there prevailed an uncommon level of humidity. For researchers this situation can be attributed to the humid-dry dipole at the location of maximum warming of the surface of the equatorial central Pacific Ocean. In this paper the causes of these changes are analyzed over the last two decades, and these include the average Sea Surface Temperature (SST) anomalies that are weakened towards the west in direction of the central Pacific; this represents an indicator that needs more observation [8].

Traveling in the Amazon region on the great river that crosses the entire northern portion of South America without the aid of a GPS or GLONASS would be, without a doubt, a difficult task, and could only be possible with the use of paper maps and a good, native navigator. The scenario since its beginning in the Peruvian Amazon up to the mouth of the great river in the Brazilian Amazon is very similar in terms of water, climatic variation, vegetation, fish, human presence, and atmospheric characteristics. This South American mosaic is singular, and these qualities make the use of navigation by satellite technology highly recommended. The most interesting example from this study was the enormous gap in internet access (approximately 90%), but Google Map, the smartphones and the GPS / GLONASS receivers continued to inform the ship's position and route in real time. This facilitated the labeling of samples, and the recording of meteorological data and georeferenced images taken by the camera at the visited sites.

This paper is structured as follows. In Section II, we present the research site, the path taken in the North of South America, the instrumentation and the steps followed in the data collection. Section III presents the results, through maps, graphs, tables of data, comments and finally

Section IV, we conclude this paper in the form of contribution of the Present State of the Amazon River to the regional warming.

II. MATERIAL AND METHODS

The northern mosaic of South America (Fig. 1) was examined in this research expedition. The average depth of the channel of the Amazon River was described in 2014 [9], (Fig. 2), maintaining or decreasing this condition between 2014-2017 [10]. In the upper deck of the boat, a digital weather station was installed for climate monitoring.

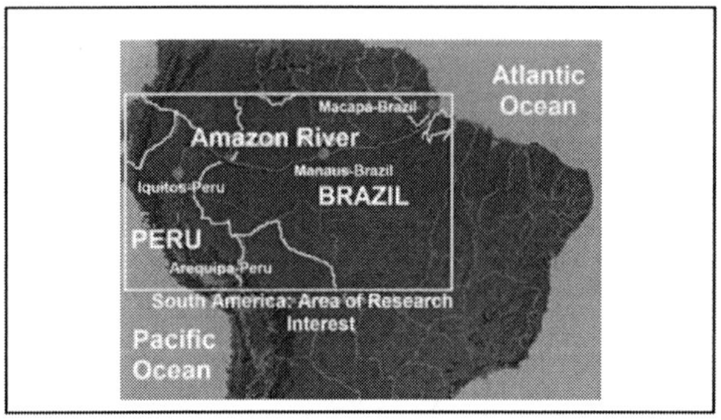

Figure. 1: Image of the mosaic of regions of tropical South America and the 2016 route of the Amazon River Expedition from Peru to Brazil (solidline), and the 2017/18 route (dotted line) (3rd phase, modified route). Source: (Adapted from Google Earth, 2016).

The station was free from obstacles that would impede accurate measurement of the variables of interest (temperature, humidity, pressure, wind speed and direction, dew point, and rainfall). The georeferencing was performed with a GPS and satellite images to identify the metadata of the water points and cities along the route (latitude, longitude, altimetry and photography).

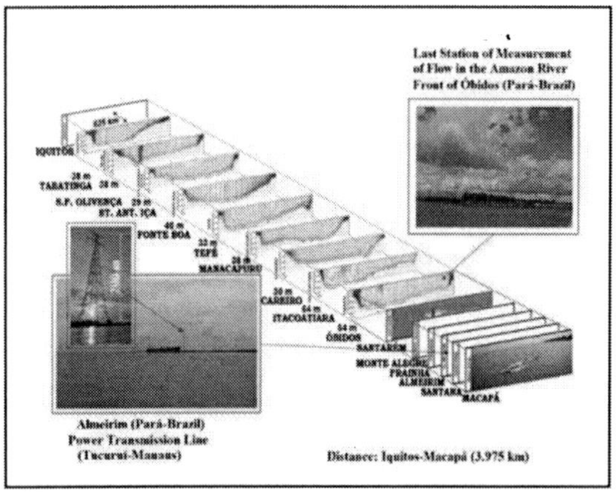

Figure. 2: The main cities of Iquitos (Peru) to Macapá (Brazil). The average depth of the river is shown in the dry season. Source: Adapted from Project Integrated and Sustainable Management of Cross – Border [9].

A. *Sampling and Chronogram*

For monitoring of weather and climate during the period of the research, a FLIR E60 thermal imager, Mira digital thermometer (LASER) and Minipa MT 360 sensors were used. Measurement of ambient air temperature, and the temperature at the edge of the river, middle of the channel, and at 1.0 m below the river´s surface was done using a Digital Weather Station with uninterrupted recording (15 days + 15 days) with data collection (ambient air temperature, humidity, pressure, wind speed and direction, dew point) which were measured every 5 minutes, and *in situ* two liter water samples were taken at each sampling point along the entire river. Temperature values are a composite of 10 *in situ* readings taken at each sampling point. The geographic coordinates of the sampling points were taken along with a description of the weather (climate) and the time at the moment of collection (water), and samples were labeled accordingly, using GPS/ GLONASS and satellite images, (Steps 1 and 2 of the Amazon River Expedition protocol).

B. *Applications and Sensors*

We worked with remote sensors (GPS/GLONASS) during the journey (Amazon Peruvian and Brazilian, Atlantic Ocean-Brazil), with Smartphones for localization (Google Map), with or without internet support in the cities we could connect in the Amazon River. We manipulate data from Aqua-Terra (Modis Sensor - Earth Observing System (EOS)) through the Web to understand the current conditions]of land and water use, for reference only.

The instrumentation used was two GPS/GLONASS (with camera and image software with digital georeferencing), to determine the points and locations visited and also to record the route of the entire trip. The data were deposited in the thematic maps; a Digital Weather Station with GPS/GLONASS, to collect the weather conditions of the trip. Camcorder and camera, for documentation purposes. Water collection in all localities for analysis of the Present State of the Amazon River during drought and El Niño prolonged phenomenon, data also deposited in thematic maps. In some cities panoramic drone flights were performed for documentation purposes. Office work was done to createthematic maps (ArcGIS-ESRI) and digital image manipulation. With treatment of field information.

Figure 3 shows the time series of temperature that was taken at three positions (ambient temperature at the ship – 100 m from the edge of the channel – middle of the channel) during the first stage of the expedition (Iquitos/Peru – Manaus/Brazil), using the FLIR E60 thermal imager and weather station. The image next to the time series shows SST in Real Time Global (RTG), High Resolution (HR) and was obtained by NOAA/NCEP/NWS by analyzing satellite images, ocean floats, sea ice cover, salinity, and conducting mathematical modeling in a second-degree polynomial series (Branch analysis method) [11].

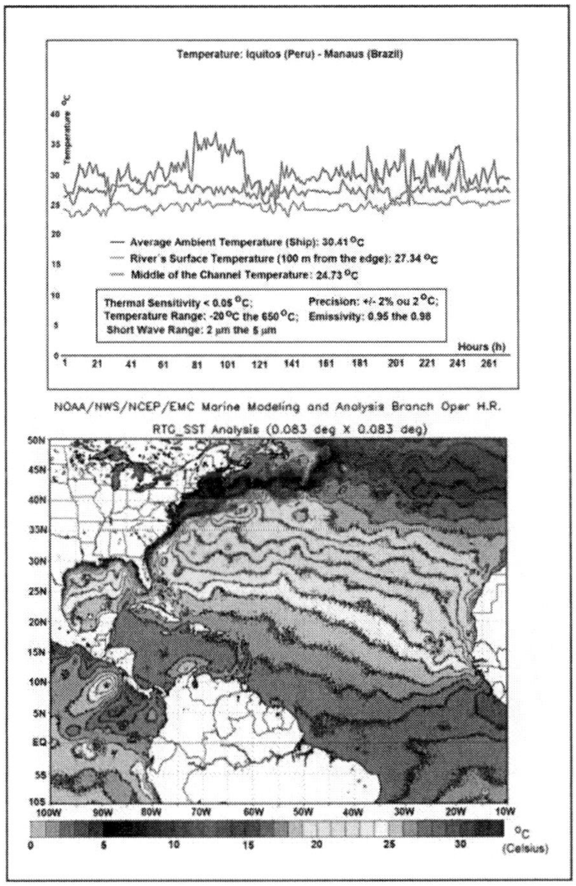

Figure. 3: Time series of temperature along the Amazon River during the first stage of the Expedition (Iquitos/Peru – Manaus/Brazil), and compared to data from the *Marine Modeling and Analysis Branch Oper. H. R.* (Verification Ensembles) of NOAA/NWS/NCEP/EMC. Source: Amazon River Expedition and NOAA, 2016.

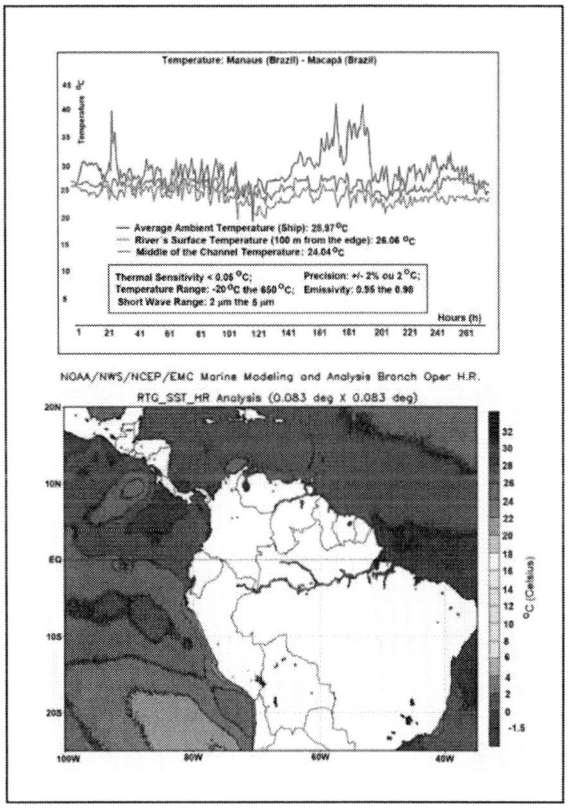

Figure. 4: Time series of temperature along the Amazon River during the 2nd stage of the Expedition (Manaus/Brazil – Macapá/Brazil) and compared to data from the *Marine Modeling and Analysis Branch Oper. H. R.* (Verification Ensembles) of NOAA/NWS/NCEP/EMC. Source: Amazon River Expedition and NOAA, 2016

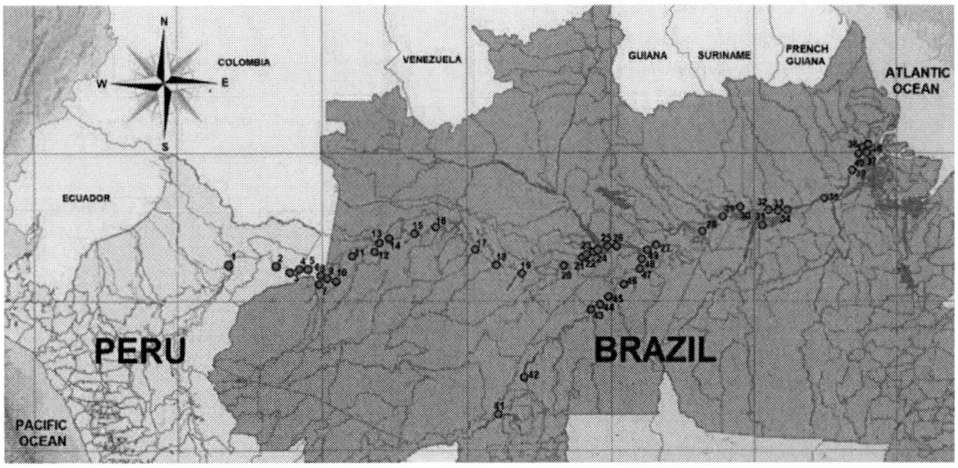

Figure 5. Map of localities in the Amazon River Expedition (PERU-BRAZIL).

TABLE I. WATER SAMPLE ANALYSIS – STAGE ONE OF THE AMAZON RIVER EXPEDITION (PERU-BRAZIL) JULY, 2016

Samples	Geographic Coordinates		Water	Temp.
	Latitude	Longitude	pH	°C
1	S 03° 43' 37.6"	W 073° 14' 23.8"	6.61	28.8
2	S 03° 48' 18.8"	W 071° 34'25.4"	7.31	26
3	S 04° 00' 59.6"	W 071° 06' 07.5"	7.29	26
4	S 03° 55' 40.8"	W 070° 47' 10.4"	7.22	25
5	S 03° 53' 49"	W 070° 30' 19.1"	7.79	26
6	S 04° 06' 39.7"	W 070° 03' 13.8"	6.92	29
7	S 04° 13' 04.7"	W 069° 57' 19.1"	6.89	27
8	S 04° 13' 44.4"	W 069° 56' 41.0"	7.2	27
9	S 04° 22' 19.5"	W 070° 01' 34.3"	7.15	26
10	S 04° 18' 31.2"	W 069° 33' 27.5"	6.6	24
11	S 03° 27' 42.2"	W 068° 57' 26.4"	7.17	24
12	S 03° 21' 14.5"	W 068° 11' 04.2"	7	24
13	S 03° 06' 29.1"	W 067° 56' 39.6"	5.81	23
14	S 02° 51' 47"	W 067° 46' 13.4"	6.15	26
15	S 02° 44' 33.8"	W 066° 46' 19.5"	6.16	25
16	S 02 ° 29' 40.6"	W 066° 04' 05.1"	7	25,5
17	S 03° 16' 32.1"	W 064° 43' 12.1"	6.87	25.5
18	S 03° 47' 18.3"	W 064° 02' 19.8"	6.93	27
19	S 04° 03' 17.1"	W 063° 04' 54.0"	6.89	26
20	S 03° 47' 17.2"	W 061° 37' 05.8"	6.76	25
21	S 03° 33' 34.6"	W 060° 53' 16"	6.75	24.5
22	S 03° 28' 34.8"	W 060° 45' 22.9"	6.76	26
23	S 03° 19' 17.3"	W 060° 37' 00.6"	6.81	23
24	S 03° 19' 17.3"	W 060° 37' 00.6"	6.77	27
25	S 03° 08' 11.1"	W 059° 53' 59.1"	5.53	28

III. RESULTS AND DISCUSSION

In this section we show the results that were obtained with the aid of sensors remotely positioned in a network of satellites (GPS, GLONASS and MODIS) that were described using a geographic information system (GIS) map with thematic layers in tables (water and temperature), graphs, and figures, and with correlations with other studies.

Figure 3 shows the time series of temperature that was taken at three positions (ambient temperature at the ship – 100 m from the edge of the channel – middle of the channel) during the first stage of the expedition (Iquitos/Peru – Manaus/Brazil), using the FLIR E60 thermal imager and weather station. The image next to the time series shows SST in Real Time Global (RTG), High Resolution (HR) and was obtained by NOAA/NCEP/NWS by analyzing satellite images, ocean floats, sea ice cover, salinity, and conducting mathematical modeling in a second-degree polynomial series (Branch analysis method) [11]. These results indicate correlation with those obtained by the Amazon River Expedition.

The observations from this study suggest regional warming of temperature gradients in the stretch between Iquitos-Peru to Manaus-Brazil in July, 2016, (dry season), with average ambient temperature at the ship (in the shade) of 30.41 °C, at the river's surface (100 m from the edge) of 27.34 °C, and at the middle of the channel of 24.73 °C (Fig.3). During the 2nd stage of the Expedition (Manaus-Brazil to Macapá-Brazil) in December 2016, the rainy season had already begun and average temperatures were slightly reduced, with average ambient temperature at the ship of 28.97 °C, at the river's surface (100 m from the edge) of 26.06 °C, and at the middle of the channel of 24.04 °C. The interval between the first and second stages was taken in order to be able to verify the effect of drought on the river due to the time necessary for water to flow across the large distance from Iquitos-Peru to Macapá-Brazil (Figs. 3 and 4).

The analyses of the water samples from both stages of the expedition are listed in Tables I (1st stage) and II (2nd stage), and these data describe the "actual state" of the Amazon River in 2016 during the dry season in the Amazon. The effects of this drought were clearly visible during the entire voyage along the river from Peru to the Atlantic, principally due to the marks left on trees in the *várzea* areas at the river's edge by the previous high-water season. However, the quality of the water from the Amazon River at the 39 georeferenced sample points (Fig. 5, Tables III and IV) was satisfactory and within the standard for potable water for human consumption by communities adjacent to the river's edge from the western portion of the basin to the Atlantic, although basic sanitation services are a preoccupation for all the communities located at these 39 sampling points, including for Iquitos (Peru), Manaus, Santarém and Macapá (Brazil).

Figure 5 shows the georeferenced map of the 39 cities of the Amazon river expedition from Iquitos in Peru to Macapá in Brazil (Table III). The cities from points 41 to 49 are the main tributary (Madeira river) on the right downstream of the river Amazonas, but it is not the focus of this work.

Table IV indicates the water quality of the Amazon River during the prolonged heating of El Niño in the Amazon region in 2016.

TABLE II. WATER SAMPLE ANALYSIS – STAGE TWO OF THE AMAZON RIVER EXPEDITION (PERU-BRAZIL) DEC., 2016.

Samples	Geographic Coordinates		Water	Temp.
	Latitude	Longitude	pH	°C
26	S 03° 08' 21.3"	W 60° 01' 35.1"	5.14	27.6
27	S 03° 08' 54.3"	W 58° 26' 54.1"	6.56	27
28	S 02° 38' 01.6"	W 56° 45' 21.7"	6.7	27
29	S 02° 09' 05.9"	W 56° 05' 43.1"	6.54	27
30	S 01° 55' 22.2"	W 55° 30' 55.3"	6.75	27
31	S 02° 24' 52.1"	W 054° 44' 13.8"	6.16	27
32	S 02° 25' 00"	W 054° 43' 22.2"	6.07	27
33	S 02° 00' 35.1"	W 054° 04' 10.0"	6.54	27
34	S 02° 00' 35.3"	W 054° 04' 11.8"	6.41	26.6
35	S 01° 31' 58.7"	W 052° 34' 34.5"	6.45	28
36	S 00° 03' 27.4"	W 051° 10' 42.1"	6.5	27
37	N 00° 01' 37.4"	W 051° 02' 55.1"	6.6	26.3
38	N 00° 02' 00.2"	W 051° 02' 43.1"	6.44	27
39	S 00° 31' 20"	W 051° 29' 59.7"	6.81	26.6

TABLE III. THE 39 CITIES OF THE AMAZON RIVER (PERU-BRAZIL) DECEMBER, 2016.

Point	Place of Collections
1	PUERTO IQUITOS (PERU)
2	SAN ANTÔNIO (PERU)
3	SAN PABLO (PERU)
4	CIEN BOTE (PERU)
5	CABALLO COCHA (PERU)
6	PUERTO ALEGRIA (PERU)
7	PUERTO SANTA ROSA (PERU)
8	TABATINGA HARBOUR (BRAZIL)
9	BENJAMIN CONSTANT HARBOUR (BRAZIL)
10	FEIJOAL (BRAZIL)
11	SÃO PAULO DE OLIVENÇA HARBOUR (BRAZIL)
12	AMATURÁ CITY (BRAZIL)
13	SANTO ANTONIO DO IÇA CITY (BRAZIL)
14	TONANTINS HARBOUR (BRAZIL)
15	JUTAÍ HARBOUR (BRAZIL)
16	FONTE BOA HARBOUR (BRAZIL)
17	TEFÉ OF LAKE (BRAZIL)
18	BIG CATUÁ ISLAND (BRAZIL)
19	COARI (BRAZIL)
20	ANAMÃ (BRAZIL)
21	MANACAPURU RIVER (BRAZIL)
22	MANAQUIRI LAKE (BRAZIL)
23	IRANDUBA INPUT
24	IRANDUBA
25	MANAUS (BLACK RIVER) (BRAZIL)
26	MANAUS HARBOUR - AM (BRAZIL)
27	ITACOATIARA - AM (BRAZIL)
28	PARINTINS HARBOUR (BRAZIL)
29	JURITI HARBOUR (BRAZIL)
30	ÓBIDOS HARBOUR (BRAZIL)
31	DOCAS HARBOUR (BRAZIL)
32	TIRADENTES SQUARE HARBOUR
33	MONTE ALEGRE HARBOUR (BRAZIL)
34	PRAINHA HARBOUR (BRAZIL)
35	ALMEIRIM HARBOUR (BRAZIL)
36	SANTANA HARBOUR (BRAZIL)
37	FORT HOTEL (MACAPÁ-BRAZIL)
38	STATION *BONDE* (MACAPÁ-BRAZIL)
39	MARACÁ RIVER (BRAZIL)

In [12], there is more information about the "actual state" of the Amazon River in 2016, not only with respect to climatology, but also with respect to the life of people in the communities in this region.

TABLE IV. WATER QUALITY OF THE AMAZON RIVER (PERU-BRAZIL) DECEMBER. 2016.

Samples	Conductivity μS/cm	Alkalinity (mgHCO3/L)	Dissolved Oxygen		Turbidity (NTU)
			%	mg/L	
1	48.3	22.57	113.5	9.5	15.6
2	112	51.24	117.6	10.02	104
3	123.7	48.19	105.7	8.46	83.72
4	119.9	46.36	103.7	8.27	53.56
5	117.4	47.58	111.8	8.81	50.18
6	78.1	36.6	108.1	9.31	8.84
7	106.5	48.19	108	8.56	79.56
8	103.7	44.53	109.2	9.44	75.4
9	104.3	47.58	110.2	8.36	73.06
10	28.3	13.42	115.8	9.29	41.08
11	100.3	42.09	124	9.85	83.98
12	98.1	43.31	113.2	9.75	82.42
13	9.51	4.27	99.8	9.71	6.24
14	17.45	9.15	117.5	9.61	21.06
15	17.92	9.76	109	8.99	10.92
16	75	32.33	119.5	9.48	54.6
17	68.5	29.89	118.9	9.92	63.44
18	69.3	31.72	108.3	9.07	42.12
19	64.2	30.5	110	9.42	44.2
20	54.4	25.01	100.7	8.34	29.38
21	50.7	23.79	103.8	7.79	44.46
22	48.1	22.57	119.1	9	20.8
23	48.5	22.57	129.7	10.45	29.38
24	48.6	22.57	108.5	9.11	24.44
25	9	3.66	114.8	9.61	3.64
26	7.92	2.44	77	5.76	3.9
27	53.3	17.08	76.6	5.35	35.36
28	51.3	16.47	69.3	5.66	44.46
29	51.2	15.25	70.5	5.63	37.44
30	52.8	18.3	68.8	5.64	38.48
31	13.8	7.32	74.9	5.68	4.68
32	13.92	6.1	82.5	6.36	2.6
33	45.7	16.47	67.2	5.29	57.46
34	50	17.69	64.05	4.98	41.34
35	47.5	21.96	71.2	5.28	33.28
36	53.1	23.18	58.4	4.70	27.56
37	53.3	22.57	71.9	5.96	27.56
38	56.5	25.01	67.7	5.37	27.3
39	45.9	21.35	65.3	4.94	36.92

IV. CONCLUSION

The oceans and enormous body of water are the main source of thermal inertia in the climate system [13]. In the current study, we contribute information on temperatures during an El Niño event. With georeferenced sample sites, since the Amazon River is an enormous body of water, and together with the Amazon forest and the equatorial Atlantic and Pacific Oceans models the climate of the South American climate.

The Amazon River, during the dry season of 2016, was influenced by a prolonged El Niño climatic tendency (2014, 2015 and 2016). With the help of georeferencing, it was possible to show the correlation between temperature measurements and satellite images throughout the trip from the city of Iquitos in Peru to the Brazilian city of Macapá, near the interface of Brazil and the Atlantic Ocean. The sea surface temperature stimulated the establishment of an increasing temperature gradient in the equatorial region along the river, combined with a tendency for regional warming during the El Niño event of 2016.

ACKNOWLEDGEMENTS

The authors are grateful to the Lutheran University Center of Manaus (Centro Universitário Luterano, Manaus, (CEULM/ULBRA)) for the help with setting up this bi-national research trip, the Brazilian Navy in the Amazon (western and eastern regiments) for information that helped with navigation, and the Foundation for the Support of Research of the State of Amazonas (Fundação de Amparo e Pesquisa do Amazonas (FAPEAM)) that provided a student scholarship to conduct the water analyses. The authors also thank the Max Planck Chemistry Institute (Mainz-Germany) for support with the chemical analyses, and the Mauá group at INPA in Manaus/Brazil. Furthermore, we thank the Secretary of Education and Quality of Teaching of the State of Amazonas, that through the DEPPE, provided logistical support in sampling areas in the State of Amazonas, Brazil and the collaborators Eliomar Oliveira, Maurício Benzecry, Abrahão Barros, Gilberto Carvalho, and Francisco Santana.

REFERENCES

[1] M. Mohtadi; M. Prange; E. Scfub; T. Jennerjahn. Circulation in Southeastern South America and it's influence from El Niño events. Journal of the Meteorological Society of Japan, 80, 21-22. Article number: 1015 (2017) doi: 10.1038/s41467-017-00855-3n, *Nature Communications*.

[2] J. A. Marego; J. Tomasella; C. R. Uvo. Trends in streamflow and rainfall in tropical South America, eastern Brazil, and northwestern. Journal of Geophysical Research Atmospheres. 103: (D2) 1775-1783 (1998).

[3] CCEE – Electric Energy Trading Chamber. https://economia.uol.com.br/noticias/Reuters/2017/09/20

[4] CPTEC – INPE: Center for Weather Forecasting and Climate Studies - National Institute of Spacial Research: (Access in: http://satelite.cptec.inpe.br/home/index.jsp, (Access in: 2016, july and december).

[5] J. Jiménez-Muñoz; C. Mattar; J. Barichivich; A.Santamaria-Artigas; K. Takahashi; Y. Malhi; J. A. Sobrino; G. Schrier. Record-breaking warming and extreme drought in the Amazon rainforest during course of El Niño 2015-2016. Scientific Reports. 33130 (2016) doi: 10.1038/srep33130.

[6] A. Erfanian; G. Wang; L. Fomenko. Unprecedented drought over tropical South América in 2016:significantly under-predicted by tropical SST. Scientific Reports. 5811(2017) doi: 10.1038/s415998-017-05373-2.

[7] G. Poveda; O. J. Mesa. Feedbacks between hydrological processes in tropical South America and large-scale ocean-atmospheric phenomena. Journal of Climate. 2690-2702 (1997).

[8] S. Hu; A. V. Fedorov. Cross-equatorial winds control El Niño diversity and change, *Nature Climate Change* volume 8, pages798–802 (2018).

[9] N. Fenzl; N. Filizola. Project Integrated and Sustainable Management of Cross - Border Water Resources in the Amazon River Basin, Considering the Variability and Climate World. ACT / GEF / UNEP, (2014).

[10] ANA – CPRM - SIPAM: Hydrological Monitoring. National Water Agency - Geological Survey of Brazil - Protection System of the Amazon. Bulletin no. 18 (2016). (Access in; https://www.cprm.gov.br/sace/boletins/Amazonas/20160513_19-20160513%20-%20191650.pdf)

[11] NOAA/NCEP/NWS/EMC: ftp://ftpprd.ncep.noaa.gov/pub/data/nccf/com/gfs/prod. (Access: July/December,2016/July, 2017).

[12] N. S. Lima, N. Rio Amazonas – Expedição Fluvial – PERU/ BRASIL. ISBN 978-85-64914-76-6 (Brazil). ISBN 978-94-92633-00-2 (Netherlands). p94. Ebook at: https://sites.google.com/vew/amazonriverexpedition.

[13] IPCC. Intergovernmental Panel on Climate Change. *Climate Change 2013: The Physical Science Basis* (Stocker, T. F. et al.) (Cambridge Univ. Press, Cambridge, 2013).

EPOS: European Plate Observing System

Keith G Jeffery
Keith G Jeffery Consultants
Faringdon, UK
Email: keith.jeffery@keithgjefferyconsultants.co.uk

Daniele Bailo
EPOS Office
INGV
Rome, Italy
Email: daniele.bailo@ingv.it

Kuvvet Atakan
Department of Earth Science
University of Bergen
Bergen, Norway
Email: kuvvet.atakan@uib.no

Matt Harrison
Director Informatics
British Geological Survey
Keyworth, UK
Email: mharr@bgs.ac.uk

Abstract—**The European plate observing system (EPOS) addresses the problem of homogeneous access to heterogeneous digital assets in geoscience of the European tectonic plate. Such access opens new research opportunities. Previous attempts have been limited in scope and required much human intervention. EPOS adopts an advanced Information and Communication Technologies (ICT) architecture driven by a catalog of rich metadata. The architecture together with challenges and solutions adopted are presented.**

Keywords - geoscience; information; metadata; CERIF; distributed databases; research infrastructures

I. INTRODUCTION

First, we introduce the challenges facing the EPOS project and cover briefly previous relevant work.

A. *Overview*

Information pertaining to geoscience in Europe is heterogeneous in language, structure, semantics, granularity, content precision and accuracy, method of collection and more. However, there is an increasing demand for access to and utilisation of this information for decision-making in industry and government policy. EPOS is providing a mechanism for homogeneous access to - and utilisation of - this heterogeneity.

EPOS may be considered a journey. During EPOS Preparatory Project (EPOS-PP) domain communities discovered their commonality and differences and – particularly - their digital assets offered as Thematic Core Services (TCSs). These were documented in a database which demonstrated clearly (a) that considerable assets existed (more than 400); (b) that the organisations (covering more than 250 research infrastructures (RIs)) owning the digital assets were willing to make them available (sometimes subject to conditions); (c) that there was overlap of assets between some communities; (d) that multidisciplinary geoscience could be achieved by providing appropriate interoperation mechanisms to make the assets available to all. The task of EPOS Implementation Project (EPOS-IP) is to build a geoscience environment (including governance, legal, financial, training and social aspects as well as technical ICT contributions) for the community. This Version 1.0 of the EPOS platform will then be maintained and extended by the EPOS ERIC European Research Infrastructure Consortium (EPOS-ERIC), the legal body set up by the supporting Member States providing greater sustainability for maintenance, coordination and access into the future.

There are currently 10 different TCS communities (with an additional one pending approval) with distinct and variable but complementary coverage over the entire spectrum of solid Earth sciences. While some of the TCSs are discipline specific such as seismology, geodesy, geomagnetism, geology, others are more cross-disciplinary in their origin such as near-fault observatories, volcano observations, satellite observations of geohazards, anthropogenic hazards, multi-scale laboratories and geo-energy test-beds for low-carbon energy. TCSs have variable histories of developments where some have longer history (>100 years) and hence more mature than the others. They have established their own distinct ways of working, data and software specifications. They have local domain-specific standards (although some are International or European) and constraints especially relating to their interoperation with other International organisations in their specific domain. A real issue is the harmonisation of the descriptions of the TCSs' assets as metadata both in syntax (structure) and semantics (meaning of terms used). The intention is to assist interoperation of the TCSs assets within and between communities by means of the Integrated Core Services

(ICS) which forms the entry-point to EPOS and the view over the EPOS assets made available within the TCSs.

The key requirements are as follows:

1. Minimal interference with existing communities' operations and developments including IT;
2. Easy-to-use user interface;
3. Access to assets through a metadata catalog: initially datasets but progressively also services, workflows, software modules; computational facilities, instruments/sensors all with associated organisational information including experts and service managers;
4. Progressive assistance in composing workflows of services, software and data to deploy on e-Infrastructures to achieve research infrastructure user objectives.

B. *Interoperability Challenge*

EPOS comprises 10 communities of users characterised by domain of interest (TCSs) which supply the metadata describing the assets to the ICS. These communities have varying levels of expertise in the use of ICT for their scientific domain. The processing techniques used vary from domain to domain. With differing domains, the data models used for data collection and processing, and the metadata associated with that data, vary greatly. Across many domains geo-coordinates (including both space and time) are common, but not necessarily using the same coordinate system. Similarly there are multiple metadata standards used.

The software used for processing in each community is different, although there is some commonality where several communities use satellite imagery. The data processing – from validating raw data, summarising, analytics, simulation and visualisation – varies from community to community. The more advanced communities have sophisticated workflows integrating data and processing with advanced computing facilities addressing key scientific challenges with big-data analyses and modelling.

Most of the domains have organised computing and observational (sensor-networks) infrastructure for their purposes at institutional, national and trans-European levels. However, additionally it may be necessary to utilise supercomputing facilities which require procurement or agreements for use as well as mechanisms to deploy the processing workflow. Progressively, EPOS is working more closely with European Open Science Cloud (EOSC) to provide such facilities, although the EPOS architecture is designed to be independent of e-Infrastructure.
e-Is (e-Infrastructures) continue to provide a level of services common to – and used by - many Research Infrastructures (RIs) and other research environments. The major e-Infrastructures of relevance to EPOS-IP are:

1. GEANT: the academic network in Europe which brings together the national computational networks [1];
2. EGI: a foundation and organisation providing infrastructure computing and data facilities for research [2];
3. EUDAT an EC-funded project to provide infrastructure services for datasets including curation, discovery [3];
4. PRACE: a network providing resources on supercomputers throughout Europe [4]
5. EOSC: the European Open Science Cloud which aims to provide infrastructure services for research with the first pilot project starting in January 2017 [5] and subsequently the EOSC-Hub which is soliciting services;
6. OpenAIRE: an EC-funded project to provide metadata to access research publications and – started recently – related datasets [6];

Participant organisations in EPOS have been involved to a greater or lesser extent in all of these activities. In particular EPOS TCSs (with support from the ICS team) have been conducting pilot projects with EGI, PRACE and EUDAT and EPOS is involved in the EOSC pilot.

The level of expertise in both the science and the use of IT varies from community to community. There has been quite some education effort from the central IT team towards the domain communities to explain current computing techniques – especially for cross-domain interoperability which previously had not been a consideration.

C. *Previous Work*

EPOS provides an original approach to the provision of homogeneous access over heterogeneous digital assets. Previous work has been within a limited domain (where standards for assets and their metadata may be consensual thus reducing heterogeneity) and involving much manual intervention with associated costs and potential errors. An early attempt for geoscience information was Filematch [7} which exhibited those problems. NASA has a Common Metadata Repository (CMM). In 2013 NASA decided it could not persuade every data provider to use ISO19115 so developed the Unified Metadata Model (UMM) [8] to and from which other metadata standards are converted. This follows the approach used in EPOS already and provides some assurance of the direction being taken. The Open Geoscience Consortium (OGC) has produced a series of standards. GeoNetwork [9] has established a suite of software based around the OGC ISO19115 metadata standard; however, despite its open nature this software 'locks in' the developer to a particular way of processing and does not assist in the composition and deployment of workflows and the metadata is insufficiently rich for automated processing. Some major projects run parallel to EPOS: EarthCube [10] is a collection of projects providing designs and tools for geoscience including interoperability in USA which investigated the brokering approach - encountering the 'explosion problem' of many bilateral brokers and is now following a metadata-driven brokering mechanism like that used in EPOS; Auscope [11] is a set of related programmes in Australia with one (AuScope GRID) providing access to assets and using ISO19115 as the metadata standard with the deficiencies mentioned above; GEOSS [12] is developing interoperation through a system or systems approach which naturally requires many bilateral interfaces to be maintained with consequent difficulties and maintenance costs as systems evolve.

Thus, the EPOS solution overcomes the major problems associated with previous or parallel work namely: many-to-many interfaces between software brokers or systems and insufficiently rich metadata for automation while enabling interoperability across multiple asset sources.

The rest of the paper is organized as follows: Section II describes the architecture, Section III discusses the importance of metadata and Section IV gives the current state and outlook.

II. ARCHITECTURE

The ICT architecture of EPOS is designed to facilitate the research community and others in discovering and utilizing through the ICS the assets provided by the TCS communities.

A. *Introduction*

In order to provide end-users with homogeneous access to services and multidisciplinary data collected by monitoring infrastructures and experimental facilities (and to software, processing and visualization tools as well) a complex scalable and reliable architecture is required. A snapshot of the architecture is outlined in Figure 1. It includes three main layers:

Integrated Core Services – ICS, the e-Infrastructure designed and run by EPOS; this is the place where the integration of data and services provided by the TCS, Community Layer occurs. Integrated Core Services are characterized by a Central Hub (ICS-C), whose main goal is to host the metadata catalog and orchestrates external resources (e.g., HPC), and the Distributed Services (ICS-D), whose goal is to provide resources (e.g., computational, visualisation).

Thematic Core Services -TCS made up of pan European e-Infrastructures which disseminate data and services of a single discipline (e.g., seismology with ORFEUS/EIDA)

National Research Infrastructures - NRI, made up of RIs providing data and services,

Starting from the latter, NRI represent the wealth of assets provided by national or regional institutions or consortia, and are referred to as DDSS, i.e., Data, Data-products, Software and Services. The asset descriptions are collected first as DDSS in the DDSS master table which also records the state of maturity and management parameters. They are subsequently harvested as metadata for population of the EPOS ICS-C catalog.

TCSs enable the integration of data and services from specific scientific communities. The architecture of the services provided by the individual communities is not prescribed, what is required is that the

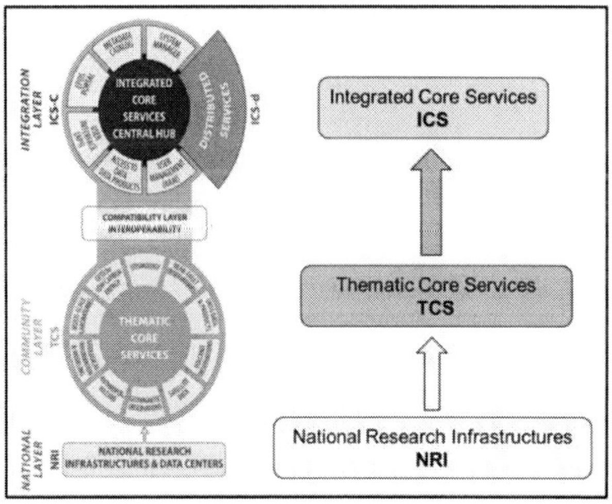

Figure 1. EPOS Architecture

metadata describing the data and services available is in a form that can be consumed by the ICS, allowing the ICS to integrate with those services and data (Figure 1).

B. *ICS*

The EPOS-ICS provides the entrypoint to the EPOS environment. The ICS consists of of the ICS-C and distributed computational resources including also processing and visualisation services (ICS-D) of which a specialization is Computational Earth Science (CES). ICS-C provides a catalog of, and access to, the assets of the TCSs. It also provides access to e-Infrastructures (e-Is) as ICS-Ds upon which (parts of) workflows are deployed (other parts may be deployed within the computing capabilities of RIs within EPOS). EPOS has been involved in projects with e-Is to gain joint understanding of the interfaces and capabilities ready for deployment from ICS-C. EPOS has also been involved in the VRE4EIC project [13} (and cooperating with EVER-EST [14]) to ensure convergent evolution of the EPOS ICS-C user interface and APIs for programmatic access with the developing Virtual Research Environments (VREs). EPOS partners are also participating in is the recently approved ENVRIFAIR project which will assist in building linkages between EPOS ICS-C and European Open Science Cloud (EOSC) (Fig. 2).

The linkage between ICS-C on the one hand and the e-Is and TCS local computing resources and assets on the other as ICS-Ds will be constructed in the ICS-C and managed in the deployment phase. The workflow for the deployment (which may be a simple file download or a complex set of services including analytics and visualisation) will be generated within the ICS-C by interaction with the users. The workflow will be checked by the end-user before deployment. However, the detailed content/capability of the

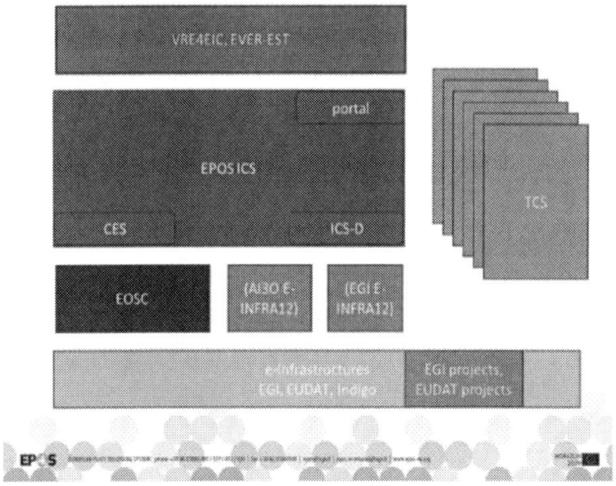

Figure 2. EPOS Positioning

assets might not be known, e.g., the dataset may not contain the relevant information despite its metadata description or the software may not execute as the user expects despite the metadata description. The execution of the deployment is monitored and execution information is returned to the end-user. The workflow may be deployed in one of two ways: (a) directly with no user interaction during execution of the deployment; (b) step-by-step with user interaction (so-called computational steering) between each step. Deployments of type (a) will have better optimisation (for performance) and security but could possibly execute a workflow the components of which do not behave as the user expects. Deployments of type (b) lack optimisation but allow the user to stop the workflow deployment at any step, examine the results and – if not as expected – reorganise the workflow (by changing components) to meet more closely the requirement.

The ICS represents the infrastructure consisting of services that will allow access to multidisciplinary resources provided by the TCS. These will include data and data products as well as synthetic data from simulations, processing, and visualization tools.

C. *ICS-C*

The ICS-C consists of multiple logical areas of functionality, these include the Graphic User Interface (GUI), web-API, metadata catalogue, user management etc. A micro-service architecture has been adopted of the ICS-C, where each (micro) services is atomic and dedicated to a specific class of tasks. The ICS-C is where the integration of other services from ICS-D and TCS takes place. The architectural constraints for the ICS-D are elaborated as a metadata model within the ICS-C CERIF (Common European Research Information Format) [15] catalog and are being implemented.

The ICS-C System is the main system that manages the integration of DDSS from the communities. On top of such system, a Graphic User Interface (GUI) enable the user to search, discover, integrate data in a user-friendly way.

The EPOS ICS-C system architecture (Fig. 3) was designed and developed with the aim of integrating data and services provided by TCS. In order to a) enable the system to run in a distributed environment, b) guarantee up-to-date technological upgrades by adopting a software-independent approach, c) proper scaling of specific system functionalities, the chosen architecture followed a microservices paradigm.

The Microservices architecture approach envisages small atomic services dedicated to the execution of a specific class of tasks, which have high reliability [16], [17]. Such architecture replaces the monolith with a distributed system of lightweight, narrowly focused, independent services. In order to implement the microservices paradigm, Docker Containers technology was used. It enables complete isolation of independent software applications running in a shared environment. In particular, each microservice is developed in Java language and performs a simple task, as atomic as possible. The communication between microservices is done via messages received and sent on a queueing system, in this case RabbitMQ. As a result, a chain of microservices processes the requests.

The current architecture includes AAAI. This has been implemented using UNITY [18] and has involved close cooperation with CYFRONET. However, in May 2018 an integrated authentication system for academic communities was announced and this has now been adopted. Authorisation is more complex and depends on rules agreed with the TCS (within the context of the financial, legal and governance traversal workpackages of EPOS-IP) for each of their assets and included further metadata elements into the CERIF catalog to control such authorisation. AAAI will be continuously evolved and updated to ensure appropriate security, privacy and governance. Related to this, the GUI now provides a user notification pointing to a legal disclaimer for the EPOS system.

A major requirement of the system, after asset discovery, is the construction of workflows that can be used to access /

process data. This has implications for the entire software stack; visually designing the workflows, managing and persisting inputs and outputs, scheduling and execution of processes, access to metadata, access to data and service

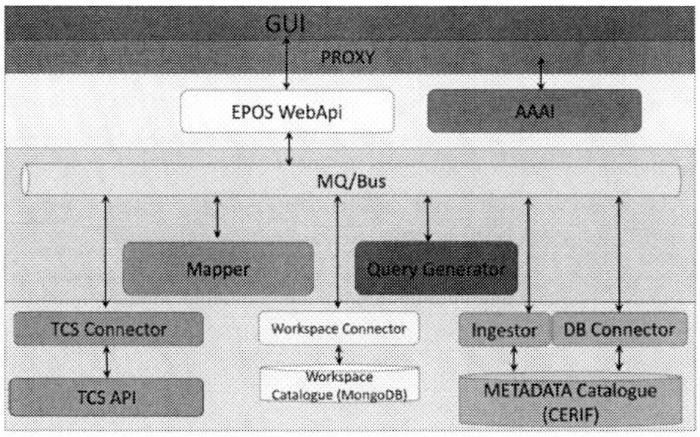

Figure 3. ICS-C Architecture

from the TCS. The topic as whole required significant analysis of requirements and available technologies. Working in cooperation with the VRE4EIC project we have the basic components for (a) a general workflow manager interface; (b) interfaces to specific workflow managers such as Taverna [17].

Beyond simple map visualisations that consume web map services the ICS-C user interface may be required to support additional types of visualisation. This set of supported visualisation types and associated data formats needs confirmation as it will not be practical to support all formats of data for all types of visualisation.

D. *ICS-D*

The distributed services offered by the ICS-D facet of the architecture ties-in with the workflow management, as the distributed services in question beyond just being discoverable are likely candidate for inclusion in processing workflows. A specification of the metadata elements required for ICS-D has been produced and forms part of the architecture. ICS-D will appear to the workflow, or to the end-user, as a service accessed through an API. However, the choice of which ICS-D to use and the deployment of a workflow across one or more ICS-Ds requires optimisation middleware. Results from the PaaSage project [18] are relevant and the concurrent MELODIC project [19] offers optimisation including that based on dataset placement and latency. Further refinement of requirements and the architectural interfaces continues.

III. METADATA

Metadata is the key to discover and utilise the heterogeneous assets of EPOS in a homogeneous way thus facilitating cross-domain, interoperable science.

A. *Introduction*

The metadata catalogue is the key technology that enables the system to manage and orchestrate all resources required to satisfy a user request. By using metadata, the ICS-C can discover data or other digital objects requested by a user, contextualise them (for relevance and quality) access them, send them to a processing facility (or move the code to facility holding the data) depending on the constructed workflow, and perform other tasks. The catalogue contains: (i) technical specification to enable autonomic ICS access to TCS discovery and access services, (ii) metadata associated with the digital object with direct link to it, (iii) information about users, resources, software, and services other than data services (e.g., rock mechanics, geochemical analysis, visualization, processing). The data model used for the catalogue is CERIF

Metadata describing the TCS DDSS are stored using the CERIF data model which differs from most metadata standards in that it (1) separates base entities from linking entities thus providing a fully connected graph structure; (2) using the same syntax, stores the semantics associated with values of attributes both for base entities and (for role of the relationship) for linking entities, which also store the temporal duration of the validity of the linkage. This provides great power and flexibility. CERIF also (as a superset) can interoperate with widely adopted metadata formats such as DC (Dublin Core) [20], DCAT (Data Catalogue Vocabulary) [21], CKAN (Comprehensive Knowledge Archive Framework) [22], INSPIRE (the EC version of ISO 19115 for geospatial data) [23] and others using convertors developed as required to meet the metadata mappings achieved between each of the above standards and CERIF The metadata catalogue also manages the semantics, in order to provide the meaning of the attribute values.

The use of CERIF provides automatically:

(a) The ability for discovery, contextualization and (re-)use of assets according to the FAIR principles [24]
(b) A clear separation of base entities (things) from link entities (relationships);
(c) Formal syntax and declared semantics;
(d) A semantic layer also with the base/link structure allowing crosswalks between semantic terminology spaces;
(e) Conversion to/from other common metadata formats;
(f) Built-in provenance information because of the timestamped role-based links;

(g) Curation facilities because of being able to manage versions, replicates and partitions of digital objects using the base/link structure;

The catalog is constantly evolving with the addition of new assets (such as services, datasets) but also increasingly rich metadata as the TCSs improve their metadata collection to enable more autonomic processing.

B. TCS Metadata

The process of populating the catalog is crucial in the EPOS vision. Indeed, populating the catalog means to make available all the information needed by an end user to perform queries, data integration, visualisation and other functionalities provided by the system.
Greater interaction with TCS communities to ensure that their metadata, data and services are available for harvesting in the appropriate format and to populate the CERIF data model has been achieved and will be continued.

C. ICS Metadata

The EPOS baseline, presents a minimum set of common metadata elements required to operate the ICS taking into consideration the heterogeneity of the many TCSs involved in EPOS. It has been implemented as an application profile using an extension of the DCAT standard, namely the EPOS-DCAT-AP. It is possible to extend this baseline to accommodate extra metadata elements where it is deemed that those metadata elements are critical in describing and delivering the data services for any given community. Indeed, this has happened when the original EPOS-DCAT-AP was found to be inadequate and a new version with richer metadata was designed and implemented.

The metadata to be obtained from the EPOS TCSs as described in the baseline document (and any other agreed elements) will be mapped to the EPOS ICS CERIF catalog. The process of converting metadata acquired from the EPOS TCS to CERIF will be done by in consultation with each TCS as to what metadata they have available and harvesting mechanisms.

The various TCS nodes have APIs or other mechanisms to expose the metadata describing the available DDSS in a TCS specific metadata standard that contains the elements outlined in the EPOS baseline documents better described in the following sections. It also requires ICS APIs (wrappers) to map and store this in the ICS metadata catalogue, CERIF. These APIs and the corresponding ICS convertors collectively form the "interoperability layer" in EPOS, which is the link between the TCSs and the ICS

In order to manage all the information needed to satisfy user requests, all metadata describing the TCS Data, Datasets, Software and Services (DDSS) is stored into the EPOS ICS, internal catalog. Such a catalog, based on the CERIF model, differs from most metadata standards used by various scientific communities in that it is much richer in syntax (structure) and semantics (meaning). For this reason, EPOS ICS has sought to communicate to the TCS communities the core elements of metadata required to facilitate the ICS through the EPOS Metadata Baseline. This baseline can be considered as an intermediate layer that facilitates the conversion from the community metadata standards such as ISO19115/19, DCAT, Dublin Core, INSPIRE etc. describing the DDSS elements and not the index or detailed scientific data (**Figure 1**Fig. 4).

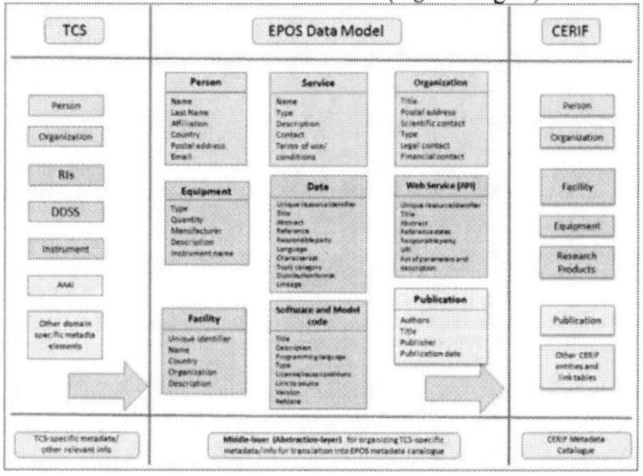

Figure 4 EPOS Metadata Baseline

D. DDSS and Granularity Database

As a part of the requirements and use cases collection (RUC) from the TCSs, a specific list was prepared to include all data, data products, software and services (DDSS). This DDSS Master Table was used as a mechanism to update the RUC information as well as providing a mechanism for accessing more detailed IT technical information for the development of the ICS Central Hub (ICS-C). The DDSS Master Table was also used for extracting the level of maturity of the various DDSS elements in each TCS as well as providing a summary of the status of the TCS preparations for the ICS integration and interoperability. The current version of the DDSS Master Table consists of 363 DDSS elements, where 165 of these already exist and are declared by TCSs to be ready for implementation. The remaining DDSS elements required more time to harmonize the internal standards, prepare an adequate metadata structure and so are available for implementation soon. In total, 21 different harmonization groups (HGs) are established to help organizing the harmonization issues in a structured way. TCSs are preparing individual TCS Roadmaps which will describe the development and implementation plans of the remaining DDSS elements including a time-line and resource allocations. In addition, user feedback groups

(UFGs) are being established in order to give constant and structured feedback during the implementation process of the TCS-ICS integration and the development of the ICS.

The DDSS Master Table was constantly being updated as new information from the TCS WPs arrive. The older versions are also kept in the archive for future reference. The DDSS master table is being transformed to the granularity database because of the problems of referential and functional integrity using a spreadsheet; relational technology provides appropriate constraints to ensure integrity.

The TCS requirements and use cases (RUC) collection process was designed carefully, taking into account the amount and complexity of the information involved in all 10 different TCSs. An increasingly detailed RUC collection process is formulated and explained through dedicated guidelines and interview templates. A roadmap for the ICS-TCS interactions for the RUC collection process was prepared for this purpose and distributed to all TCSs.

In this approach, a five-step procedure is applied involving the following:

- Step 1: First round of RUC collection for mapping the TCS assets;
- Step 2: Second round of RUC collection for identifying TCS priorities;
- Step 3: ICS-TCS Integration Workshop for building a common understanding for metadata
- Step 4: Third round of RUC collection for refined descriptions before implementation;
- Step 5: Implementation of RUC to the CERIF metadata;

Planning for the requirements and use cases (RUC) elicitation process started with the pre-project meeting held during the period July 8-9 2015 at the BGS facilities in Nottingham, UK. The first version of the guidelines level-1 for the ICS-TCS integration was prepared soon after this meeting and was distributed to the TCS leaders and the relevant IT-contacts. A second, more detailed guidelines level-2 was prepared in September 2015 and distributed in the EPOS-IP project kick-off meeting held in Rome, Italy, during the period October 5-7 2015. Prior to the kick-off meeting, a preliminary collection of the RUC was requested from each TCS, which was then presented during the meeting.

In parallel with the guidelines for the ICS-TCS Integration, a dedicated RUC interview template level-1 was prepared to be used during the first site visits to the TCSs. The site visits were conducted during the time period between November 2015 and March 2016. All four steps are now completed, whereas step 5 with metadata implementation has started in January 2017 and is ongoing.

Work is almost complete in converting the DDSS tables (in Excel) to the granularity database using Postgres. This will (a) facilitate finding particular DDSS elements, eliminating duplicates and checking the progress of getting DDSS elements into metadata format; (b) actually harvesting to the metadata catalog.

IV. CONCLUSION

Currently 103 distinct services from the domain communities are represented by CERIF metadata in the EPOS ICS-C catalog. These services, described by the metadata, can be discovered, contextualised and utilised individually or composed into workflows and hence become interoperable. A GUI (Graphical User Interface) provides the user view onto the catalog, and it also provides a workspace to collect the metadata of the assets selected for use (Fig. 5). From the workspace a workflow may be constructed and deployed.

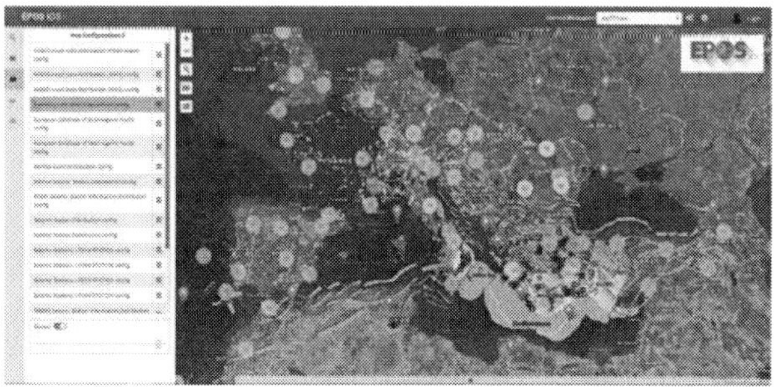

Figure 5. EPOS-ICS graphical user interface.

Future plans include:

(a) Harvesting of metadata describing more assets: not only services but also datasets, software, workflows, equipment;
(b) Improving the GUI to allow workflow deployment with 'fire and forget' technology or single-step with user checking and adjustment at each step;
(c) Completion of the software to permit trans-national access to laboratory and sensor equipment;
(d) Improved AAAI (Authentication, authorisation, accounting infrastructure) to give the domain communities finer control over utilisation of their assets;
(e) The inclusion of virtual laboratory-type interfaces (virtual research environments) allowing users access and connectivity including open-source frameworks such as Jupyter notebooks [25] which are increasingly being used in some scientific communities.

The architecture outlined and demonstrated (in successive prototypes) in EPOS-IP has found favour (not without some criticism of course – leading to agile improvements) from the user community. Furthermore, the prototype system has passed Technological Readiness Assessment procedures within the governance of the EPOS-IP project. Currently the ICS is undergoing validation tests. The architecture meets the requirements, it is state of the art and has a further development plan.

ACKNOWLEDGMENT

The authors acknowledge the work of the whole ICT team in EPOS reported here and the funding of the European Commission H2020 program (Grant agreement 676564) and National Funding Councils that have made this work possible

REFERENCES

[1] GEANT: http://www.geant.org/ (Accessed on December 14, 2018)
[2] EGI: https://www.egi.eu/ (Accessed on December 14, 2018)
[3] EUDAT: https://eudat.eu/ (Accessed on December 14, 2018)
[4] PRACE: http://www.prace-ri.eu/ (Accessed on December 14, 2018)
[5] EOSC pilot: https://eoscpilot.eu/ (Accessed on December 14, 2018)
[6] OpenAIRE: https://www.openaire.eu/ (Accessed on December 14, 2018)
[7] P G Sutterlin, K G Jeffery, E M Gill: 'Filematch: A Format for the Interchange of Computer-Based Files of Structured Data' Computers and Geosciences 3(1977) 429-468.
[8] UMM: https://earthdata.nasa.gov/about/science-system-description/eosdis-components/common-metadata-repository/unified-metadata-model-umm (Accessed on December 14, 2018)[9] GeoNetwork https://geonetwork-opensource.org/ (Accessed on December 14, 2018)
[10] EarthCube: https://www.earthcube.org/ (Accessed on December 14, 2018)
[11] AuScope: http://www.auscope.org.au/ (Accessed on December 14, 2018)
[12] GEOSS: https://www.earthobservations.org/geoss.php (Accessed on December 14, 2018)
[13] VRE4EIC: https://www.vre4eic.eu/ (Accessed on December 14, 2018)
[14] EVEREST: https://ever-est.eu/ (Accessed on December 14, 2018)
[13] CERIF: https://www.eurocris.org/cerif/main-features-cerif (Accessed on December 14, 2018)
[14] Newman, Sam. "Building Microservices", O'Reilly Media, Inc., 2015
[15] International Journal of Open Information Technologies ISSN: 2307- 8162
[16] UNITY: http://www.unity-idm.eu (Accessed on December 14, 2018)
[17] Taverna: https://taverna.incubator.apache.org/ (Accessed on December 14, 2018)
[18] PaaSage: https://paasage.ercim.eu/ (Accessed on December 14, 2018)
[19] MELODIC: melodic.cloud/ (Accessed on December 14, 2018)
[20] DC: http://dublincore.org/documents/dces/ (Accessed on December 14, 2018)
[21] DCAT: https://www.w3.org/TR/vocab-dcat/ (Accessed on December 14, 2018)
[22] CKAN: https://ckan.org/ (Accessed on December 14, 2018)
[23] INSPIRE: https://inspire.ec.europa.eu/ (Accessed on December 14, 2018)
[24] FAIR: https://www.force11.org/grohttps://ckan.org/up/fairgroup/fairprinciples (Accessed on December 14, 2018)
[25] Jupyter: https://jupyter.org/